THE
HURRICATS

Painting by James Goulding

THE HURRICATS

THE FIGHTERS THAT COULD NOT RETURN

Ralph Barker

TEMPUS

First published 2000

PUBLISHED IN THE UNITED KINGDOM BY:

Tempus Publishing Ltd
The Mill, Brimscombe Port
Stroud, Gloucestershire GL5 2QG

PUBLISHED IN THE UNITED STATES OF AMERICA BY:

Arcadia Publishing
Tempus Publishing Inc.
2 Cumberland Street
Charleston, SC 29401

Tempus books are available in France, Germany and Belgium
from the following addresses:

Tempus Publishing Group	Tempus Publishing Group	Tempus Publishing Group
21 Avenue de la République	Gustav-Adolf-Straße 3	Place de L'Alma 4/5
37300 Joué-lès-Tours	99084 Erfurt	1200 Brussels
FRANCE	GERMANY	BELGIUM

British Library Cataloguing in Publication Data.
A catalogue record for this book is available from the British Library.

ISBN 0 7524 2005 4

Typesetting and origination by Tempus Publishing.
PRINTED AND BOUND IN GREAT BRITAIN.

Contents

Acknowledgements

I should like to acknowledge first my great indebtedness to John Pickwell, formerly a fighter direction officer with the Merchant Ship Fighter Unit and since the war an energetic if unofficial reunion organiser, who put me in touch with many surviving members of that colourful unit. He also read the finished draft of this book and made many valuable amendments and suggestions, though the final responsibility of course remains mine.

Mrs Ann Lance, secretary of the Fleet Air Arm Association, helped me similarly to find surviving naval pilots of No. 804 (F.A.A.) Squadron, amongst whom I must especially mention Alan Marsh, who passed details of his own researches into the history of that squadron on to me.

By far the most prolific sources of information overall were the Air and Admiralty files now available for study at the Public Record Office. I am also greatly indebted to various branches and directorates of the Ministry of Defence, particularly the Naval and Air Historical Branches and the Libraries.

Individual acknowledgements for information and help, often extensive, are listed below:

General
Lord Balfour of Inchrye MC; Reg Barlow, formerly editor of the official journal *Coastguard*; Captain Jack Broome DSC; Denis S. Clark; District Officer, HM Coastguard Holyhead; Dick Evans, formerly of HM Coastguard; Philip Lucas GM; Miss Norah Marks; Militararchiv, Akte R.L. 10/563 (from German Federal Archives, Military Archives); Volkhard Matyssek; Air Chief Marshal Sir John Whitworth Jones, GBE, KCB.

Fleet Air Arm
Maurice A. Birrell, DSC, Leslie H. Kemp, G.P. Magwood, the late R.B. Mancus MBE, Alan Marsh, John E. Scott DSC, Cecil A. Walker DSC.

MSFU

Graham W.B. Austin OBE AFC, Harry Ball-Wilson, John H. Davies, Deryck K. Faulks, Roy C. Ford, Mowbray Garden DFC, A.W. Giggins, H. Norman Gostelow, G.S.K. Haywood, Deryck F. Lamb, T. Bryn Lewis, Anthony S. Linney OBE, Air Vice-Marshal M.D. Lyne AFC, Alec Lumsden, John E. MacDonald, Peter G. Mallett, Charles M. Morbey, Patrick D. O'Sullivan, John G. Pickwell, G.C. Pinkerton OBE DFC, J.A. Sabourin, A. Vernon Sanders DFC, R.L. (Peter) Spurdle DFC, James A. Stewart DFC, Basil T. Tatham, D.R. Turley-George DFC, George W. Varley DFC, S.L. (Peter) Ward.

Books and Newspapers

Aircraft in Profile, Volume V (Profile Publications, 1967)

Becker, Cajus, *The Luftwaffe War Diaries* (Macdonald, 1966)

Broome, Captain Jack, *Convoy is to Scatter* (William Kimber, 1972)

Churchill, Winston S., *The Second World War*, Volume III (Cassell, 1950)

Conradis, Heinz, *Design for Flight: The Kurt Tank Story* (Macdonald, 1960)

Forbes, Wing Commander Athol, and Allen, Squadron Leader Hubert, *Ten Fighter Boys* (Collins, 1942)

Green, *William, Famous Bombers of World War II* (Macdonald and Jane's, 1975)

Griffith, Hubert, *The R.A.F. in Russia* (Hammond and Hammond, 1942)

Lloyd, F.H., *Hurricane* (Harborough, 1945)

Poolman, Kenneth, *The Catafighters* (William Kimber, 1970)

Price, Alfred, *German Bombers of World War II*, Volume I (Hylton Lacy, 1968)

Robertson, Terence, *Walker R.N.* (Evans Bros., 1956)

Smith, J.R., and Kay, Anthony L., *German Aircraft of the Second World War* (Putnam, 1972)

Smith, J. Richard, *Focke-Wulf: An Aircraft Album* (Ian Allen, 1973)

Aircraft Illustrated Extra, No. 14

Royal Air Force Review, January 1952

Sunday Express

The Times

I

The Scourge of the Atlantic

Seated facing each other in the high-backed walnut chairs of the Air Council Room in King Charles Street were the top brass of the Royal Navy and the Royal Air Force. The man who had called the conference was Air Chief Marshal Sir Charles Portal, the newly appointed Chief of the Air Staff. Confronting him across the square walnut table was the First Sea Lord, Admiral of the Fleet Sir Dudley Pound, Chief of the Naval Staff. The highly polished furniture, the rich velvet of the curtains, the thick pile of the carpet, the solid permanence of the stone fireplace, and the graceful aerobatics depicted in the First World War paintings on the panelled walls, failed to create the usual atmosphere of relaxation and confidence. The date was Tuesday 12 November 1940, the time four o'clock in the afternoon.

The Battle of Britain had been won, but Britain still stood alone against a powerful, ruthless and impatient enemy. Four days earlier, Hitler had sworn to intensify the air and U-boat war. Britain was to be bombed and starved into submission. The November fogs that might have blanketed London as a target had failed to materialise, and the gales that had restricted enemy air activity the previous night had blown themselves out. The sky was clear and the moon was full. Across the English Channel the *Luftwaffe* were preparing to renew their onslaught, with London the main objective.

As the conference deliberated, the lights in the room were switched on and the curtains punctiliously drawn. From a score of heavily sandbagged Government departments in adjacent Whitehall, drably attired civil servants scurried off home to beat the blackout. As night fell sirens wailed and within minutes the guns of the barrage thundered. Soon, from the outskirts of the city, the first bombs reverberated. But the men closeted in the luxurious isolation of the Air Council Room paid no heed. They did not allow the bombing to interrupt their proceedings. In any case the bombing, for the moment, was not their prime concern. Nor were the U-boats, though they were headache enough. To the unrelenting battle of attrition in the Atlantic, in this first winter of the shooting war, a new dimension had been added and the brass-hats had been caught off their guard. They faced what seemed an insoluble problem, yet it was one to which they had to find the answer. 'If we fail in this,' said one of them, 'we lose the war.'

Before the German conquest of Norway in April 1940, Britain's trade routes were menaced by U-boat and surface raider only. The threat from the air was confined to the routes along the east coast. Even after Norway fell, Britain's merchant shipping crossing the Atlantic, or plying to and from the southern hemisphere, could safely use the south-western approaches, rounding Southern Ireland before passing through St George's Channel and into the Irish Sea. But with the fall of France in June 1940, Germany commanded the entire Western European seaboard from Norway to the Pyrenees. Former French airfields were occupied by the *Luftwaffe* and it was from one of these airfields, Bordeaux-Merignac, that the Nazis unleashed a new threat to Britain's lifelines in the Focke-Wulf 200, or Condor, soon to be described by Prime Minister Winston Churchill as the 'scourge of the Atlantic'.

The Condor, aptly named despite its genesis as a peacetime airliner, began its depredations against Allied merchantmen in August 1940 and in two and a half months these huge four-engined bombers, hurriedly converted from the civil version, sank nearly 90,000 tons of Allied shipping. With dimensions and wing area roughly equivalent to the Lancaster and Halifax bombers of later years, they were capable of reaching more than a thousand miles out into the Atlantic, far beyond the range of Britain's shore-based fighters. At once it was clear that the Germans had found one of Britain's weakest links.

Under the command of the experienced and dedicated *Oberstleutnant* Edgar Petersen, the Condors of the newly formed I. *Gruppe/Kampfgeschwader 40* exploited it eagerly. Frustrated in their invasion plans, the Nazis abandoned their efforts to attain air superiority over the English Channel and concentrated their resources first on the destruction of Britain's industry and morale by night bombing and second on the severing of her vital trade lifelines. Patrolling at 2,000 feet and 190 miles an hour, searching for single ships or stragglers, the Condors that autumn began to sink ships almost at will. In vain did the British Admiralty close all southern ports to heavy shipping, switch convoys to the Clyde and the Mersey, and re-route their ships as far as possible away from Bordeaux. On 26 October the 42,000-ton Canadian Pacific luxury liner *Empress of Britain*, operating as a troopship but sailing without escort, was bombed and set on fire 80 miles west of Bloody Foreland, by a pilot named Bernhard Jope on his first operational flight. Sailing from Cape Town to Liverpool, she had encountered good weather and was a day ahead of schedule. Jope sighted her, circled and flashed a recognition signal; but he was fairly certain that in this position she must be an enemy vessel. He worked round to her stern, then turned in suddenly on the same course, opened fire and dropped his first bombs. Until the last moment the crew of the liner thought the aircraft was friendly. In two further attacks Jope met heavy return fire from the troopship's three-inch and Lewis guns and his Condor was severely damaged, but he managed to limp back to Bordeaux. Next day the 5,000-ton *Alfred Jones* was bombed and badly damaged 150 miles west of Malin Head; and six more ships were bombed and in some cases abandoned off the west and north-west coast of Ireland in the next ten days. Although medium bombers like the Heinkel 111 and the Junkers 88 had operated successfully in the North Sea, the range of these types was restricted and in every case the attacking aircraft was a Focke-Wulf Condor.

The loss of the *Empress of Britain* – she was given the *coup de grâce* two days later by a passing U-boat while a tow was being attempted – stood out as a devastating blow. She had taken three years to build and in wartime she was irreplaceable. Some defence against the new predator had to be found.

The man sounding off most shrilly in the corridors of Whitehall was an RAF air commodore named Donald Stevenson, Director of Fighter Operations at the Air Ministry. Denouncing what he saw as the Admiralty's complacency, he kept thumping home the message that the Western Approaches were Britain's lifeline, without which the war was lost. East coast traffic, which he felt the Admiralty were treating as of equal importance, was not comparable in his view. There was no alternative to the Atlantic route, whereas east coast traffic, in the last resort, could always be transported by road or rail. In any case losses in coastal waters, which had reached a peak during the first phase of the Battle of Britain in July, had fallen off considerably since then. No doubt this was an over-simplification; but Stevenson argued with some force that the naval staff be invited to review their routeings and priorities so that fighter protection in the Atlantic to the greatest practicable range could be provided.

In an impassioned plea to Portal, Stevenson submitted that the Condor bomber was one of the most serious problems of the future. It could find ships and convoys at great distances, and it was unrealistic to suppose that shore-based fighters could help. They would only be effective against the shorter-range He111 and Ju88. The overseas convoys must face the fact that they must rely on local protection only – their own guns, plus anything that the Navy could provide in the way of carrier aircraft. Stevenson did offer Portal one crumb of comfort, but he warned that it was a crumb upon which Britain might choke. The Germans had started the Condor war on Britain's trade, he said, with a small unit backed up by a very limited production programme. Indeed, essentially the Condor was not a war machine at all. It still followed the structural lines of its predecessor, hastily strengthened for war purposes. Even the new Condors that were coming off the production line of the Focke-Wulf factory at Bremen followed the same constructional principles, so that the machines, although well armed, were far more susceptible to damage from enemy defences and from minor accidents than the average robust operational type. The Condor might well be decisive, warned Stevenson, in a maritime war against Britain's trade, but only if it were employed in considerable numbers before Britain could find an antidote. 'It looks as if Germany has repeated the same kind of mistake as she made in 1914-18 with her U-boats,' conjectured Stevenson. This was very fortunate for Britain; but it could not be expected to last. Germany had ample bases and production was bound to increase. By the spring of 1941, Britain's arrangements to secure her vital trade against this form of attack must be completed.

Detail from an Air Staff assessment of November 1940 of the radii of action of German bombers, assumed a base on Brest. Stimulated by these and other outpourings from Stevenson, Portal called a conference to discuss fighter protection for Britain's convoys, to which he invited Sir Dudley Pound and his vice-chief, Admiral Tom Phillips (Fifth Sea Lord and Chief of Naval Air Services), and the commanders-in-chief of the two RAF commands most closely concerned – Fighter and Coastal. The agenda was prepared by Stevenson; and even on the morning of the conference he was sending urgent minutes to Portal. This was the conference that met on that fateful afternoon of 12 November 1940 in the Air Council Room in King Charles Street.

The meeting began with a discussion of the various methods by which the activities of the Condors might be countered. The Condor factory at Bremen and the Condor base at Bordeaux must be singled out for bombing attack. Anti-aircraft armament for merchant ships must be substantially improved, even if it meant – as it assuredly would – denuding shore defences. But no one believed that these measures were more than palliatives. The obvious requirement was for high performance fighters capable of making interceptions to the limit of Condor range; but the only way of achieving this was by providing them as an integral part of convoy escorts, which meant aircraft carriers. With the sinking of the *Courageous* and the *Glorious* in the early months of the war and the demands of the Mediterranean theatre, the aircraft carrier cupboard was bare.

Second best seemed to be to transfer squadrons of the new twin-engined Beaufighter to Northern Ireland. But there were objections. The Beaufighters, helped by ground radar stations which vectored them on to their targets, were doing a good job in a defensive role where they were and could ill be spared. Attempts to locate Condors in the wide-open spaces of the Atlantic were not likely to succeed. It was one thing for a Condor to locate a convoy, it was quite another for a Beaufighter to track down a Condor, even with the aid of Intelligence gleaned from the secret radio intercept service at Cheadle. Nevertheless the Admiralty favoured above all else the strengthening of the long-range fighter force in Northern Ireland. The Air Staff had assessed the requirement as a minimum of three Beaufighter squadrons, and the transfer was duly made. It was nothing like enough. There might be as many as four convoys in the danger zone at any one time, to say nothing of unescorted vessels, and to maintain continuous patrols would have required ten times as many aircraft, equivalent to the entire Beaufighter output for the next twelve months. Even then some of the attack areas would have remained out of reach.

Arising from this discussion, however, the Assistant Chief of Naval Staff (Training), Rear Admiral H. R. Moore, interposed a suggestion. If special ships in each convoy were equipped as mobile radar sector stations, they could guide the Beaufighters on to their Condor targets. This sounded like good sense; and an unnamed Air Ministry representative at the conference went one better by suggesting a refinement – 'to fit such a ship with a catapult so that two or three fighters could be carried for interception purposes'. The notion of the expendable fighter, flown by a pilot on a one-way ticket, had been anonymously born.

Even in the rarefied atmosphere of the Air Council Room, it was difficult enough to take decisions and make recommendations; and when it came to translating these policies into reality, the complications multiplied tenfold. However, the Condor crews themselves, by further bombing attacks off the west and south-west coasts of Ireland, concentrated the thoughts of one man's mind wonderfully. After producing a further paper for Portal immediately after the conference, Stevenson was writing to him again within a week. Since the meeting, he said, several more ships had been bombed. He listed the *Apapa* (9,000 tons), the *Fishpool* (5,000 tons) and the *Empire Wind* (7,500 tons); two sunk, the third on fire and sinking. Even as he was compiling his list, news reached him of the bombing of two more ships. One of them, the 10,000-ton *Nestlea*, the convoy commodore's ship, lay abandoned and sinking. Both, Stevenson alleged, had been routed within a hundred miles of the south-west point of Ireland, where they were 'easy money'. Why were the Admiralty still routeing ships in this way?

For the Admiralty, of course, the routeing of convoys presented a ceaseless dilemma. Especially vulnerable were the routes to and from Gibraltar, where the flank was continually exposed to the Condor base. The Admiralty's answer was to route convoys further and further west to stretch the Condors to the uttermost; but this had the disadvantage of widening the gap between shore-based air cover from south-west England and Gibraltar. While the right compromise was being sought, convoys continued to suffer. Another factor that angered Stevenson was the Admiralty's attitude, expressed in the conference, towards warning their convoys of the known approach of Condors. So vital to Britain's conduct of the war was the knowledge she gained from her intercept service that no one dare risk compromising it. But surely, argued Stevenson, it was not beyond the wit of the Admiralty to devise a safe method of passing the necessary information? The screw was being turned and the effect of shortages was already becoming apparent on the industrial scene. Stevenson recommended that all convoys should approach from the north-west, where Condors from both France and Norway were at the limit of their range, pass into the danger area in darkness, and rely on protection from land-based fighters from dawn. But the Admiralty, with the menace of U-boats and surface raiders still the major threat, thought otherwise. For the long term, however, Stevenson pinned his faith on the expendable fighter. 'We should get moving on this at once.'

Thus fertilised, the idea of the expendable fighter took root in Portal's mind, and he sounded Pound out on the practicability of allocating a ship fitted with radar, catapult and fighter to accompany each convoy. Pound approved in principle; but in a situation where shortages were endemic, the catapults, the radar equipment, and above all the ships and the aircraft, had to be found. It was thought at first that tankers, with their lengthy fore-deck, would be the type most easily adapted to mounting a catapult rail; and it was believed that the aircraft most likely to be available in numbers was the single-engined twin-seat Fairey Fulmar. But tankers, it was soon realised, were too slow. A speed of 10-12 knots would be needed to assist the launch and another requirement was the ability to turn quickly into wind for launching, which the tanker lacked. The Fulmar was also dismissed as too slow, except as a stopgap; its margin of speed over the Condor was reckoned to be not more than 10 mph. After a flirtation with a new light-weight wooden aircraft, the Miles M.20, which would have been easy to catapult but which never reached the production stage, investigations began into modifying the Hawker Hurricane. This tough little aircraft, in the process of being superseded in fighter squadrons by the Spitfire, seemed likely to prove the ideal choice.

As for the catapult, the type normally used to launch aircraft from ships was hydraulically operated and had a cordite cylinder, but it was too cumbersome, too sophisticated and too expensive for general use in merchant ships, while the lighter naval type could not launch a fighter of the weight of the Hurricane at the velocity required. The alternative was the simple rocket catapult, propelled by banks of 3-inch rockets; and the rockets happened to be available. All these matters, however, remained for the moment in the realm of investigation and no decisions could be taken until the results of preliminary trials were known.

One measure that could be quickly implemented, however, was the bombing of the Condor base and on the night of 22/23 November a sizeable force from Bomber Command set out to attack Bordeaux-Merignac. Of the forty-three crews detailed in eighteen Wellingtons, eleven Whitleys and fourteen Hampdens – thirty claimed to have dropped their high-explosive and incendiary bombs in the target area, and they reported explosions and fires amongst hangars and buildings. But although German accounts confirm that the raid did considerable damage, further raids were less successful and the activities of the Condors were never interrupted for long.

While the air marshals continued to pursue the idea of the expendable fighter with optimism – 'Bert' Harris, Deputy Chief of the Air Staff, and Wilfred Freeman, Vice-Chief, among them – the admirals on the whole were not enthusiastic. They still preferred to see the strengthening of Coastal Command. Churchill agreed with the air marshals. 'The eight-gun fighter,' he wrote, 'will be a powerful deterrent.' Yet it was the Admiralty who were the first to take action operationally. They ordered HMS *Pegasus*, a former seaplane carrier that was being used as a catapult training ship, to sail on 9 December with the next outward bound convoy, carrying two Fulmars for catapulting. Tom Phillips thought little of their chances because of their speed limitations, but believed it was the best that could be done at short notice.

The priority the Admiralty were giving the problem, however, did not satisfy Churchill. 'What have you done,' he demanded of Pound on 27 December, 'about catapulting expendable aircraft from ships?' Three days later, on 30 December, a final decision was taken – although still only in principle – to fit out an unspecified number of merchant vessels for the catapulting of one or more unspecified types of aircraft. They were to be known as Catapult Aircraft Merchant Ships, or Camships, and their numbers were to depend on trials and an operational experience. These Camships were to sail as an integral part of convoys; they would fly the Red Ensign, and they would carry normal freight. Since they would be in the danger zone for no more than a few days at a time, once during the outward journey and once on the return, the watch-keeping was unlikely to be so onerous that one pilot could not cope with it. But where were the vessels to come from? To withdraw freight carriers from convoy service for the fitting of catapults and radar equipment and for training, would impose an unacceptable reduction of working tonnage, so only vessels under construction, big enough to take a 75-foot steel runway mounted over the forecastle head, were to be fitted. This meant a delay of several months before the scheme could start operating.

Meanwhile, as a stopgap, four ships that were being fitted out for service as auxiliary naval vessels were to be adapted for catapult work. These ships, which had been banana boats in peacetime, were the *Ariguani*, the *Maplin*, the *Patia* and the *Springbank*, and they were to be known as Fighter Catapult Ships. Each was to carry two expendable fighters, one hoisted in readiness on a catapult trolley and the other stored as a reserve, with the necessary gantries to hoist it into position. As naval auxiliaries they would fly the White Ensign and form part of the convoy escort; they would not carry freight. They would be employed in the danger zone only, accompanying convoys to the western limit before returning with incoming convoys. With approximately seventeen days of concentrated watch-keeping in prospect, and a spare aircraft, they would need three pilots to cope.

While the British sought to improvise an antidote to the Condor, the Germans aimed to capitalise on a weapon that was itself an improvisation. Before the war the Focke-Wulf Condor, designed by the firm's technical director Kurt Tank, had broken many records on the commercial air routes and had gone into service with Lufthansa and Danish Air Lines. An order from Japan early in 1939 had stimulated design work on a reconnaissance version and this proved useful when, on the outbreak of war, Germany found herself lacking any long-range reconnaissance aircraft. Göring, urged by Udet, had cancelled production of a projected long-range bomber, and Hitler, believing that he could avoid war with Britain, had trusted to the blitzkrieg for a quick and easy victory. The only suitable aircraft on the drawing board was the Heinkel 177, but it was nowhere near production. The Luftwaffe thus found itself obliged to look for a suitable aircraft to fill the gap. It was Edgar Petersen, formerly Director of the Instrument Flying School at Celle and a flyer with much long-range peacetime experience, who suggested the Condor. Some progress had already been made with the training of crews. With the increasing risk of war against Britain if Poland were invaded, an investigation was ordered in the spring of 1939 which revealed that all combat units lacked experience of flying over water and a special course was established at Oldenburg to which Petersen was appointed Director. Then on 1 August 1939, with the formation of the new *Fliegerkorps X*, Petersen was transferred to its staff.

Summoned soon afterwards to General Hans Jeschonnek, the *Luftwaffe* Chief of Staff, Petersen was ordered to prepare proposals for the formation of a long-range unit for attacking marine targets in the Atlantic. An examination of available types showed Petersen that the FW 200 alone had sufficient potential range and he submitted his proposals accordingly. Jeschonnek approved, the Focke-Wulf company were duly asked to produce a military version and ten machines were ordered. Four of these were earmarked for transport work, but the remaining six were fitted with defensive armament and bomb-racks. Auxiliary fuel tanks built into the fuselage increased their maximum range to over 2,000 miles. To prepare for the delivery of these six modified Condors (or Kuriers, as the military version was called, though the name Condor soon reasserted itself), a *Staffel* was formed under Petersen at Bremen on 1 October.

Petersen was careful to choose pilots who were expert in blind flying and navigators who had specialised knowledge of astro navigation. Most of them had served as instructors at the instrument flying schools and the *Staffel* soon developed the discipline and charisma of an elite corps.

While the Condors underwent conversion, the crews passed the winter in training flights over the North and Baltic Seas. Then in the spring of 1940 the unit was redesignated I./KG 40 and began operations, flying armed reconnaissance in support of the German invasion of Norway and bombing sorties against British shipping engaged in the campaign. Following the Allied debacle the unit was expanded into two *Staffeln*, redesignated I.*Gruppe* KG 40, and re-equipped with an improved mark of Condor, the 200 C–1, which differed from its predecessor principally in that the ventral, or belly, gondola was considerably lengthened, allowing a 20-millimetre cannon to be fitted to the forward section to silence the guns of target vessels, firing forward and down. The ventral armament was completed by a 7.9-millimetre machine-gun in the rear of the gondola, firing aft and down. The dorsal armament consisted of a 7.9-millimetre machine-gun in a forward turret, with an all-round field of fire, and a similar weapon to the rear. The four BMW engines, as in the earlier version, each developed 850 hp, and they could lift five or six 250 kg (551 lb) bombs and a crew of five. These consisted of pilot, co-pilot, navigator (who also served as radio-operator, bomb-aimer and gunner), engineer-gunner, and rear dorsal gunner. The economical cruising speed was approximately 180 mph and the radius of action with a full bomb-load about 1,100 miles.

Early in July, following the fall of France, the transfer of the new *Gruppe* to a newly acquired airfield at Bordeaux-Merignac was begun; but its true metier was still not fully understood, except perhaps by Petersen. The first phase of the Battle of Britain had started and it was perhaps inevitable that KG 40 should be thrown into the fray. With two big aerial mines suspended externally, the Condor crews, operating in darkness, began a mine-laying campaign against Britain's east coast ports; but, thus handicapped, the Condors suffered disastrously in speed and stability and became too vulnerable a target for the ground defences. When two Condors were lost on mine-laying operations on the night of 19/20 July, Petersen urged that such operations be discontinued. Unable to get permission through the 'usual channels', he bypassed them and appealed by telephone direct to Jeschonnek. 'This wasteful business of mining will have to stop,' he told Jeschonnek. 'Otherwise we shall lose all our planes and crews.' Although taken aback at Petersen's outburst, Jeschonnek knew his man and agreed. (The two men had served together in the secret air force in Russia in 1929.) Petersen went on to urge that the *Gruppe* be allowed to begin the work for which it was formed, equipped and trained, and Jeschonnek was sympathetic. But with the Battle of Britain rapidly approaching its climax, the *Gruppe* was next recruited into the night bombing of Britain's cities and missions were flown to the Liverpool-Birkenhead area on four successive nights in August. By this time, however, the Condors had begun operating against Allied merchant shipping, mostly in the North Atlantic, and they soon began to enjoy spectacular success. Co-operating with *Marine Gruppe West* at Lorient, the Condors took off singly from Bordeaux in the early morning and flew out across the Bay of Biscay as far as 24 degrees west before describing a right-hand semi-circle that took them north of Scotland on their way to a landing in Norway, returning by the same route two days later. Any convoys cut by this huge arc thus came under surveillance and single ships and stragglers were attacked on sight.

Lacking any sophisticated form of bomb-sight, the Condor crews attacked their targets visually from abeam at low level, diving down to masthead height, where the guns of escort vessels were powerless to interfere. 'You could hardly miss,' says Petersen. 'Even without a bomb-sight at least one of the bombs would find the ship provided you kept low enough.' Some pilots, learning from experience that what little armament the merchant ships themselves carried was invariably mounted astern, directed their bombing runs along the length of vessels from the bow, pulling up steeply after they had dropped their bombs to avoid collision with masts. It was in this period, from late August to mid-November 1940, that the Condors sank nearly 90,000 tons of Allied shipping, and damaged a good deal more. These were the sinkings that first stimulated the search for a counter-measure by the British naval and air staffs. But they did not satisfy Petersen. Despite well-earned awards of the Knight's Cross to pilots like Captains Fliegel and Daser and Lieutenants Verlohr and Buchholz, as well as to Jope and himself, and despite the posting-in of the cream of the bomber training schools, Petersen could not contain his frustration. At just about the time that Stevenson was warning Portal that an intensification of the Condor threat must be anticipated, Petersen was appealing to Hitler for a dramatic increase in Condor production. 'If I had enough aircraft to send out between forty and fifty a day,' he is reported to have said, 'the blockade of England could be really effective.' Clearly Petersen was not given to over-statement, a characteristic which may have told against him in Nazi Germany. Anyway, for the moment at least, he was no more successful in his pleadings than Stevenson had been. Throughout 1940 only thirty-six Condors were built and although an improved variant – the 200 C-3, incorporating four 1,000 hp Bramo-Fafnir radial engines and other refinements – was in preparation, production was still limited to four or five machines a month. Indeed throughout the winter of 1940/41 the *Gruppe* continued to operate two *Staffeln* on about fifteen aircraft, of which rarely more than eight were serviceable at any one time.[1]

This problem of serviceability, which was to dog the Condor for many months, was directly traceable to the haste with which the military version had been adapted from the commercial. The basic structure of the Condor, as has been noted, was not designed to meet the demands of continuous operational flying, and the chosen methods of attack, often involving violent evasive manoeuvres at low level, imposed too great a strain. The most frequent faults were that the rear spar failed and the fuselage aft of the trailing edge of the wing cracked. Despite these drawbacks, however, the two Condor *Staffeln*, backed up by one small factory with an output of little more than one aircraft a week, continued to sink ships and exert an influence on the sea war out of all proportion to their size. The short-term measures taken against them proved inadequate, further bombing raids on their bases found defences strengthened and dispersal effective and the expendable fighter, coupled with strong defensive armament on all merchant ships, seemed the only hope of relief.

This relief, though, was still a long way off and meanwhile the Naval Air Division of the Admiralty put forward an imaginative proposal to erect dummy aircraft on selected ships on a simulated catapult. The Intelligence Division would then spread a rumour that merchant ships were being equipped with fighters and it might be some time before the bluff was called, providing a deterrent effect meanwhile. Objections were that the deception would be so obvious at the ports of embarkation that the enemy would soon get to know the truth and that even if the ruse didn't fail completely it might only attract Condor attack. But with real fighters and real catapults in prospect, the enemy might well

---

[1] The nominal strength of a Staffeln was nine aircraft. The nominal strength of a Gruppe was three Staffeln.

guess wrong at a later date. Five old Fokker seaplanes and two dummy biplanes were sent to Liverpool and Glasgow, but only two had been fitted when, in June 1941, the idea lapsed on the introduction of the first Camships. It was, however, resuscitated later on the Russian convoys.

The need for fighters at least equal in performance to the Hurricane was underlined on 11 January when a *Fulmar* was catapulted from *Pegasus* to attempt an interception. This launching, the first of the so-called expendable fighters, took place 250 miles off the Irish Coast and the pilot was able to reach land, so it lacked an essential element; but there were important lessons to be learnt from it. The ship being attacked was five miles distant from *Pegasus* on the port beam, clearly visible, and although the Fulmar got off quickly the ship was bombed and hit and the Condor pilot already heading for the sanctuary of cloud when the Fulmar began the chase. Indeed the cloud conditions were such that a launching would hardly have been ordered had the pilot not been within reach of land. In the short pursuit that developed, the Fulmar was exposed as far too slow. The Fulmar pilot, Petty Officer F.J. Shaw, landed safely at Aldergrove in Northern Ireland.

By this time the Condors were finding it more profitable to head out into the Atlantic to a point about 25 degrees west, carry out a two-hour search, and return to Bordeaux, rather than continue to Norway; and their tactics paid off so well that forty-three ships suffered attack by Condor in the first two months of 1941, of which twenty-six were sunk. The worst day of all was 9 February, when five Condors led by Captain Fritz Fliegel sank five freighters in the same convoy, 400 miles south-west of Lisbon and over a thousand miles from Bordeaux. The Condor crews were claiming 363,000 tons of Allied shipping sunk to date, eighty-five ships in all. Nineteen of these were sunk in February alone. The British knew only too well that, unlike some of the bragging of the Nazi leaders, the claims of the Condor crews were soundly based.

In these early months of 1941, sorties by German surface raiders, among them the battle-cruisers *Scharnhorst* and *Gneisenau* and the cruiser *Hipper*, wrought further destruction, while the U-boats, which as in 1914 had begun the war underprepared, were known to be building up for a decisive campaign. On 30 January Hitler boasted that a combination of sea and air power would soon encompass Britain's starvation and surrender. 'In the spring,' he promised, 'our U-boat war will begin at sea and they will notice that we have not been sleeping. And the Air Force will play its part.'

Early in March 1941 the *Luftwaffe* established a new anti-shipping command under *Fliegerführer Atlantik*, with a headquarters near the U-boat base at Lorient. Its task was to direct air operations against Allied shipping in the Atlantic in close co-operation with the C-in-C Submarine Fleet. Up to this time it had been rare for Condors to shadow convoys in order to call up U-boats, but now the arrival of a Condor often presaged attack by U-boat. Churchill's reaction was typical. 'We have got to lift this business to the highest plane, over and above everything else,' he told Pound. Nine months earlier, on 18 June 1940, he had heralded the Battle of Britain. Now he proclaimed the Battle of the Atlantic.

In view of various German statements [he announced in a historic directive of 6 March 1941], *we must assume that the Battle of the Atlantic has begun…We must take the offensive against the U-boat and the Focke-Wulf wherever and whenever we can. The U-boat at sea must be hunted, the U-boat in the building yard or in dock must be bombed. The Focke-Wulf and other bombers employed against our shipping must be attacked in the air and in their nests.*

Extreme priority will be given to fitting out ships to catapult or otherwise launch fighter aircraft against bombers attacking our shipping. Proposals should be made within a week…

Preparations for the employment of the expendable fighter after nearly four months of uncertainty and delay, were at last given the impetus that was needed. Within three months of this directive, four Fighter Catapult Ships were operating and the first of the new Camships was about to sail.

II
Frustration and Failure

Long before any Naval or RAF pilot came anywhere near to getting his feet wet, the admirals and the air marshals and even Churchill himself were suffering from a different form of discomfort – *cold* feet. Had they, under the pressure of events, made an error of judgement? Was the Camship an economic use of resources? Visions of a fleet of 200 such ships – the number suggested – crossing and re-crossing the Atlantic, Hurricanes at the ready, might or might not frighten the enemy; but they certainly posed frightening problems of supply. Allowing for a reserve in Canada to replenish any Hurricanes launched or damaged on the outward voyage, how many pilots, aircraft, and not least Merlin engines, would this absorb? Churchill eventually decided that the figure was unrealistic and he reduced it to fifty, then later to thirty-five. The scheme was an experiment, and any further expansion must await results. Even then the doubts persisted.

The intention was that the first Camships should be employed between eastern Canadian ports and the west coast ports of Britain, thus ensuring the quickest turn round while keeping them in the danger zone for as long as possible. The Fighter Catapult Ships, it was thought, would be employed on the Gibraltar run. Since it was mandatory that Camships should have a minimum distance of eighty-five feet between bow and foremast, the ships selected consisted almost entirely of large freight carriers of up to 9,000 tons. The freight carrying would remain of equal importance and the fitting of catapults was so arranged as to cause minimum interference with cargo capacity.

Even with maximum utilisation, however, it was calculated that, allowing for periods for repairs and for loading, training and leave, Camships and their pilots and crews were unlikely to spend more than thirty days a year in the areas where protection from air attack was needed. Wouldn't it be better, it was asked, to arm a smaller number of these vessels purely as antiaircraft ships and earmark them for escort duties only, greatly increasing their effective operational cover? But the combination of the protection of a Hurricane fighter and the retention of importing capacity was held to justify the allocation of pilots and crews. Churchill was sceptical of the claim that importing capacity would not be reduced and he suggested a compromise in which the first ten Camships should be made available for continuous patrolling in the danger area. From experience with these, a decision could be taken on the remainder. But the Admiralty stood firm. 'We recommend adherence to the original plan.'

Trials with the Hurricane, and with the rocket-propelled catapult, had meanwhile been satisfactorily completed, at least on land, and by the end of March sixty Hurricane Mark Is, with Merlin III engines, had been allocated for use in the new role. Orders had meanwhile been given to fit the ships with the rocket catapults and to begin modifying the planes, which soon became known as Hurricats. Much as he regretted the diversion of aircraft and pilots from his squadrons, Sholto Douglas, the C-in-C Fighter Command, did not resist it. He judged – rightly – that by co-operating he would keep the organisation in his own hands. Some decentralisation, however, was necessary and he formed a new unit to act as parent station for controlling aircraft and crews. A new Fighter Command group, No. 9, situated near the headquarters of the C-in-C Western Approaches in Liverpool, was well placed to study the requirements of the new unit, advise on tactics, and help train and administer personnel. This group was already in constant touch with the local naval authorities, Liverpool would probably be the main port of embarkation for the Hurricanes and a maintenance unit and a fighter sector station were already operating there. The new unit, to be named the Merchant Ship Fighter Unit (MSFU), was set up at the old Liverpool civil airport at Speke on the Mersey, with a regular officer, Wing Commander E.S. Moulton-Barrett, to command. The unit establishment included a headquarters and a practice flying flight, two mobile loading parties, and thirty-five ship detachments. The Hurricanes were made available for conversion from early May.

Although the Navy had accepted the task of manning the Fighter Catapult Ships as an emergency measure, they did not have the resources to provide pilots or maintenance crews for the Camships and this responsibility fell to the RAF. The ground detachments, known as the sea crew, consisted of a fitter, a rigger, a radio-telephone operator and an armourer. The Navy did agree, however, to provide the fighter direction officers – the men who would direct the pilots on to their targets and home them back to the convoy after combat – also the radar operators and the seamen-torpedomen who would service the catapults. Completing this embryo example of combined operations were the Army volunteers who manned the anti-aircraft guns. The Camship crews, of course, were merchant seamen.

The fighter direction officers (FDOs) were already being recruited when, in mid-March, a conference was held at the Air Ministry to discuss the provision of pilots. What special qualities would be demanded? Pilots, it was envisaged, would be in command of a small specialised team in whose efficiency they would have a strong vested interest; this, it was thought, ought to be enough to ensure responsible leadership. They must be experienced operational pilots, capable of performing well and aggressively after long periods of inactivity. In order to have some sort of status in the ship's hierarchy, they should be officers. It was not the sort of job that every pilot, however skilled, would be fitted for; therefore they should be volunteers. It went without saying – almost – that these paragons of fighter-boy virtue must be first and foremost good sailors.

On 2 May 1941 Fighter Command issued a circular to all their groups and stations advertising for 'officer volunteers who must be fully operational pilots'. A brief description of the work was given. 'Once released, the fighter cannot return to the ship, and the pilot must alight in the sea unless he is within range of land.' What would persuade established fighter pilots, privileged to enjoy the most exciting and glamorous flying in the RAF, to apply for such hazardous and uncertain work?

There were, of course, many reasons. Some people are natural volunteers. To them it was a challenge they had to answer. Some, preferring the exercise of self-discipline to the restrictions of squadron routine, saw an opportunity to be more their own master, in an occupation where a streak of youthful irresponsibility might find expression. Some NCO pilots, foreseeing a shortage of officer volunteers, seized the chance of a short cut to a commission. Many joined just for the hell of it. Others were merely bored or unhappy where they were.

If there was a sense of anti-climax in Fighter Command after the Battle of Britain, there were plenty of dedicated characters out to dispel it. Fighter sweeps over the Channel and over occupied France were an exhilarating form of aggression, designed to bring a reluctant enemy to combat; but fundamentally they amounted to little more than going out looking for trouble. Those who were motivated by impatience to strike at the enemy enjoyed it; others didn't find it much fun. Most of the men who volunteered for MSFU had joined up for the duration and, although in 1941 it was too early to let the mind dwell on thoughts of surviving the war, they couldn't work up much enthusiasm for getting 'chopped' on one of these parties over France. At least in the catapult fighters they would be going out in a blaze of glory, doing what they felt was a vital job. In the back of some minds, too, was the glittering attraction, in those days of austerity, blackout and blitz, of the bright lights of New York. To cross the Atlantic meant to get to Canada at the very least and, if one played one's cards right, to America too. It is difficult to imagine how infinitely desirable the glamour of a great American city seemed to a young Englishman then.

By contrast, the Fleet Air Arm pilots in the Fighter Catapult Ships were given no choice. They were transferred to 804 Squadron at Sydenham, Belfast – the supply squadron whose task it was to man the planes – on a normal posting. There was no question of asking for volunteers – not, presumably, because it was feared that they might not be forthcoming, but because the prospect of being launched in mid-ocean with no hope of dry return was not expected to daunt members of the Senior Service. Similarly, fighter direction officers for the Camships were selected arbitrarily on a normal posting.

Few of the FDOs had any experience of aircraft interception, but they were trained in radar plotting and fighter control at the Fighter Command Controllers' School at Clamp Hill, Stanmore and at the Naval Air Station at Yeovilton. At Stanmore they took turns to play fighter pilot, Condor pilot, and FDO, riding heavily blinkered round the centre of the spacious lawn of a local mansion in the saddle of a Wall's Ice Cream tricycle, specially fitted with voice radio (R/T), and with a metronome for synchronising pedal speed, while another similar tricycle, cast as the dreaded Condor, powered in on fast metronome from the perimeter to attack the supposed convoy, and a third trainee, safely above the battle, vectored one tricycle on to the other, with all the Fighter Command R/T procedure being employed from 'Bandit' to 'Tally-ho!' With an experienced broadcaster named Ernest Lush to teach them microphone technique, they thus familiarised themselves with their new trade.

Whereas the hydraulic catapult launched pilots at a modest 2.5G, the rocket catapult approached 3.5G and was 'a much more physical experience' both for the pilot and for those left behind on ship or shore. There was a deafening sibilance and a blinding coruscation of light and the area behind the rockets had to be protected against fire and blast, while everyone in an exposed position took cover. For the pilot, the acceleration was such that he needed to force his skull back against a heavily padded head rest to absorb the jerk that might otherwise injure his neck; and a slight impairment of vision and faculties was generally noticeable. Most pilots found their first launching a novel and slightly alarming experience. Also the Hurricane, with its directional swing to the left, and its known longitudinal instability at slow speeds, presented undoubted problems for catapulting. The drill was to use one-third starboard rudder and one-third flap, keep the elevator and trimming tabs central, and jam the right elbow into the hip so that the hand on the stick didn't pull back as the plane shot forward. The Hurricane showed a tendency to sink when launched into a light wind and most pilots noticed a slight drop. But although the catapult platform used on the ground had only six feet or so of clearance, any easing back on the stick as the plane left the rail had to be gentle in the extreme. The margin above the stall at this point could be narrow and the temptation to haul back on the stick had to be resisted. With a fully loaded aircraft under operational conditions, there was a real danger of losing flying speed and stalling into the sea. The tendency to sink on leaving the catapult rail was not expected to be such a problem at sea, where there was a clearance of up to 40 feet available beyond the bows. But in training it was better to risk brushing the ground with the wheels (which were kept extended for ground launchings), than to develop habits which might have unpleasant consequences later. Immediately after the initial drop the Hurricane climbed away strongly.

After the shock and surprise of the initial launch, most pilots took the process in their stride. But due to variations in pilot reaction and skill, the speed and characteristics of individual aircraft, fluctuations in wind speed and direction, and the conditions of lift, no two launchings were exactly alike. For most pilots, every launching held its own moment of truth.

The early training was done in Fulmars at the Experimental Catapult Flight of the Royal Aircraft Establishment at Farnborough, where the man in charge of the launching pad, Mr Charles Crowfoot, brought a touch of incongruity by discharging his duties in a bowler hat. But the distance to travel from MSFU and the restriction to Fulmars was unsatisfactory, so on 6 July a rocket catapult was erected at Speke. There a squadron leader named Louis Strange, forty-nine years old and holding the DSO, MC and DFC from the First World War, took charge of catapult work. At first he had the assistance of the bowler-hatted Mr Crowfoot. Strange was an outstanding character, very much admired by the young men of MSFU. One of the first flying 'aces' of the First World War, he had survived a bizarre incident when changing the ammunition drum on the Lewis gun of his single-seater Martinsyde scout. Steadying the control stick between his knees, he had been using both hands to change the drum, which had jammed, when he lost control and the Martinsyde whipped over on its back. The jerk snapped the seat harness, which was slightly loose, and Strange fell out of the cockpit, still gripping the jammed drum. Had the drum, with the perversity of mechanical things, now come adrift, he would have fallen to his death. But it stayed jammed. Eventually Strange succeeded in freeing his legs, which were caught up in the broken harness, and reaching the control stick with his feet. Somehow he righted the machine, then slid back into the seat.

At the start of the Second World War he had achieved a feat almost as remarkable, flying an abandoned and unarmed Hurricane out of a French airfield under the noses of the advancing German Army, with no previous experience of high-speed aircraft. Driving off enemy fighters by a series of mock attacks, he had brought the Hurricane safely back to Britain. For this exploit he had been awarded a bar to his DFC. Before being posted to MSFU, Strange had set up the first RAF parachute training school at Ringway and the story of his methods there had preceded him to Speke. He had done the first few jumps himself, from Whitley bombers, to show his pupils how it was done and he adopted a similar policy at Speke. To the youngsters of MSFU, this slightly grizzled Great War hero looked positively elderly; but they soon fell under his spell.

Two months short of his fiftieth birthday, in the first launching to take place from Speke, Strange was rocketed off in a Hurricane. 'If an old boy like me can do it,' he told the assembled pilots, 'it won't mean a thing to lads like you.' The launching, according to one account, was a great occasion which was witnessed by everyone who could possibly attend. Squadron Leader Strange did a magnificent launch in which the blast screen suffered severely, being partially stripped of its metal facing, the woodwork being set on fire and the whole being left in a shaky condition. After this exhibition of what the firing of the catapult could do in the way of blast the screen was greatly strengthened. Unlike many men less than half his age, Strange suffered no momentary blackout. 'In the rush down the runway, I realised everything but was powerless to act, until automatically I found myself quite normally at the controls.' His experience was not untypical, though, as one of his pupils, Harry Ball-Wilson, remembers: 'I could feel the G distorting my face, forcing the jowls of my cheeks back against the bone. Next thing I knew I was 200 feet over the Mersey! 'How did you like it?' asked Strange afterwards. 'Marvellous. They should put one of those things on every aerodrome. Save a lot of taxying.' Nevertheless he declined Strange's invitation to have another go right away. His description of the launching – 'Flash – and I was 200 feet over the Mersey' – earned him the nickname of 'Flash Harry'.

The mature Strange warned pilots and FDOs not to crew up together too casually, but to get to know each other first over a few drinks in the relaxed atmosphere of the Mess. Thrown together in close proximity for weeks and even months on end and depending on each other for much more than a few minutes of highly charged operational excitement, they needed to find a basis of compatibility. It was sound advice, and workable friendships were soon formed.

The training syllabus at Speke covered an understanding of the work of KG 40 and a study of the armament and capabilities of the Condor, so that pilots could anticipate the likely evasive tactics the Condor crews would adopt. In a surprise attack, even below 500 feet, the Hurricane was expected to have a decided speed advantage. But if the Condor pilot knew his approach had been seen, he was expected to climb if cloud cover was available and to dive down to sea level if not. The latter manoeuvre was in practice much the more likely as the Hurricane would not normally be sent off into a lowering, overcast sky. 'Once a Focke-Wulf is down to sea level,' wrote Squadron Leader D.E. Gillam, a distinguished Battle of Britain pilot then working on air tactics at Fighter Command Headquarters, 'destruction becomes much more difficult.' The chief aim must always be to kill the pilot; at low level the Condor would probably strike the sea before the second pilot could take over. This meant head-on attack; but if that proved impossible through lack of speed, a beam attack would have to be made. The aim should be to kill pilot and crew. To stop the engines might be good enough, but there were four of them. It was fairly certain, thought Gillam, that the Condor pilot would turn in towards any threatened beam attack and this should be allowed for in the approach. The breakaway should be erratic and at sea level until out of range. A stern attack should be avoided at all costs on account of the heavy armour and armament aft.

Included in the pilots' training programme were such elementary subjects as air firing, cross-country navigation, and aircraft recognition; pilots were liable to meet a wide variety of machines from the Coastal squadrons and might even sight aircraft being flown across from Canada under the Atlantic Ferry Organisation. They were also given special instructions in dinghy drill and survival at sea.

All previous experience with fighters alighting in the sea had shown that such aircraft tended to go straight to the bottom and the Hurricane, with its huge air scoop under the fuselage, had the worst reputation of all. As soon as the scoop churned into the sea the machine turned over on its back. So the recommended escape drill was to leave the aircraft at about 2,000 feet by inverting it and falling out, rigging it slightly tail heavy and pointing it away from the convoy so as not to be a danger, and judging the moment so as to land as close as possible ahead of the selected escort vessel. While the vessel was steaming towards him, the pilot would get into his 'K'-type dinghy, the one-man dinghy attached to the parachute which by this time had been introduced into Fighter Command. If for some reason a pilot was forced to ditch, he was recommended to alight with straps tight and hood open, as slowly as possible but with engine on so as to make the tail touch first.

Control and homing practice for FDOs, maintenance at sea for airmen (with special attention to preventive and remedial measures against corrosion) and catapult maintenance for naval ratings, were other matters in which pilots had a vested interest. Finally, on completion of training, individual teams were despatched to the ports of embarkation – generally Liverpool or Glasgow, but sometimes Cardiff or Avonmouth – where they assisted in the loading of their aircraft. For Glasgow, pilots flew their machines to Abbotsinch, near Paisley, where the wings were removed, transfer to the docks being effected by means of a motorised transporter. The machines were then reassembled at the dockside and lifted by crane on to the catapult trolley. Many pilots, obliged to sit in their cockpits during the lift in order to raise the landing gear before the aircraft could be lowered on to the trolley, found this and the moment when they climbed out of the cockpit and stared at the drop below, the most frightening experience of all.

Although the Camships were to carry radar, it was realised from the start that it would be absurd to launch the Hurricane on a radar plot alone, however menacing. Once release was effected, protection was short-lived and the deterrent effect too was gone. Thus the FDO's principal role was likely to be homing the pilot after combat; but he was no less valued for that. The breakdown of responsibility on board ship was inevitably a complex one. The MSFU crews signed ship's articles, either as supernumerary officers or as deck-hands, according to rank, and they thus came under the jurisdiction of the master; for stops in neutral ports they were issued with civilian papers and wore civilian clothes. The chief engineer was responsible for the serviceability of the catapult and the mate did the actual firing (unless a relief pilot was available), from a blast shelter or firing hut forward. Thus when it came to the launch, four men had to signify their agreement:

1 The decision to launch was the responsibility of the master.
2 The decision whether conditions were fit for flying was the responsibility of the pilot.
3 The approximate timing of the launch was the responsibility of the FDO.
4 The launching of the aircraft on an upward scend, sometimes on a signal from the pilot, was the responsibility of the catapult firing officer (CFO).

The senior officer of the escort, too, or the commodore of the convoy, with their superior overall picture of the convoy's dangers, might feel they ought to have some say in the matter. The chain of command, as might be expected, did not always work smoothly.

Throughout the initial training period at Farnborough, involving over sixty launches, there was not a single accident. But these had all been ground launches, most of them on Fulmars, and it remained to be seen how pilots would cope with a ship-board launching in a Hurricane. The rocket take-off gear, too, was entirely untried at sea and no one knew how the rockets would react or what would happen if one or more of the rockets misfired.

The first pilot to leave Speke with an MSFU crew for operational trials in a Camship was Pilot Officer H.J. Davidson. A cheerful self-reliant young man from a Lancashire mill town, he was of practical bent and was keen to get on with the job. Although he was the first pilot to be posted to the unit, he had never been rocketed in a Hurricane before, either on land or afloat. Joining the S.S. *Empire Rainbow* at Greenock on the Clyde on 31 May 1941, he was hoisted on to the catapult trolley, the rockets were placed in position and the circuits were tested. Then the ship weighed anchor and steamed downriver at 10 knots into a 2-knot breeze. On the bridge, at the catapult, and in the firing hut, all the recommended preliminaries were punctiliously followed and with a startling eruption of pyrotechnics and blast the Hurricane rocketed on its trolley along the rail. Watching from the starboard side of the bridge, clear of the blow-back (the rail ran very slightly across the fore and aft axis of the ship, from port to starboard), two staff officers who had come to observe this seaborne initiation, and to record every detail of it with the aid of notebooks and stopwatches, were dismayed to see the Hurricane drop its port wing beneath the bows of the ship and lurch into a staggering turn to the left.

When they next caught sight of the Hurricane it was right down low on the water, a hundred yards ahead of the ship. They saw its port wing touch the water, winced at the splash and shared Davidson's desperation as he battled with the controls. It was not until the Hurricane reached full flying speed and was climbing away at right angles to the ship that they remembered their notebooks and stopwatches. Was there something inherent in a rocket launching at sea that had been overlooked? On consideration it did not seem so. For some reason only eleven of the thirteen rockets had fired, while in the nervous excitement of the moment Davidson had forgotten to wind on the recommended 30 degrees of flap, thus reducing the lift, or to make any rudder correction to prevent the swing to port. The observers noticed, too, that the cover plate of the rocket stowage had blown off and had struck the tail-wheel during the launching, which might have had a retarding effect. These faults, it was thought, had combined to cause the aircraft to take off in a stalled condition. The damage done was not serious, however, and Davidson landed safely at Abbotsinch.

A test pilot from Farnborough – Squadron Leader H.J. Wilson CO of the Experimental Catapult Flight – flew up to the Clyde to test the *Empire Rainbow*'s catapult himself. Sceptical of the reasons advanced for the mishap, he found, on running up the Hurricane's engine, that when he removed his hand from the throttle to test the switches, the throttle slipped back to half-way. Part of the launching drill, after the throttle had been fully opened, was for the pilot to raise his left hand – the hand on the throttle lever – to signify that he was ready, then drop it sharply as the signal to the firing officer to rocket him off. Wilson felt that here, rather than in the failure of the two rockets or the omission to use flap, lay the true cause of the mishap. He advanced a plausible reason for Davidson's aberrations: 'Too many cooks standing around with stopwatches made pilot "flap".' He discounted the blow from the cover plate altogether.

Those who witnessed the launch did not agree with Wilson and they continued to believe that the cover plate had had a good deal to do with the trouble. But the tightening of the throttle friction nut was made mandatory in the pre-launch and firing sequence laid down for MSFU crews. In practice, most pilots found it easier to signal to the firing hut, which was forward to their right, with the right hand.

Feeling, perhaps, that Wilson might be right in attributing the pilot's mistakes to the atmosphere they themselves had created, the two staff officers did not report adversely on Davidson and when the *Empire Rainbow*, the first of the regular Camships, sailed for Halifax, Nova Scotia on 8 June 1941, Davidson retained his place as pilot.

A second Camship, the *Empire Moon*, with Pilot Officer A.R.M. Campbell as pilot, sailed soon afterwards for the same destination, and meanwhile two more ships embarked their aircraft and crews and completed their trials prior to being allocated to convoys. By the end of that month there were six Camships at sea.

One volunteer is said to be worth two pressed men; but for the 'conscripts' of the Fleet Air Arm, the posting to 804 Squadron for attachment to the Fighter Catapult Ships was generally welcomed. Because they were operating in the danger zones only, their work was more concentrated and they escaped the tedium of spending days and even weeks outside the danger zone with no prospect of being fired off. They returned more frequently, too, to their base and thus they knew each other better. Whereas the MSFU crews lived and worked amongst merchant seamen under the Red Ensign, the 804 Squadron men enjoyed the reassuring propinquity of the Senior Service and the White Ensign. Whereas MSFU was a collection of colourful individuals struggling to find a corporate identity, the Fleet

Air Arm men drew strength from the abstracts of a squadron image and an *esprit de corps*. Yet the distinction was only one of degree. Like the RAF men they rarely flew together and never as a squadron, and if they were not individualists when they began they soon became so.

One distinction that they did enjoy was being first in the field. When *Empire Rainbow* sailed on 8 June, *Pegasus* had been operating in the Western Approaches for exactly five months, while three of the four banana boats, *Springbank, Ariguani* and *Maplin* in that order, had joined the convoy escorts a month earlier. The fourth boat, *Patia*, had been sunk on the first day of her sea trials, on 27/28 April, in a scrap with an enemy bomber that proved to be a fight to the death. *Patia* put up a tremendous fight and eventually shot down the bomber, but the enemy proved equally resolute, causing fatal damage to the *Patia* before succumbing to return fire. Seven officers and thirty-one ratings on *Patia* were killed.

Neither RAF nor Fleet Air Arm pilots, perhaps, needed this kind of example; but the crews of the *Luftwaffe* were continually providing it. The men of the Condors, however, had soon shown their respect for *Pegasus* by keeping their distance. From the launching of Petty Officer Shaw on 11 January to the sinking of *Patia*, not a single catapulting in anger had taken place.

A fortnight before the loss of *Patia*, the first two Fleet Air Arm detachments left Yeovilton for Sydenham, Belfast, where 804 Squadron was to establish its base. These two parties were earmarked for *Springbank* and *Ariguani*, which like *Pegasus* were to carry Fulmars. Next day, to fulfil another commitment, Sub-Lieutenant M.A. Birrell flew a modified Hurricane I – a Sea Hurricane Mark IA, to use the official nomenclature – to Belfast for installation in the Camship *Michael E*. The modifications were mostly confined to local reinforcement of the airframe to withstand the extra loads imposed by catapult acceleration and the fitting of catapult spools. The *Michael E* was the first of all the Camships, but with no RAF pilot yet trained for the job, the Fleet Air Arm agreed to underwrite this particular voyage and Birrell was chosen. Birrell was one of twenty-five naval pilots who had been lent to the RAF for the Battle of Britain. Trained on Spitfires, he was immediately posted to Biggin Hill on Hurricanes. Within a fortnight, because of squadron losses, he had risen to flight commander, but then the squadron was pulled out of the line and he was posted back to the Navy.

Thus, in May 1941 [he writes], *after we had heard that Churchill urgently required pilots for the first Camship, I found myself, as a twenty-one-year-old acting sub-lieutenant, commanding the flight attached to the steamship* Michael E *destined for New York.*

On 24 April I had catapulted for the first time – from the light naval cordite catapult at Gosport, in a Hurricane at maximum boost. 50 knots end-speed left much to be desired, but my main worry, the tail-plane, stayed on and apart from hitting the ground the take-off was OK. After this I went to Farnborough, was introduced to the 'P'-type catapult, and did one launch in a Fulmar. I was then adjudged ready to join the ship at Belfast.

May I was catapulted in a Hurricane from the Michael E *in Belfast Lough, but only half the rockets fired and disaster seemed certain. Somehow I hauled the aircraft out of the sea and got back to Sydenham. Since our destination was a neutral port I was signed on as fifth mate, and I flew in civilian clothes, with a bowler hat at the ready.*

We sailed on 28 May and joined the convoy, and although there were Condors about they were spotting for U-boats and none came near enough for me to be fired off. My crew consisted of a relief pilot, a fitter, a rigger, a radar controller and a radar technician. Five days after sailing, when we were outside Condor range, we secured the aircraft, and the convoy dispersed. But then the work of the Condors bore fruit: we were torpedoed by a U-boat.

Sunk in the early evening, the survivors were picked up next day. Birrell, together with his crew, came through safely and lived to fight again. Such, though, was the ignominious fate of the first of the Camships.

The Fighter Catapult Ships were meanwhile having no better luck. *Patia*, as related, had been sunk; and on 11 May Sub-Lieutenant F.M.C. Harvey, fired off *Ariguani* in a Fulmar, found his supposed speed advantage totally insufficient in a stern chase. Too far to the north to reach the British Isles, he made for the recommended emergency haven of Kaldardanes in Iceland and got down safely. The Condors, then, were still operating; but the knowledge that the occasional single-engined fighter might be met and that the armament of most merchant ships had been improved, was making the crews more cautious. It was co-operation with the U-boats that they concentrated on now, and in this role they proved elusive.

Two more launchings in early June continued the frustration of the naval pilots, who were still the only men in action. On the 8th Lieutenant B.F. Cox was fired off *Pegasus* in a Fulmar, but all he ever saw after launching were some very stale, dissolving bursts of flak that marked the spot where the Condor had been. The Condor itself had dissolved even more quickly and no one could direct him to it. Hampered by poor radio communication, he made a few despondent circuits of the convoy and then turned to the task of reaching land.

In poor visibility he made a landfall near Malin Head, pinpointed his position, and aimed for the RAF airfield at Limavady, 15 miles west of Londonderry. But low cloud and mist blotted out Limavady and with his radio receiver still crackling unhelpfully he was faced with a problem. If he climbed up through the cloud and headed across country for an alternative airfield, would he be able to descend safely through the cloud when the time came? Checking his gauges, he decided he had enough fuel to coast-crawl all the way round to Belfast Lough, staying under the weather. The first anyone at Sydenham knew of it was when they saw a Fulmar do a split-arse turn overhead and land in a hurry. His fuel had just held out.

A similar experience befell Petty Officer Shaw, the man who had first catapulted off *Pegasus* in January. Now transferred to *Springbank*, but still flying a Fulmar, he was rocketed off at 09.30 on the morning of 10 June 250 miles out in the Atlantic to chase a Condor. Misinterpreting recent orders not to cross over convoys because of the risk of being fired at, he circled briefly instead of going straight for the Condor at full throttle and thus lost valuable seconds. The German pilot naturally made for cloud, and although Shaw chased after him and sprayed him with machine-gun fire from long range, it was a desperate, impotent gesture. He too faced a fuel problem, but he had better luck than Cox with the weather, and he scraped into Aldergrove with five gallons left.

By the end of the first week in July, twenty-five modified Hurricanes had been delivered to MSFU and sixteen Camships had sailed, but opportunities for launching had been nil. Meanwhile 804 Squadron were still making do with Fulmars in all the Fighter Catapult Ships except *Maplin*, which had begun her maiden voyage with three pilots and two Hurricanes on 9 May. The decision to equip *Maplin* with Hurricanes was a thoroughly sensible one and, so far as these ships were concerned, was long overdue. The Fighter Catapult Ships were first in the field and spent longest in the firing line, they should surely have been given the improved type of plane directly it was available. More than one inconclusive stern chase might thereby have been changed into a combat and perhaps a victory.

Whether the newly delivered Sea Hurricanes would really produce the desired improvement, however, was soon questioned, especially amongst the naval pilots. Those with experience of Fighter Command, and those who took enough interest to read their aircraft log books, could hardly fail to realise that their machines were RAF cast-offs. It was true that in most cases the RAF had been flying them operationally right up to the moment of transfer, but some were ex-Battle of Britain aircraft which had been extensively damaged before conversion and even those aircraft that were practically new were often in a lamentable state when they reached General Aircraft Limited at Hanworth Air Park for modification. 'All aircraft received here which have been in service with the RAF,' complained General Aircraft, 'show many signs of neglect and bad maintenance.' This was a serious indictment, but the company backed it with an appalling list of defects. The Air Ministry, sensing the threat to morale, deplored the dubbing of these aircraft as cast-offs, obsolescent as they might be in Fighter Command, and they moved quickly to correct wrong impressions and restore confidence.

Pegasus, still operating Fulmars, fired off Lieutenant T.R.V. 'Cocky' Parke at 07.58 on 7 July and the familiar frustrating chase ensued. This was the fifth unsuccessful firing of a Fulmar, each time exposing pilot and telegraphist/gunner to a situation of considerable hazard, especially when convoys were hundreds of miles out in the Atlantic and the weather was uncertain. Everyone in both convoy and escort, of course, was exposed to hazard; but these were hazards that pilots and their back-up crews shared, as Birrell and others had soon discovered.

Everything was done on the Fighter Catapult Ships, and later on the Camships, to help a pilot find his way back after a launching, either to land or to convoy. While on stand-by he was given hourly positions and distances from land, he had the frequencies and call-signs of all appropriate radio stations and he carried the co-ordinates of all airfields available to him in emergency, running from the Outer Hebrides to Iceland. His weather reports were slanted to focus on the conditions at the airfields he might make for after combat and he was also given a forecast of conditions within a hundred miles of the convoy, in case, after a combat, he had no hope of reaching land.

All these measures were conscientiously applied for the launching of 'Cocky' Parke on 7 July. However, it was an atrocious day, characterised by low cloud, poor visibility and rain. The RAF airfields at Aldergrove and Limavady were both alerted to stand by for a call, but they listened in vain. Wireless reception was poor and Parke's radio may have been faulty, since there is no evidence that he or his telegraphist tried to contact anyone. Some time after midday Parke's zero hour for endurance passed, and it was realised that he must have come down.

There was every hope that he had force-landed somewhere and would be on the telephone soon; but during the afternoon news came through that a Fulmar had flown into high ground south of Campbeltown, on the Mull of Kintyre. Both Parke and his gunner were killed.

The men of the Fighter Catapult Ships, and of the Camships too for that matter, badly needed a victory.

III
Bob Everett and HMS *Maplin*

The best news that came the way of the Fighter Catapult Ships in the spring of 1941 was the decision to equip *Maplin* with two Hurricanes; and after an uneventful first trip she sailed again in mid-July with a convoy outward bound for Halifax, Nova Scotia. This time, with Lieutenant R.W.H. Everett and Sub-Lieutenants C.W. Walker and J.E. Scott as pilots, there was rather more action.

If the RAF pilots tended to be the more aggressively extrovert, there was no more colourful character in either Service than Lieutenant Bob Everett. One might not have guessed it from a casual look; but even that was revealing. He wore a shabby, threadbare uniform the gold braid on which was bleached and muddied a murky yellow. From his wrinkled cap the greying hair sprouted untidily, while the First World War medal ribbons on his tunic accentuated the hint of anachronism. An oddly dry character, his curt manner was sometimes mistaken for rudeness and, when he chose, he could be extremely outspoken. At various times Bob Everett had broken or bruised nearly every bone in his body. But at the age of forty he had kept his ascetic, Gary Cooperish good looks. Six feet tall, he had a slimness of hip and a litheness of leg that suggested the physical adroitness of the matador. A bachelor, he was equally popular in male and female company. Born in Australia, where his father had taken an appointment as an engineer, Everett had entered the naval training school at Osborne as a cadet in 1915 and he spent two years afloat as a midshipman before the end of that war.

Relinquishing his commission in 1920, he farmed in South Africa in a casual way for some years. His abiding passion, stemming from his childhood in Australia, was for riding. 'Almost born on a horse,' according to his brother, he took to riding racehorses in South Africa and when he returned to England in 1927 he began riding under National Hunt rules. On 26 October 1928, after riding his tenth winner, he turned professional. For a steeplechase jockey, then as now, the race of the season was the Grand National; but when it came to engaging jockeys for the fancied runners, the little-known Everett, not surprisingly, was overlooked. 'I wish I could get a decent ride in the National,' was the burden of his talk that spring and to his friend Ted Leader, a top National Hunt jockey, and son of Newmarket trainer Tom Leader, he said: 'I'll ride anything.'

Tom Leader had five horses in the race that year, and one of them, Gregalach, had fallen at Sandown Park the previous week. Although a genuine chaser, he wasn't expected to make much of a show at Aintree and the bookmakers had made him a 100–1 outsider. When the jockey engaged to ride him was hurt in a fall, Ted Leader rang his father. 'I've found you a jockey for Gregalach. Bob Everett. He's sound rather than brilliant, but he's keen. Above all, he's brave.' That was enough for Tom Leader. Thus it was that Bob Everett lined up at the start on Gregalach for the 1929 National with sixty-five other runners, the biggest field ever. But Tom Leader didn't have a bet on the horse himself and neither did anyone in the stable.

The favourite, the top-weight Easter Hero, led from the start and by the Canal Turn second time round he was one of three horses clear of the field. One of these horses fell at the fence after Valentine's, leaving the other two, it seemed, with the race to themselves. But amongst half a dozen horses in a second group a tangerine tunic with black striped sleeves and white cap was beginning to show. Riding a patient race and biding his time, Everett brought Gregalach through two fences from home and easily outpaced the tiring Easter Hero to win by six lengths.

His victory was greeted with stunned silence. What was Gregalach's history? Who was Everett? In the next ten years Bob Everett frequently made the sporting headlines. Sometimes it was through success, as when he won the Irish Grand National in 1934. Sometimes it was through failure, when he broke a limb or a collar-bone in a heavy fall.

In the off-season he turned professional on a different kind of mount. Learning to fly at the old Hanworth Air Park near Feltham, where General Aircraft were later to modify the catapult Hurricanes, he took a blind flying course, got a licence to carry passengers and spent his summers as an air taxi pilot, ferrying charter parties all over Britain and to and from the Continent. There were spills in this game, too, but he survived them. He still made more money steeplechasing than flying.

When the war came he went to Lee on Solent and applied personally to join the Fleet Air Arm, succeeding in getting himself recalled for full flying duties, and on 18 April 1941 he was posted to 804 Squadron. Then came the attachment to *Maplin*.

The 8,000-ton *Maplin*, filled with empty fuel drums for buoyancy, and painted a pale strawberry pink for camouflage, carried one Hurricane on the catapult at bridge height forward of the mast and a second Hurricane stowed immediately forward of the bridge in No. 2 Hatch, ready to be hoisted into position when needed. A diary, kept illicitly by John Scott, one of the three pilots, gives details of *Maplin's* escort task that July.

Thursday 17 July. *Was called at five this morning for my early watch. I handed over to Bob at 6.30 and retired to bed again without undressing. I'd just started breakfast when the flap started. A large unidentified aircraft appeared flying low, later identified as a Whitley with one motor out of action. After flashing 'SOS' for a bit this aircraft sank lower and lower till it finally stalled a wing just above the water and pancaked into the drink. The crew all appeared to get away in their dinghy and were picked up by a corvette. Later we discovered that this Whitley had had an engagement with a Condor about twenty miles away and had come off worse. We did not see the Condor from Maplin*

Friday 18 July. A day of tremendous excitements, all too much in so short a space of time. To begin with, yesterday evening when we thought all activities were over for the day, two unidentified aircraft appeared during Walker's watch. These were later identified as Condors. They did not come any closer than fifteen miles but hovered about just below the cloud base. They disappeared just before I took over my watch.

Today, however, things really began to happen. While I was having my breakfast and Bob was in the aircraft, a Condor arrived and started to circle the convoy at much closer range. We were tempted to fire off, but restrained ourselves since he didn't attack. He continued to circle the convoy at varying stages for about an hour before retiring in a southerly direction. We had scarcely lost sight of him in the distance when there was a tremendous rumpus aft, where they had spotted another Condor at sea level, approaching the convoy point blank and already close in. We immediately fired Bob off in the Hurricane, but before he had time to turn round and close with the Condor, it had dropped a stick of bombs across another ship and set the bridge on fire.

It was 09.40 when Everett was catapulted off, and although his launching was directly away from the Condor, he soon swung round and got into position for a head-on attack. Lining up his sights, and with the distance closing rapidly, he was about to open fire when he blinked in amazement as a segment of the Condor's starboard wing came slowly adrift and spiralled down. For the gunners on board the *Norman Prince*, who had scored the hit, and indeed for the entire convoy, it was a moment of great jubilation. After the appalling losses that merchant seamen had suffered at the hands of the Condors here at last was revenge and according to Scott the cheering was audible for miles. For Everett, though, it was a moment of strange disappointment, compounded by the fact that he found himself under fire from his own side. 'Some damned fools opened fire on Bob,' was Scott's comment in his diary. Fortunately they weren't such good shots as the men on the *Norman Prince*.

For the crew of the Condor, however, it was the end. The plane rolled over on its back and dived inverted into the sea, and no survivors were found. Circling the spot where the Condor had gone in, Everett was still half-bemused by the turn events had taken. Scott, calling him up on the voice radio, learned that he had decided to make for Lough Erne, inland from Donegal Bay, a distance of 300 miles. With the combat thus truncated he had plenty of fuel and he landed safely at St Angelo, on the shores of the Lough, at 11.37, having been airborne just under two hours.

There were casualties on the bombed ship, but the fire on the bridge was quickly put out. There was a casualty, too, on *Maplin*, when during the hoisting of the second Hurricane from the well-deck to the catapult, one of the derricks broke loose and a crewman suffered a broken thigh. Eventually, however, the Hurricane was lifted on to the catapult and the two remaining pilots shared the watch. 'It means nine hours each per day from dawn till dusk,' noted Scott. (For the Camship pilots, of course, the watch at this time of year – although only for a limited period – was eighteen hours a day.)

Returning with a homeward-bound convoy to Bangor, Scott and Walker learned for the first time that Everett had got back safely. 'Had a great time shooting a line about our experiences,' confided Scott to his diary. But on 31 July, again with Everett and Scott, but with another pilot – Dickie Mancus – replacing Cecil Walker, *Maplin* joined a convoy from Liverpool numbered OG 70, outward bound for Gibraltar. There were no air attacks on this convoy, thus *Maplin's* striking power remained intact for the return trip,

At 21.30 on Saturday evening, 2 August, while Convoy OG 70 continued to Gibraltar, *Maplin* headed south-west with three destroyers to meet Convoy SL 81, homeward-bound from Sierra Leone. The destroyers in attendance on *Maplin* were the Norwegian-manned *St Albans* to starboard, the four-stacked American lease-lend *Campbeltown* to port, and *Wanderer*, carrying the senior officer of the escort, dead ahead, each at a distance from *Maplin* of about half a mile. When daylight came on Sunday 3 August, the weather was foggy, but during the morning the air warmed up and by noon the horizon had cleared. The wind was westerly, Force three, and there was some light wispy cloud, but visibility was extensive, impaired only by the dancing mirage in the middle distance where the surface of the sea reflected the sun. As they continued to head south-west, the three pilots on *Maplin* took turn and turn about in the cockpit of the Hurricane, two hours on and four hours off.

At two o'clock on that Sunday afternoon Bob Everett, taking over from the tall, angular Dickie Mancus, climbed the 30-foot ladder to the top of the catapult and stepped into the cockpit for his second vigil of the day. *Maplin* was now 450 miles from Land's End, so there was no chance, in the event of a launching, of saving the Hurricane. Perched high in the bows of the ship, but loosely strapped in for the moment, Everett adjusted his reflector mirror until he could focus comfortably on the radar scanner at the masthead aft. So long as that rotating eye continued its measured, hypnotic sweep he could relax. When the radar operator got a contact he would start hunting for it. The movements of the scanner would become erratic, precisely reflecting the anxious concentration of the operator. That was the time to tighten one's straps.

He ran his eye along the 75 feet of catapult rail ahead of him. Beyond that lay the sheer drop into the sea. In the distance was the ruled line of the horizon; but between that and the bows of *Maplin* was a vast expanse of heaving sea. It was like looking down the barrel of a naval gun from the breech-block end. At 14.10 *Wanderer* signalled that she had sighted a dark object in the water to the south. It looked like a U-boat. Almost simultaneously, Everett tensed as the radar scanner suddenly halted its rhythmic, monotonous sweep. Four minutes later, just above the horizon eight miles to the south, the crews of all four ships picked out the unmistakable silhouette of a Focke-Wulf Condor.

The Condor was acting as contact plane for a pack of U-boats. In many ways this was its most dangerous role. Although not in direct contact with the U-boats, the Condor crew would report any sightings of ships to Flag Officer Submarines at Brest, who would then vector the U-boats on to the target. Thus the destruction of the Condor would strike a double blow towards protecting the approaching convoy. At 14.45 *Campbeltown* and *St Albans* were ordered by *Wanderer* to take up position five miles on either beam of *Maplin*. *Wanderer* kept ahead of *Maplin* to pick up the Hurricane pilot in case of a launching. But the Condor pilot, still acting the part of shadower, kept his distance.

The presence of *Maplin* and the destroyer escort could only alert the wolf-pack to the imminent approach of a convoy and *Wanderer* ordered a change of course to intercept SL 81 at the nearest point. Nine hundred miles from his base at Bordeaux, the Condor pilot was beginning to worry about his fuel situation. Soon he was forced to abandon his role of shadower and the men of the escort vessels watched him head back for Bordeaux. But at 15.15, with the four warships still heading south-west, a second Condor was sighted ten miles astern. Approaching low down from the north, it lay on *Maplin's* starboard quarter. It seemed that either the pilot hadn't seen the four warships or he had made up his mind to attack.

Everett had already tightened his straps. Catapult and aircraft crew were standing by. Fourteen 3-inch rockets had been loaded, all securing gear had been removed and firing circuits connected. The engine, warmed up earlier, was ready to start. Whether the Condor was attacking or not, the chance of depriving the wolf-pack of its long-range contact patrol looked too good to miss. *'Stand by to launch.'* On this order, from the captain of *Maplin*, the aeroplane flag was hoisted as a warning to the destroyers. Everett made his switches and the engine started first time.

In his steel shelter in the bows, the catapult firing officer signalled to the captain that the Hurricane was ready for launching. Keeping one eye on the Condor, the captain began the turn to starboard that would head the ship – and the catapult runway – dead into the wind. *'Take cover!'* The din of the alarm bells warned the crew of the imminence of the blast and burning cordite that would envelop the fore-deck at the firing of the rockets. *'Launch as soon as ready!'* Alerted by a flag signal from the firing officer, Everett pushed the throttle lever forward and tightened the throttle nut. He could feel the engine's power, but the breaking point of the strip of metal that connected the rear of the trolley to the catapult itself would not be reached until the rockets fired. Raising a hand towards the steel cab, he waited for the bows to come up on an upward scend, then cut his hand down in an imperious gesture. *'One... two...'* As the firing officer began his three-second count, Everett clenched his fist on the stick and jammed his elbow into his hip to prevent the backward jerk that would otherwise be involuntary as the aircraft accelerated down the rail. *'Three.'* As the firing officer closed his switch, Everett forced his skull back against the head-rest and fought to keep the stick well forward. For a moment he felt a slight dizziness under the force of the G and feared he might black out. Then he was clear of the bows and sinking towards the swell. Holding the Hurricane clear of the water, he selected flaps up and began the turn to port that would bring him right round from the westerly direction of his take-off, back towards the point where he judged he might make the interception.

The Condor was still heading almost due south and Everett soon sighted it. Despite the pyrotechnic display that had accompanied the Hurricane's take-off, the German crew did not seem to be aware of its presence. Everett crept in to about one and a half miles' range and was hoping for a quick interception when the Condor pilot, warned presumably by his crew, sheered off to port.

The chase was on and although Everett kept his throttle wide open it took him nine minutes to get within 600 yards of the Condor. By this time, with the Condor heading south-east for Bordeaux, he was well out of sight of *Maplin*. Then, flying at 200 feet, which gave him a small height advantage, he began to overtake on the starboard quarter. He was aware that the defensive armament of the Condor, formidable enough already, had recently been strengthened by the introduction of sliding beam panels that masked a 7.9 millimetre machine-gun on either side. Going into action there were three and sometimes four gunners available to man the guns. Against this the Hurricane boasted eight .303 machine-guns but no cannon. These guns could only be fired straight ahead.

A curved diving attack from dead ahead was the tactic recommended by Denys Gillam, but Everett soon found that the Hurricane did not have the speed to get into that position. Attacking from astern, he knew, was reckoned to be throwing away good ammunition on armour plating, as well as giving the Condor gunners an easy target. The best alternative was a beam attack, though the breakaway point could be a vulnerable moment. All this passed through Everett's mind as he came up on the Condor's starboard quarter. As he did so the gunner manning the stern gun opened fire.

Everett reckoned he was thirty miles or more from *Maplin*. If he was shot down now they would never find him. Indeed, as he knew well enough, they were most unlikely even to look for him. But even Everett did not realise how precarious his situation was. Seven minutes after his take-off, a conning tower had been sighted to the south. Increasing to twenty knots, *Wanderer* had altered course to close the U-boat, while *St Albans* took station on her beam. Simultaneously the homeward-bound convoy, consisting of seventeen ships, was sighted and *Campbeltown* was ordered to escort *Maplin* towards it. All four ships were fully committed to urgent tasks.

It was not that Everett was forgotten. A lookout was being kept and when he got back, someone would put down a boat to pick him up. But first he had to get back.

The fire from the stern cannon of the Condor was passing underneath the Hurricane, or falling short of it. Intent on getting into a good attacking position, Everett ignored it and continued the chase. Glancing at his air speed indicator he saw he was doing 244 mph. The Hurricane was absolutely flat out, yet he still could not get abeam of the Condor. He judged that the German must be doing at least 235.

As he crept up almost abeam and to starboard he saw that the forward cannon was now firing at him. Again the rounds were passing underneath or short. But they were getting closer. Sooner or later they were bound to find the range.

Rather than start firing at medium range he decided on a determined attack aimed at the cockpit, as he had been taught in training, closing right in and expending all his ammunition in a single assault of maximum ferocity. This, he felt, was the best way to make use of such advantages as the Hurricane had. But he still could not get properly abeam of the target and to turn in before he did so would be to drop astern too soon. As on a past occasion, he had to be patient, and bide his time.

Suddenly the Condor pilot, perhaps reading Everett's intention, turned sharply to port, throwing Everett astern. Then the German pilot, apparently changing his mind, came back on to his original course. The manoeuvre was accompanied by a burst of fire from the Condor's forward cannon and a barrage from the machine-guns firing abeam. But Everett found his problem had been solved for him. In the turn the Condor pilot had lost considerable ground, surrendering to Everett the position he had been striving for. He was well placed now for a beam attack. Indeed he had almost reached the starboard bow. Seizing his chance, he flipped the Hurricane to port and tore straight into the attack, holding his fire until the range was down to 200 yards, then firing a succession of bursts aimed at the cockpit. But as the Condor pilot turned again to port the main weight of his attack developed abaft the beam. He kept on firing five-second bursts until he had dropped forty yards astern, but his guns seemed to be having no effect whatever. A final burst at point-blank range from dead astern and his guns were empty. In the same instant his wind shield and hood went opaque with a huge splash of engine oil. His oil system must have been hit. Breaking away to port, he throttled back and put the airscrew into coarse pitch to save fuel, then slid back the hood to try to see what had happened.

The Condor was still flying strongly ahead of him, but its camouflage seemed to have undergone a subtle change. Turrets and gondolas and beam hatches were glowing like a Chinese lantern. It was not only the Hurricane that was exuding oil. The Condor was leaving a trail of oil on the water ten feet wide that stretched for three-quarters of a mile. Whether or not his own machine would survive the combat, Everett was satisfied that the Condor was doomed. For the first time since the combat started he called up his ship. 'The Condor's definitely in trouble. It looks alight inside.' Before he could switch from transmit to receive, the Condor dropped a wing and then plunged into the sea. 'She's down!' As Everett flew low over the top, the water where the Condor had gone in seemed strangely quiescent. There was no sign of plane or survivors. All that was visible was a tell-tale residue of smoke where the Condor's fires had been dowsed.

'Well done. Are you all right?' This reply from *Maplin*, coming up loud and clear, gave Everett immense comfort. He had no more than a vague idea where he was, his forward view was still obscured by oil and he was going to need all the help he could get to regain the convoy.

'My engine oil system's been hit. My windscreen's covered with oil.'

'Where are you?'

'About forty miles to the south-east'

'What height?'

'200 feet'

'Climb to 2,000 feet and we'll give you a bearing.'

The bearing, when it came, put him less to the south than he had imagined. He was almost due east. He would never have located the ship without it. But uppermost in his mind now was concern for his engine. There was a huge patch of oil out on the starboard wing and without oil his engine was finished.

After five or six minutes on a course of 280 degrees he was given a 20-degree correction to 260 and a distance from the ship of 16 miles. His engine was still pulling well, and a few minutes later he spotted the unmistakable silhouette of *Campbeltown*, her four straight stacks transformed for him into something incredibly beautiful in the sunlight. He could still see almost nothing straight ahead. Fearing that at any moment his engine might seize, he decided to bale out while he still retained control. He looked around for *Wanderer*, the ship that, according to his briefing, was to pick him up.

Wanderer, accompanied by *St Albans*, was well ahead of the other two vessels. Ten minutes earlier the U-boat they had been chasing had dived, but an Asdic sweep had picked up positive echoes and the two ships had started depth-charging. All this was unknown to Everett as he began a circuit of the ship to indicate his intention. *Wanderer*, despite her preoccupations, prepared to accept him, while *St Albans* swept round her defensively.

Aiming to bale out half a mile ahead of *Wanderer*, Everett released his straps, pulled back the cockpit hood, and wound on forward trim. Then he rolled the Hurricane over on its back. In the inverted position the forward trim was supposed to jerk the nose up, dropping the pilot out backwards under gravitational pull. Everett was half out of the cockpit, upside down, when the nose of the Hurricane dropped instead of lifting, forcing him back into his seat.

Bringing the Hurricane back to straight and level flight, he tried again. The same thing happened. He was half out when the machine nosed down and deposited him back in the cockpit. Some of those in *Maplin* thought Everett was making a very bad fist of a victory roll. But Dickie Mancus realised what was happening. He guessed that Everett was either losing too much speed or wasn't winding on enough forward trim. To Everett, still half blinded by the oil on his windscreen and anticipating an engine failure at any moment, the important thing seemed to be to get down as soon as possible. Two abortive attempts to bale out had induced the fear that he might never succeed. Accustomed to spills of considerable violence, he did not doubt that he would somehow survive a ditching.

Advice from *Maplin*, when he told them his intention, was immediate: 'Don't ditch!' But Everett, although knowing full well the reputation of the Hurricane for somersaulting immediately on ditching, had made up his mind. Keeping the cockpit hood open, but refastening his harness, he brought the Hurricane down low over the water ahead of *Wanderer*. In an effort to avert the somersault, he then throttled right back and let the plane drop towards the water in a stalled attitude, tail well down. But immediately the tail touched the water the nose fell forward and the scoop dug in.

The Hurricane didn't even float the 1.7 seconds guaranteed by Hawkers. It sank like a brick with Everett inside it.

All Mancus saw, watching from *Maplin*, was a monstrous cascade of water that hid the Hurricane completely. When the water subsided there was nothing to be seen of pilot or plane.

Down in the inky blackness that the Hurricane quickly reached, Everett struggled to free himself from his harness. The shock of the impact had driven the breath from his body, and already his lungs were starved of air. By the time he had fought his way out of the harness and scrambled clear of the cockpit, he was down to a depth he could no longer estimate and his lungs were bursting. He was not a powerful swimmer and his strength was ebbing, but he struck out in a desperate dog-paddle, seeking the growing opalescence above him that was giving him hope. Choking and gasping, his limbs still flailing the water to assist his ascent, he somehow broke surface and sucked in lifesaving breath.

Inflating his lifejacket, he sat back on his unused parachute and felt in his pocket for a cigarette. He needed something to steady his nerves. But the packet was soaked. While *St Albans* continued to circle protectively, *Wanderer* dropped a boat and picked him up. For being the first man to destroy a Condor in this way, he was awarded the DSO.

Congratulated later by the Duke of Kent, he admitted that catafighting was his most exciting experience so far, beating Valentine's, Becher's, the Open Ditch and the Water Jump rolled into one.

Just under six months later, on Monday 26 January 1942, Bob Everett was detailed to fly the squadron hack – Hurricane P.3452 – from Belfast to Abingdon for a major inspection, using Tern Hill in Shropshire as an intermediate stop if required. He took off at 12.30 and was duly wired out to Abingdon, but he never got there, nor did he call in at Tern Hill. Yet through some unaccountable oversight, proper overdue action was not taken. As it happened, the Hurricane had been seen and its last moments of flight witnessed and recorded. At 13.13 that afternoon the Coastguard officer on duty at Penmon, on the eastern rip of the Isle of Anglesey, received a message from a coastwatcher at Carreg Onnan that a plane had crashed in Red Wharf Bay. 'It was coming from a northerly direction and losing height,' said the coastwatcher, 'with the engine making banging noises. It nearly reached the beach and when quite low, dived into the sea.' Visibility was poor and the cloud layer was low, and although the aircraft was only 150 yards out to sea it was not identified.

High speed launches from Holyhead and Menai Bridge, both capable of thirty knots, were quickly launched, the Moelfre lifeboat was within five miles of the crash, and a third motor launch was soon ordered to the position. But the sea was rough, and it was not until 15.20 that the wreck was located. It was in three fathoms of water, and there was no sign of survivors. The search continued until dark, but all that was recovered was a sponge-bag containing shaving-kit, and an aircraft panel. There was nothing to identify pilot or plane. 'No more information was received,' said the Coastguard log. 'The plane was assumed to be totally destroyed, and all the authorities were informed.'

No report reached Sydenham that Everett had failed to arrive, however, and no one linked these eye-witness accounts with the 804 Squadron Hurricane. It was not until three days later, on Thursday 29 January, that news reached Belfast via an Air Ministry round-robin signal that Everett had failed to arrive at Abingdon and had been missing since the Monday. Enquiries at airfields flanking Everett's route drew blanks, and no one had any plot of his movements.

On Sunday 1 February the squadron learned of the spongebag and aircraft panel picked up in Red Wharf Bay, also of the coastwatcher who had seen an unidentified aeroplane crash into the sea at about 13.15 on the Monday, 'just when Everett would have been there,' as the squadron log noted. But there was consolation in the knowledge later revealed that everything had been done by the men on the spot to save the pilot.

'I never did trust that aircraft,' said Dick Mancus recently. 'I thought it was clapped out. There was something fishy about the oil pressure – it was abnormally low. Worn bearings, probably.' Dick Evans, the only survivor today of the Coastguard men, remembers that a fishing boat with a grappling line was eventually sent out and that divers went down at low water with air bags and pumped air into the sunken wreck, after which the plane was lifted to the surface. The pilot was not in the cockpit, and the Sutton harness was undone. When Everett's body was eventually washed ashore several months later, a post-mortem revealed that he had drowned.

Both Dick Mancus and another squadron pilot, Alan Marsh, believed that Everett, remembering his difficulties on a former occasion, would have preferred to attempt a ditching rather than bale out. But in any case, to parachute into the Irish Sea in poor visibility in January would surely have been to abandon all hope. Everett's best chance was to try to reach the nearest land, and he very nearly made it. It was a poignant end to a colourful life.

A moving tribute to Bob Everett came from his squadron commander, Pat Havers, in a letter to Everett's mother:

> *We all missed him more than we would have missed anybody else. He was the most experienced aviator on the squadron and quite the most liked of the whole lot. I am not exaggerating when I say that the squadron was quite different and very gloomy for a long time after.*
>
> *We were all delighted when Bob got the DSO. He so richly deserved it and was completely unspoiled by it. I don't suppose there has ever been a chap who was so clever at flying and who did the job so well for his age, and yet managed to be so universally liked by all who knew him. He was the best pilot I had, and a great friend.*

An entry in the squadron log for 8 December 1941 is indicative of Everett's approach to his job. 'Everett was seen as usual heading Linkwards [i.e., to the Link Trainer], as there weren't any aircraft for him.' He knew the importance of keeping himself in practice and his surviving contemporaries (Havers himself was killed later) endorse the view that he was a thoroughly dedicated and professional flyer. Their general assessment of his qualities, though, is strikingly similar to Ted Leader's recommendation of him as a jockey thirteen years earlier. Sound rather than brilliant. But above all, brave.

IV
Catapult Ships under Fire

'Captain uninterested and unhelpful, tends to be nervous and excitable.'
'Captain is a most difficult man.'
'Captain is prejudiced against MSFU.'
'As a pilot, I do not wish to sail with this man again.'

These were typical of the comments of RAF Camship pilots on their return from their first crossings of the North Atlantic in the summer of 1941 and there is no doubt that many masters, with the conservatism and taciturnity of the sea, proved difficult shipmates. On the other hand, a parallel compilation of criticisms of MSFU pilots and their crews would have been readily available from the masters had they been asked. These men were acutely aware of their total command at sea and they resented the presence on the bridge of pilot and FDO. Their responsibilities, the dangers they were exposed to and the tensions inseparable from a closed community aboard ship, were severe enough and they grumbled at the additional burden.

The Hurricane and its catapult gear, besides obscuring the view ahead, acted as a sail in rough weather and impeded steerage way. In practice it inevitably meant some loss of cargo capacity and it presented an inviting target for aerial bombardment. Meanwhile the Condors suddenly, and it seemed unaccountably, disappeared from their North Atlantic haunts, depriving the Camship pilots of the opportunity to demonstrate their value. Thus there was little recognition of the fact that pilots had a duty to perform and needed co-operation to perform it efficiently. They had no recognised status in the convoy and liaison between the naval escort, the convoy commodore, and the Camship was negligible – indeed often non-existent. To increase the odds against a successful interception, Camships were often badly positioned in convoys for the quick turn into wind necessary for a hurried launching, while the appointing of a specific escort vessel to pick up pilots after launching was sometimes refused.

While in the danger area, which was taken to be up to 30 degrees west, aircraft were warmed up at dawn each day and the pilot, in full flying kit, stood by from dawn till dusk with the FDO on the bridge. Even between 30 and 35 degrees west a watch was maintained. These long hours of readiness, although lasting at the most seven or eight days outward and homeward, imposed a heavy psychological strain on the pilots, who might at any moment, perhaps after weeks of inactivity, be expected to embark on a most testing operation.

Most fighter pilots, if not exactly excitable types, were certainly used to regular excitement. The boredom of many hours of watchful inactivity was altogether foreign to them. Most of them were young men in their early twenties, some scarcely out of school, whose uninhibited individualism did not always endear them to men fighting a long war of attrition at sea, a war which had been going on for many months and which from the start had been neither phoney nor glamorous.

Another basic difficulty was that, in the eyes of the Merchant Navy, the armed forces were considered badly organised institutions. Masters and crews told countless stories of the stupidity and irrelevance of actions and orders emanating from the Services. Ship's crews proved indifferent and even at times hostile and pilots did not always make allowances for the natural antipathy of merchant seamen to a breed of men who, in the general estimation, belonged to the officer class. One team who were later to make their mark on the Russian convoys, pilot John Kendal, a Battle of Britain man, and his FDO, Peter Mallett, noted that a strong sense of humour and a talent for diplomacy were essential. Most captains and their crews did respond to a tactful approach and this method was quickly adopted by the more mature personalities. 'Studied acquiescence,' wrote Cranwell-trained Mike Lyne, later to become an air vice-marshal, 'will accomplish anything.'

Although all MSFU men were subject to the Merchant Shipping Act and came under the master's orders, the master had no powers under the Air Force Act, and the senior serving officer on board, pilot or FDO, was granted the powers of an officer commanding a detachment, with certain limitations, and was directly responsible to the master for the discipline of the detachment. But however carefully masters and pilots were instructed in their status and the division of duties, misunderstandings occurred. At least one master signed on his pilot and FDO as deck-hands, as a reminder of their inferior status; and some masters tended to think that if they told the pilot to launch then he must launch, regardless of professional considerations. This attitude brought a reminder to all Camship captains that the pilot was the sole judge of conditions for launching.

As time went by, however, phrases such as 'very good indeed', 'very cordial', and 'affable' began to appear in the pilots' reports on relationships, and often it was the ship's own engineers who carried out necessary repairs to the catapult and ancillary equipment. When a real effort was made by the entire MSFU crew, led by the pilot, to observe ship's customs and orders, the atmosphere was generally good. 'The Merchant Service skippers were a grand bunch,' writes former FDO, T. Bryn Lewis, 'from whom I personally learnt much about the sea.' It was mostly a question of adapting to the skipper's personality.

One pilot who had reason to be grateful that he had established a good relationship with his captain was twenty-one-year-old Battle of Britain pilot Dickie Turley-George. A member of 54 Squadron at Hornchurch during the battle, he had been shot down twice in August 1940 and the second time a bullet in the face had virtually blinded him in the right eye. Tall, slim and gangling, Turley-George coupled an amused contempt for rules and regulations with a cool determination to get back to flying, and under a sympathetic commanding officer he sneaked some unofficial local flying before travelling down from Yorkshire to a medical board in London. His method of travel, as the medical board somehow discovered, was by air, flying alone. 'How about giving me a flight?' asked the eye specialist, whom Turley-George happened to know, and the trip was duly made. Next day the President of the Board reminded Turley-George that to fly with a non-flying category was a court martial offence. But to save him offending further, he was given a full operational flying category, and soon after returning to his station Turley-George joined MSFU.

For his second trip to Halifax, in the Camship *Eastern City*, Turley-George was warned by Moulton-Barrett that the skipper had had an unfortunate experience with his previous pilot and that he hated everything to do with the RAF. It was up to Turley-George to do all he could to redeem MSFU. As they approached Halifax, Turley-George discovered that the ship was ultimately bound for Houston, Texas; but a signal ordered that the Hurricane be catapulted off first, to land at the Pilots' Pool that had been established at the RCAF base at Dartmouth. Pilot and aircraft would remain at Dartmouth until the ship returned from Houston, so that Turley-George could get some flying practice. Keen as he was on getting airborne, this didn't suit Turley-George at all and he got his sea crew together and persuaded them to report that the plane was unserviceable.

'That bloody aeroplane's been perfectly all right all the way across the Atlantic,' was the captain's brusque response. But a signal reporting the plane as unserviceable was sent. The reply made Turley-George the most unpopular man on board. 'SS *Eastern City* will proceed into Halifax.' He had messed it up for everybody.

It was too late to own up now. But once in Halifax, the way seemed open at least for a trip to New York and Turley-George went round to the American consul's office to get a visa. It was a Saturday and the consulate was closed, but he tried the door and it opened. On the consul's desk was a list of telephone numbers, one of which was apparently the consul's home. Turley-George dialled it.

'Is this the American consul?'

'Yes.'

Turley-George explained who he was. 'I'd like a visa.'

'Sorry, we're not open today.'

'*You* may not be open, but your office is.'

There was a pause. 'Where are you speaking from?'

'I'm sitting at your desk.'

'Don't move. I'll be right round.'

So Turley-George and his FDO set off for New York via Montreal by train and in New York they were so lavishly entertained that they decided to prolong their stay as much as possible and fly back to Dartmouth; a plane was due to go that would meet their deadline. But when the time came they couldn't get a seat on the plane. They took the train to

Montreal and arranged to fly from there – but when they got there, down came the fog. The six-hour delay that followed was just enough to cause them to miss their sailing by half an hour – a dereliction of duty that could never be lived down or forgiven.

Near the docks was a seaplane base where some Royal Canadian Navy officers had a billet or mess, and Turley-George raced round to see them.

It was Sunday morning [he says], *and there'd clearly been a party the night before. It was nearly eight o'clock by this time, and the ship had sailed at seven. One chap was asleep in the bath, another was in bed with a bird. But they pulled their clothes on, made some coffee, got a fast launch out and raced after the Eastern City. We caught them up and as I climbed the ladder and peeped over the top, the captain was waiting for me.*

Turley-George came rather raggedly to attention and saluted. 'Good morning, sir.'

'Good morning. So glad you could join us' But the captain asked no questions, and when they got back to England, he asked for Turley-George again.

Turley-George's escapades, and his manner of relating them, were always so hilarious, and the denouements so irresistible, that he invariably escaped retribution. In the opinion of a later CO of MSFU, he was one of the biggest morale-builders the unit ever had.

By 9 September 1941, three months after the sailing of the first Camship, 39 pilots and 164 men had been trained at Speke for ship detachments, there had been 37 Camship sailings and 15 Camships had completed one round trip. (Camships were being exclusively employed on the North Atlantic run.) But of the 39 pilots, 3 had been sent to Canada to set up the Pool at Dartmouth, to provide replacement pilots for the Camships and to collect and test the Hurricanes that were being made in Canada; and new volunteer pilots were not coming forward. The shortage of pilots was acute; but against that, no convoy in which a Camship had been present had been attacked from the air and indeed not a single enemy aircraft had been identified by any Camship crew. A falling off in German air activity over the Atlantic was to be expected following the attack on Russia, and no one could forecast when it might be resumed at its former level; but in a situation where Britain's resources were strained to the uttermost, it was inevitable that the whole policy surrounding the catapult fighters should come up for review.

Stimulated by Sholto Douglas, the Fighter Command C-in-C, who hated the thought of experienced fighter pilots going idle and naturally wanted them back, the Air Ministry asked: 'Is it economical to continue with the Camship proposal at all? Would it be better to cancel this scheme and convert a proportion of the merchant vessels now used as Camships to Fighter Catapult Ships entirely under Admiralty control and operation?' In this they were echoing Churchill's doubts of six months earlier. The enemy were containing the equivalent of two fighter squadrons by means of a threat that had lapsed, at least for the moment, and it certainly seemed on the face of it that MSFU as a unit was becoming uneconomic and unsound. Against this it was argued that the evaporation of the threat to British shipping might well be due, in part at least, to the deterrent effect of the Camships.

From German documents it is now clear that the policy of KG 40 in the North Atlantic, dictated by the increased firepower of merchant ships and the feared presence of catapult fighters, had been principally to shadow and report and that this was why the use of the Condor as a sort of low-level dive-bomber, the only form of attack that was suited to its armament, had fallen away. Even the most courageous and enterprising pilots were deciding for the first time not to attack when they judged convoys to be too well protected. In their minds too was the reputation of the Condor for vulnerability, the crews dubbing it 'The Tinfoil Bomber'. But to disband the Camships was to invite the Condors to resume their offensive and although it was not expected that launchings from Camships would continue to be practicable in the North Atlantic throughout the winter period, their retention in what Churchill is said to have called a 'positive/negative' role was never in serious doubt. There was also the Gibraltar run to consider. During that summer of 1941 the converging homeward runs from Gibraltar and Sierra Leone had become the focus of U-boat and Condor activity, costing Britain thirty-one merchant ships and three escort vessels in August and September alone. The Fighter Catapult Ships, all four of which were guarding this route, were unable to cope.

When the Admiralty had allocated five vessels for catapult work with convoys, the measure had been intended purely as a stopgap until the Camships were ready. They had quickly lost the *Patia* and even after the Camships had got into their stride, it was the men of 804 Fleet Air Arm Squadron who saw most of the action.

If Bob Everett's combat was the most spectacular, there were other pilots who had their excitements. Three weeks after Everett's victory, on 26 August, Maurice Birrell was shot off *Ariguani* in an abortive attempt to round up a Condor which was dodging in and out of the cloud base. Despite his microscopic speed advantage in the Fulmar, Birrell got near enough to fire one good burst at long range before the Condor disappeared into cloud and he caught glimpses of it and chased it for many miles before having to give up and make for land in filthy weather. When he finally made a landfall on the Irish coast he had no idea where he was, so he landed on a strip of sandy beach at the head of a long inlet to enquire. He found that he was near Ardara, Donegal, in neutral Eire, twenty miles from the border. The locals helped him fix his position and when he elected to take off again, despite having very little fuel, they raised no objection, although the local constabulary were gathering to intervene. The weather by this time was appalling and between Birrell and the nearest RAF airfield at Eglinton lay the Blue Stack Mountains, rising to 2,200 feet; but the thought of internment and the loss of his aeroplane appealed to Birrell still less. Taking off successfully along the beach, he got safely across the mountains and landed at Eglinton, a feat for which he was specially commended by the C-in-C Western Approaches. 'The final flight from Ardara to Eglinton with such a narrow margin of petrol and under the prevailing weather,' wrote the C-in-C, 'was a most creditable performance.'

Nevertheless yet another Condor, although diverted from its shadowing role, had easily escaped from a *Fulmar* and lived to fight another day. Nineteen days later, on Sunday 14 September, the shortcomings even of the Hurricats were demonstrated when Cecil Walker was catapulted off *Maplin* after another Condor 100 miles south-west of Eire. The twenty-six-year-old Walker, who had never been to sea in his life until he joined the Fighter Catapult Ships, was on his third trip in *Maplin*, having worked his way up from junior to senior pilot.

Maplin had left Gibraltar on 2 September as part of the escort for Convoy HG 72 and there were no incidents until 11.45 on the Sunday morning, when the lookouts reported an aircraft flying at sea level six miles to the north. *Maplin* was on the starboard bow of the convoy and there were no launching problems, but visibility was impaired by haze and it was not at first possible to identify the aircraft, which kept flying in and out of a cloud base that was ten-tenths at 1,800 feet.

After about ten minutes the aircraft reappeared at 1,500 feet seven miles to the northeast and one of the escort vessels opened fire at it, reporting it as hostile. Three minutes later, at 11.58, the machine was seen in silhouette from *Maplin* and positively identified as a Condor. At exactly noon the Condor turned towards the convoy as though coming in for a bombing run. Walker was already in the cockpit of the Hurricane and within thirty seconds the flag signals had been exchanged and he was catapulted off. He made straight for a cluster of black puffs of smoke where someone was firing at the Condor and then he saw the silhouette and climbed straight towards it for a head-on attack.

Opening fire at 200 yards, intent on killing the pilot, he got in a burst of fire at point-blank range and saw his tracer enter the nose of the Condor. The German pilot began to turn to port, but Walker continued to fire into the Condor's nose until he almost collided with it, the whole burst lasting approximately five seconds. Turning to starboard and tucking in behind the Condor, he fired a four-second burst from astern and again saw his tracer hitting the target. But the German pilot held on grimly, reaching his cloud base with the Hurricane still on his tail. Almost immediately Walker lost contact.

The whole of this part of the encounter was watched anxiously from the bridge of *Maplin*, where disappointment was intense at the failure of Walker's apparently well-aimed fire to bring the Condor down. A nice problem now faced Walker's FDO, Sub-Lieutenant G.W. Lomas. The IFF equipment – identification friend or foe, which transmitted an impulse from all British aircraft, establishing their identity – was not functioning properly on the Hurricane. Lomas also knew that there were two Sunderland flying-boats in the vicinity whose IFF was similarly out of action. That was four machines in the area, all out of sight for the moment and all on a similar bearing. How was he going to sort them out and direct an interception? The first thing, he decided, was to get the Hurricane below cloud and he ordered Walker to orbit in sight of the convoy until the two Sunderlands showed themselves. When they did he would be able to send the Hurricane after the remaining radar echo.

The Condor pilot, it seems, was an old hand. (It has not been possible to establish his identity.) Somehow he had escaped serious damage during Walker's attacks and he was not disposed to abandon the scene until he had dropped his bombs. At 12.42 he began to circle on the starboard quarter of the convoy at a distance of fourteen miles, apparently looking out for the Hurricane and weighing up the prospects for an attack.

At once Lomas sent Walker off on an interception course. But by the time the Hurricane got into position, the Condor was about to re-enter cloud. Walker could get in no more than a brief burst before the Condor was gone. Still the German pilot lingered, hoping perhaps that the Hurricane might run out of fuel. Three more times he came down below cloud for a look round and on the last of these occasions Walker nearly got him. He just had time to get in a two-second burst from abeam before the German pilot regained cloud cover.

The whole engagement had lasted nearly an hour. But now at last the German crew gave up. Jettisoning their bombs from somewhere in the cloud bank, two and a half miles to starboard of the convoy, they headed for home.

Walker still had some endurance left, but he had no hope of reaching land. He cruised around until his fuel was all but exhausted, then decided somewhat nervously that he must use his parachute. Apart from Everett's abortive attempt, his would be the first bale-out from a Hurricat. Climbing to 3,800 feet, he slowed down to just under 100 mph, pulled back the cockpit hood, released his seat harness, jettisoned the side panel that formed the starboard wall of the cockpit and turned the aircraft on its back. He fell out cleanly and once clear of the aircraft pulled the ripcord. As he descended he kicked off his shoes and watched them fall into the sea.

Casting off his parachute harness when he reached the water, he inflated his rubber dinghy and was soon picked up by the destroyer *Rochester* and returned to *Maplin*. There he began to wonder if it had all been a dream: while he was away the reserve Hurricane had been hoisted and placed in position on the catapult.

In evaluating the action the commanding officer of 804 Squadron, Lieutenant-Commander Pat Havers, put his finger on some basic weaknesses. The Condor, he thought, would have been destroyed if the Hurricane had had cannon, or if it had enjoyed the improved climb and performance given by the Merlin XX installed in the Hurricane Mark II. As it was, yet another Condor had been brought to action but had escaped. And this time a Hurricane had been lost.

Whatever the Admiralty's intentions about the future of the Fighter Catapult Ships may have been – and they were already planing to return *Pegasus* to the work of catapult training – the issue was soon decided for them. On 25 September, one day out from Gibraltar on the homeward run, there was yet another abortive launching of a Fulmar against a Condor. Petty Officer Shaw and his telegraphist/gunner got safely back to Gibraltar after the action and *Springbank* went on without them; but she never reached her destination. The shadowing Condor that had evaded Shaw had done its work and on the night of 26/27 September repeated efforts were made by U-boats to sink *Springbank*, the only Fighter Catapult Ship in the convoy. The assault culminated in an attack in which *Springbank* was hit by two torpedoes, one carrying away her screw and rudder and the other knocking a hole in her stern. Everyone was fully alert because of the earlier attacks and she floated for eighteen and a half hours, finally being sunk by gunfire from the escort; but even so, casualties were considerable, one officer and thirty-one ratings being lost. As with *Patia*, no replacement had been planned and none was forthcoming.

When *Ariguani* was torpedoed twice in two minutes 300 miles off Lisbon a month later on the same run, it seemed that the Germans were paying special attention to these ships. After being abandoned, the *Ariguani* was later reboarded and successfully towed into Gibraltar. Two of the crew and a soldier on repatriation were killed. Maurice Birrell, torpedoed for the second time (he had been the pilot on the first Camship, the *Michael E*), was among the survivors.

That left only *Maplin* of the Fighter Catapult Ships. But with her complement of two Sea Hurricanes she had always been a better proposition than her sister ships. It was decided to keep her in service, and to strengthen her striking power by adapting her to carry a third Sea Hurricane in reserve.

On 19 September 1941, even before the loss of *Springbank* and *Ariguani*, a decision had been taken to transfer six Camships to the Gibraltar run, so the enemy's attempt to clear the seas around the Iberian peninsula of catapult fighters – if that is what it was – did not succeed. The Gibraltar Camships, which would be in the danger zone for the whole fourteen days of each voyage, outward and homeward, and in generally better weather, were allotted two pilots. A pool consisting of three Hurricats and three fully-trained MSFU pilots was formed at Gibraltar, with ground crew backing, on the same lines as that in operation in Dartmouth.

The first of the Gibraltar-bound Camships, the *Empire Gale*, sailed on 3 October. Seven days later the last of the thirty-five Camships went into service. Despite the onset of winter, the North Atlantic Camships, sometimes consisting of two, three, and even four to a convoy, still plied to and fro.

V
Unhappy Landings

By the end of October 1941, after nearly five months of sailings, there had still been no operational launching from a Camship. The only firings were those made at the conclusion of voyages, as the most practical means of delivering aircraft to Speke, to the detachments operating at Abbotsinch and Fairwood Common (the latter for the Bristol Channel ports), or to the Pools at Dartmouth and Gibraltar for servicing. These launchings also gave valuable practice to pilot and sea crew. The alternative of off-loading the Hurricane and transporting it first ashore and then to the appropriate airfield was tedious and cumbersome and, except in the early stages in Canada, it was only employed when weather or unserviceability precluded a launching.

The man placed in charge of the Dartmouth Pool was a twenty-seven-year-old former Battle of Britain man named Anthony S. Linney – Tony Linney. He was one of three MSFU men who left Liverpool for Canada in July 1941 for duty as back-up pilots in case anyone was fired off on the way over and was injured or killed. Linney had only just completed his catapult training.

Before we left [he writes], *the CO, a vague and pleasant wing commander named Moulton-Barrett, said we would only be in Halifax for about six weeks and then would be replaced; in the end, the six weeks turned out to be nine months.*

We began by taking the aircraft off the ship in Halifax harbour, putting it on a barge, towing the barge to the seaplane base, then taking it off and towing it up the road to the RCAF base at Dartmouth, where it was checked and de-salted, after which we air-tested it.

After the aircraft had been taken off the Camship, the ship itself proceeded to a port in the United States to load, returning later for the Hurricane. The ships' captains did not like the run at all, as the Camships were in short supply and they got very little port time. Sometimes the pilot and FDO continued with the ship in the hope of conning the US authorities into letting them go ashore; otherwise they mostly hung around Halifax.

The maintenance unit at Dartmouth was run by a great flight-sergeant named Worrall and came under No. 1 Canadian Fighter Squadron, which had recently returned from England. We told the RCAF administration that the whole procedure at Halifax was too cumbersome and we suggested that we shoot the aircraft off the ship and land it at Dartmouth, saving much time and effort. They replied that the operation was highly secret and that nobody must see the shoot-off. We thought this was ridiculous. I was continually thwarted by the RCAF administration in this period, but I used to go out in an air-sea rescue boat to observe the launchings.

There were many shortages of parts and equipment at Dartmouth, all items that I knew were in good supply in the UK. They could have been put aboard the next Camship, but the RCAF assured me that everything had been requested months ago and that nothing further could be done. They wouldn't let me write any sort of report and they flatly refused to send signals for me, so I went to the Cable and Wireless office in Halifax and sent a commercial cable to Speke saying: 'Many detrimental actions here; request authority to report immediately.' This brought quick action – but not from the direction I expected. Next day I was sent for and told to report to a group captain in Ottawa. I flew up on Trans-Canada Airlines, saw the group captain, and had my own cable read back to me. It had been intercepted by the censor. I was told in no uncertain terms to stop complaining and mind my own business. But after that, things began to happen.

Meanwhile the three of us were going broke because of the high cost of living. The RCAF got paid twice as much as the RAF. After continual complaints we received a questionnaire from the Air Ministry asking a whole lot of asinine questions, among them the price of laundry, apples, and gin. My mess bill had grown to $450 and the station commander was getting fidgety; he thought I might be recalled suddenly and leave without paying it. Finally some smart sergeant in Accounts found a way of paying us allowances as though we were transients and this made all the difference.

As with the early abrasiveness between pilot and ship's master, there were no doubt faults on both sides in the clash between the MSFU men and the Canadian administration. One grievance of the Canadians was the manner in which MSFU pilots indulged in low flying down the streets of Halifax when they were air-testing their machines. There were so many complaints that restrictions were eventually applied which, in the opinion of the MSFU men, virtually precluded any sort of satisfactory air-test altogether. (The Canadians denied this.) One can well imagine the uninhibited flying that resulted from the sudden release of young ex-Battle of Britain pilots from the tensions and tedium of an Atlantic crossing, in a country where they imagined they were relatively free from any sort of restraint or retribution.

Even the pilots of the Dartmouth Pool were not immune from criticism, as Linney himself admits. He writes:

It was decided that we should have some spare Hurricanes delivered to Dartmouth. The Canada Car and Foundry company were building Hurricanes at Fort William, Ontario, 1,250 miles west of Dartmouth on Lake Superior, and I was sent across with Flying Officer Mitchell and Pilot Officer Bradford to ferry three aircraft back. We flew by TCA to North Bay, then caught the train round Lake Superior to Fort William.

The aeroplanes were well built, and the engines had been sent out from Rolls-Royce UK, but no fuel consumption tests had been made, the compasses were inaccurate, and we had no radios. Winter had set in, and most of the airfields along the route had rolled snow runways.

Our first trip, in which each pilot took turns to do the navigating, which mostly meant following the railroad, was fairly uneventful, although when it came to Bradford's turn he took the wrong fork and we were headed for the United States until Mitchell caught up with him and got him back on the right track.

On the second trip, after leaving Fort William on the return flight, we were dogged by bad weather, which was especially variable and treacherous at that time of year. At one small airport we were held up for three days. When we eventually reached Montreal, Air Commodore 'Taffy' Powell, the man who was running Atfero, the Atlantic Ferry Organisation, lent us a radio receiver so that we could fly the beacons and we fitted it in Bradford's aircraft. Powell was emphatic, however, that we return it next trip, and I gave my solemn promise.

From Montreal to Dartmouth was about 500 miles and we made one intermediate stop, at Saint John, New Brunswick – but not before Mitchell and Bradford had insisted on flying under a suspension bridge near Millinocket, Maine, fifty miles inside the United States border. They tried to do it in formation, but at the last moment Mitchell realised that there was not enough room for both and went over the top, bringing the traffic that was crossing the bridge to a juddering halt.

On the ground at Saint John, we called Dartmouth to get the weather and were told that if we left immediately we could make it before the weather closed in. We took off at once. I was leading and we were in cloud almost immediately so I climbed to get out of it, intending to come down to sea level after we had crossed Nova Scotia and were well out to sea. However, my oil cooler was freezing up and my oil pressure was going down.

The 'book' said that when this happened, one should climb steeply to melt it out. I did so, but understandably neither Bradford nor Mitchell realised what was happening and they dropped away from me. Without radio I had no means of enlightening them. By the time my oil pressure was back to normal, I was at 27,000 feet. I descended, flying out to sea, and I was down to 200 feet before the sea appeared beneath me.

I turned onto reciprocal and headed back to the coastline, but it did not appear and I flew and flew. What I didn't know was that above 15,000 feet I had had a tail-wind of 70 mph. When I finally hit the coast I was still thirty miles south-west of Halifax with only a few minutes' fuel left and I landed wheels up on a sandy beach. I discovered afterwards that ten miles away Mitchell had done exactly the same. Bradford, short of fuel as we were and spotting a destroyer about forty miles out to sea, elected to bale out near the ship. But when the crew reached the spot they could find no trace.

In his official report, Linney blames the weather for the fact that after this the Hurricanes were crated and sent across from Fort William by rail, to be assembled at Dartmouth. But more recently he has conceded that an ever-lengthening list of complaints about the beating-up of places in both America and Canada may have been a contributory factor.

As Taffy Powell's radio was in Bradford's aircraft, Linney was never able to fulfil his promise to return it. 'Taffy was still complaining about it,' says Linney, 'when I went to work for him at Silver City Airways eight years later.'

Human error and the flouting of regulations were not confined to the Canadian side of the Atlantic. On the homeward voyage, pilots and their support crews who had managed to get ashore in Canada or the United States were almost invariably loaded with contraband. The only way of avoiding punitive Customs dues was to pack the Hurricane to the gills, launch it at the end of the crossing, and find some excuse for a forced landing at a non-Customs airfield before proceeding to Speke.

One very large convoy, re-crossing the Atlantic on a broad front in September/October 1941, included four Camships. The pilots, all of the rank of pilot officer, were R.S. 'Spud' Spurdle (*Eastern City*), a New Zealander; Alec Lumsden (*Daghestan*); Gerry North (*Empire Spring*); and Norman Lee (*Empire Spray*). The crossing was completed without interference from the air. Then, as the convoy neared Anglesey on 6 October, it assumed a much narrower formation prior to entering the Mersey, and the four Camships were grouped together for launching.

Conditions that morning were typical of the approach of a warm front. After a sunny beginning, the high cloud thickened and lowered, and an oily swell developed. Standing orders were that pilots were to launch 'north of and in sight of Anglesey', and the first of these requirements was soon fulfilled. But did the second have to be fulfilled as well? If they were north of Anglesey, could pilots launch without actually sighting land?

The pilots themselves, almost certainly, knew what was meant. They were to wait for visual confirmation that the weather along the coast was clear. But as the four Camships steamed ten to twelve miles north of the island of Anglesey on the run past the North Wales coast towards the Mersey, visibility was poor and the coastline was obliterated by a clinging mist. While the pilots discussed the situation with their crews, or sat in their cockpits waiting for the weather to clear, the temptation, to some of them at least, was to launch if they possibly could. 'I had emptied all the ammunition out of my plane and filled the panniers with contraband,' writes Spud Spurdle, 'nylon stockings, bottles of rye and Bourbon, Scotch whisky and gin, etc. I had even taken my parachute out and left it on the ship, and I was sitting on "goodies" stored in the seat well.' For Spurdle, and possibly for some of the others, a landing at some intermediate airfield, before having to clear Customs at Speke, was mandatory.

The Camship captains, too, had reason to encourage their pilots to launch. Captain Bobbin, for instance, of *Daghestan*, was bound for Manchester via the ship canal with 7,000 tons of grain. If he had to put into dock at Ellesmere Port to off-load the Hurricane, he would miss the tide and locks he was steaming to catch. He was thus prepared to interpret the regulations freely.

The Camships were taking their lead from one of their own number, the *Empire Spring* (Gerry North); and the other Camships looked to *Empire Spring*'s captain for a decision. Several times Norman Lee, on *Empire Spray*, signalled *Empire Spring* for confirmation of the time of launch. The harassed captain, re-reading his launching instructions, found them ambiguous. One of the two alternative conditions – if they were alternatives – was clearly fulfilled. Under some circumstances he might have slowed down until the weather improved; but he too had a rendezvous to keep. He was due to cross the bar at high water, which was 14.00 hours, and he could not afford to loiter. Pressed by the flow of signals from the other Camships, he finally ruled that pilots must use their own judgement. Soon after 09.00, Gerry North was catapulted off, followed by Alec Lumsden from *Daghestan*.

No sooner had I got clear of the ship and done the customary beat-up past it [says Lumsden]
*than I ran into some embarrassingly low cloud. Then it started to rain. We had only just got off
in time. As I headed slightly north-east the warm front that was coming down from the north-
west caught up with me and I headed instead for the Flint coast. By the time I got to Rhyl,
which I knew well, I was very low down on the water.*

Lumsden had a good load of silk stockings on board, stuffed into sundry hiding places, but
he didn't think the Customs men would worry over-much about those. He had his share
of cigarettes too, but he had no liquor and he had filled up with oranges and onions, which
had been unobtainable when he left. So when he took off his intention had been to go
straight to Speke.

*But the more I aimed towards the north-east the worse it got and I didn't think I could possibly
get to Speke. I decided to make for Sealand, on the river Dee, where I had done most of my
advanced training as a pilot. The trick in this sort of weather, I remembered, was to aim for the
chimneys of John Summers' Steel Works, which were in the Sealand circuit. I flew between the
chimneys by the river and then it was a question of left hand down a bit, wheels and flaps
lowered, and I was on the approach.*

'Where have you come from?' Lumsden was asked when he landed and taxied up to the
watch office. 'Canada.' His answer went straight into the Station Line Book. 'Spud'
Spurdle, too, had a haven to make for, and with even more reason.

As Customs Officers were present at Speke [he says], *I flew to Hawarden airfield; at the head
of the Dee estuary. I'd trained there on Spitfires on my arrival from New Zealand, so I knew
the topography well. The CO was Wing Commander John Hallings-Pott DSO, AFC, the
man who led the famous raid on the Sylt Islands at the beginning of the war.*
    *Marching into his office, lugging a full parachute bag, I asked if I could leave it in his care
for a couple of days. As I made the request I stood a bottle of Bourbon on his desk. We eyed each
other for a moment in perfect understanding, and no questions were asked. He was a good sport
and a few days later I flew over from Speke on a training flight and collected the goods.*

The visibility that day was better on Anglesey than it was on the mainland, but not all the
pilots had thought to mark the airfield on the island – Valley – on their maps, nor do they all
seem to have computed the exact position of their ships before launching. With the help of
local knowledge, Spurdle and Lumsden had avoided disaster; but the other two pilots were
not so fortunate. They flew up and down the North Wales coast, where conditions were bad,
trying in vain to pick out an airfield, a quest that was not so easy in 1941 as it later became.
Gerry North searched in vain for Valley and eventually crash-landed in a field near Bangor,
while Norman Lee, unable to fix his position or find an airfield, eventually put down on the
beach at Leasowe Castle, near Wallasey, in the Mersey estuary.
    He made a good landing on a fine stretch of sands, wheels down, which was a bold
thing to do; and he then found that by good luck he had alighted near an anti-aircraft gun
battery, where there were plenty of men available to move the Hurricane higher up the

beach. This was important as the tide was making. He asked for a party of twelve, then went off to a nearby pub to telephone Speke. Put through to Moulton-Barrett, he explained that the Hurricane was undamaged, that it was being moved above the high-water mark, and that he would fly it off when the sands dried out and the weather improved. 'Are you all right?' asked Moulton-Barrett. 'Perfectly.' 'That's all right, then. I'll send someone over.'

But as Lee turned away from the telephone and looked across towards the beach, his eyes focused on a different picture. While he was on the telephone, the men on the beach had been fighting a losing battle. Lee had left his brakes on, the wheels had dug into the sand, the tide was coming in fast and the twelve men Lee had asked for were proving insufficient for the task. When Lee finally regained the beach, only the tail of the Hurricane was still showing.

A salvage party was sent down from Speke to recover the plane and the party was accompanied, inevitably, by a Customs Officer. According to legend, when the plane was dismantled, thousands of waterlogged cigarettes and hundreds of pairs of ruined nylon stockings fell out on the sands. The quantities were probably exaggerated; but an enquiry was ordered.

The man who did the investigation was a solid but worldly Scottish farmer named George Pinkerton, whose appointment as wing-commander-flying at Speke had already brought him into daily contact with MSFU. An auxiliary with No. 602 (City of Glasgow) Squadron, he had fought and distinguished himself in the Battle of Britain. Pinkerton's attitude – and in this he had the tacit agreement of the Air Officer Commanding – was that everyone indulged in a little smuggling now and again, or in some way benefited from it. Indeed Moulton-Barrett, when Pinkerton interviewed him, was sitting at his desk carving up a sizeable lump of smuggled tobacco. Lee's offence was to have been caught red-handed. Some action had to be taken, however, and Lee was quietly posted elsewhere.

Another MSFU pilot who had the misfortune to be caught – though not for smuggling – was an American named S.E. McCann. On a training flight from Speke, he took the opportunity of paying an aerial visit to his girlfriend. But after the inevitable shoot-up he discovered that he was lost. The thought of landing at an airfield to ask his way, with the embarrassment of the movement report that would certainly be made to his base, did not appeal to him; but his fuel margin gave him no choice. Then he spotted an airfield that had apparently just been built but was not yet occupied, and it occurred to him that, while the airfield construction men would tell him where he was, there would be no one there to report or expose his error. Unfortunately he failed to notice, as he came in to land, that the far end of the runway had only just been laid. As the wheels of the Hurricane sank into the soft concrete, the aircraft tipped up on its nose.

McCann was one of the first to agree that the time had come for a transfer to an American squadron.

VI
A Launching in Mid-Ocean

The pilot of the duty Camship with convoy HX 156, homeward bound from Halifax, was the twenty-one-year-old George Varley. Fair hair parted casually on the right, strong but sensitive features, and a spare but compact build, accorded well with the popular image of the fighter pilot. After the Battle of Britain he had graduated to Hurricane night-fighters, but without enthusiasm. A traumatic experience at St Eval in Cornwall, when he landed in darkness and crashed into a fresh bomb-crater, convinced him that his element was daylight. This, and a love of the sea, had directed his steps towards the catapult fighters.

One of the first men to join MSFU, he had been with the unit for five months and was on his second North Atlantic round trip. But like all MSFU pilots of that period he was desperately short of flying time. Since joining the unit he had accumulated less than twenty flying hours. Such a circumstance was hardly calculated to maintain pilot efficiency; but for George Varley, at least, it made him all the more eager for action.

Varley's fighter direction officer, as on his first trip, was a shrewd, urbane Yorkshireman named Norman Gostelow. A few months older than Varley, he nevertheless recognised him as a go-ahead young man from whom he could learn.

The captain of the *Empire Foam* was a forthright sailor named McWilliam whose earthiness was especially appreciated by Gostelow. On the afternoon of 1 November 1941, all three men were standing on the bridge and Varley was considering whether he could safely escape to the 'heads' to spend a penny, when the first radar warning of an unidentified aircraft came through.

At 16.05 on the previous afternoon, convoy HX 156 had been met by five escort vessels led by the destroyer *Broke*. The convoy had been in two sections and at daylight on 1 November the Iceland section had turned away to the north, accompanied by its own escort. The UK section, having passed through longitude 25 degrees west during the night, was now 550 miles off the Irish coast, well into Condor country. Warned that U-boats were shadowing the convoy, the senior officer of the escort, Commander W.T. Couchman, altered course. But soon afterwards the destroyer *Buxton*, which was proceeding to an anti-shadowing position astern, was missed by a salvo of six torpedoes. After a counter-attack with depth charges and a further alteration of course, it was hoped that the U-boats had been shaken off. But at 14.50 that afternoon came the warning of an unidentified aircraft in the vicinity. Assuming it was hostile, which seemed likely, it would home the U-boats back to the target unless it could be driven off quickly.

The typical Atlantic weather that the convoy had been encountering was disappearing astern and although half the convoy was still protected by a canopy of ten-tenths cloud, the leading vessels, among which was *Empire Foam*, were sailing under a vault of the palest blue, with a calm sea and a slight swell to complete what promised to develop into a perfect November day. Conditions, thought Varley, were excellent for launching. The ship was steaming straight into a 9-knot wind and they wouldn't even have to alter their heading.

At 15.05 a four-engined aircraft was sighted on the horizon dead ahead, flying at about 1,000 feet. The engine of the Hurricane had already been warmed up and as Varley disappeared down the companion way from the bridge and ran forward, the sea crew were alerted and warned to get ready to start up and clear away to launch.

'What is it?' Captain McWilliam demanded of Gostelow. 'Is it a Condor?'

'Yes.'

'Do we launch?'

'Yes – it's positively identified.'

'Action stations!'

By this time Varley too had identified the plane as a Condor. He watched for the hand signals from the first officer, who was already standing by the firing hut, opened the throttle and screwed the nut tight, cut his hand down and felt the shock of the impetus behind him as the Hurricane shot forward on its trolley. As soon as he was airborne he selected flaps up, closed the cockpit hood, did a 180-degree turn and flew down the northern flank of the convoy, heading west, looking for the Condor. There it was, a long way away to his right, on the port beam of the convoy, and he turned towards it, pushing the throttle through the gate, giving the engine full boost. Simultaneously the Condor pilot turned in towards the convoy as though to make an attack.

Varley saw the Condor's bomb-doors open and he judged that the pilot was making for a straggler astern. The black-painted machine was now clearly embossed against the sky. But Varley had scarcely got into position to attack when be realised that the Condor crew had seen him. Surprised to find what he took to be a land-based fighter out in mid-ocean, the Condor pilot straightened out of the turn, abandoned his bombing run and dived for the water. From the shocked tones of his signals, duly intercepted at Cheadle, he seems not to have heard of the catapult Hurricanes. Anyway he opened his throttles and made for the cloud bank astern.

Almost before the Condor had flattened on the water, Varley lost sight of it, the dark camouflage merging perfectly with the sea background. The position of the cloud bank, too, was providential for the Condor. Before Varley could get close enough to open fire, the Condor was clear of the convoy and heading for cloud. Varley asked Gostelow for a vector and was told to steer 270. Sighting the Condor briefly, he chased it into the cloud and stalked it for some minutes, but saw nothing more. Then a thought occurred to him. Suppose this machine was a decoy? While he was wasting time and fuel on a fruitless errand, a second Condor might be creeping in to bomb the convoy.

There were two other Camships in the convoy, but they would normally be held back while Varley was airborne. Gostelow called up these two ships, both of which had radar, and asked if they had a plot, but they could give him no help. Eventually, at Gostelow's suggestion, Varley returned to orbit the convoy, maintaining a standing patrol overhead for the next ninety minutes.

While he was orbiting, Varley was given two separate radar plots which had been passed to Gostelow, each showing unidentified aircraft five miles astern. He investigated both plots and found nothing, but the plots were firm and his presence, it would seem, kept these aircraft at a distance from which they could not attack or observe the convoy.

After Varley had been patrolling for an hour, Gostelow spotted another four-engined aircraft, which he believed to be hostile, approaching on the port bow, range ten miles and he at once alerted Varley. The first thing Varley saw was a cluster of smoke puffs left by shell bursts from a corvette, evidently aimed at the intruder, and he headed at once for these. Soon afterwards he saw an aircraft dead ahead of the convoy. But as he got into position to attack, the aircraft crew fired off the colours of the day – the prearranged recognition signal that proved their identity as friendly. Varley recognised it as a Coastal Command B-24 Liberator.

After one hour forty minutes in the air, Varley was suffering increasing discomfort through his failure to find time to go to the 'heads' before launching. To pass water where he sat was to risk soaking his seat-type parachute; and that was something he was going to need. In contrast, having been on full boost for much of the flight, his fuel tank was embarrassingly empty. He thought that both containers were good for another few minutes; but he warned Gostelow that soon he would have to bale out.

At 17.05, after nearly two hours in the air, he judged that, in both cases, the limits of endurance had been reached. After flying round *Broke* in an anti-clockwise direction and rocking his wings as the signal that he was about to bale out, and getting his signal acknowledged, he climbed to 3,000 feet and made a final call to Gostelow. Then, in preparation for the bale-out, he slid back the cockpit hood, took off his flying boots and helmet, and tipped them over the side. The boots, he thought, might fill with water and drag him down; and he didn't want his helmet and plug fouling anything in the cockpit as he left.

The next thing was to jettison the emergency side panel; when the release mechanism was operated the panel dropped away. The panel was originally introduced as a means of exit when, in a crash landing, the Hurricane turned over on its back; but it also gave more freedom of movement in a bale-out. The lever was recessed to his right, and he pulled it, but nothing happened. He jerked at it again and again, but it was stuck. Salt water corrosion, he thought. That would be it.

He would just have to climb out of the cockpit the same way as he had climbed in. He knew it would be difficult and that the slipstream would force him back, but it was the obvious way. He trimmed the Hurricane carefully to fly straight and level and began to climb out. But before he could get one leg over the side, the Hurricane began to slip out of control.

During the Battle of Britain he had read in the combat reports that pilots had sometimes knelt on their seats and kicked the stick forward, the resultant jerk pitching them out in 'jack-in-the-box' style. So he climbed back to 2,500 feet, knelt on the seat on one knee, and kicked at the stick with his free foot. Perhaps it needed a flying-boot to get the right sort of pressure. But he did the best he could in his stockinged feet. The next thing he knew he was half in and half out of the cockpit, held by the legs, but with his hands grasping for a hold immediately behind the engine exhaust pipes. The aircraft was meanwhile diving alarmingly to the left. Somehow he worked his way back into the cockpit and regained control.

There was one other way of getting out, and that was to turn the aircraft upside down; but Varley didn't think of it. Sweating with fear and frustration, he looked again at the emergency panel. Turning sideways on, facing the panel, and steadying the stick with his left hand, he kicked out violently with both feet. He bruised his feet badly, but he felt nothing. Two or three more kicks and the panel gave way.

He put his legs through the opening and worked himself outwards, still guiding the stick with his left hand, determined to retain control as long as he could. Then, with the air-speed indicator showing 120 mph, he let go of the stick, pulling himself clear of the cockpit, and ran as hard as he could along the starboard wing. He didn't get as far as the wing-tip, but he got far enough to make sure of clearing the tail. Then the airstream buffeted him off and he fell backwards, arms and legs flung wide.

Drawing his limbs together, he felt for the ripcord handle, then decided not to pull it for the moment in case the aircraft was following him down. Eventually, seeing and hearing nothing, he pulled the ripcord and for an agonising moment saw the handle loose in his hand. He had forgotten that this was the normal sequence. Then the canopy billowed.

It seemed to him that he was floating absolutely still, as though time itself were suspended. The ships below him looked so small that he thought they would be gone by the time he got down. He inflated his lifejacket and then the water suddenly came closer and he prepared to release himself from the parachute harness. He knew he was supposed to punch the quick release box just before he hit the sea, judging his height, but he was too late, and he found himself struggling in the water with the canopy on top of him, the rigging lines tangled hopelessly round one leg. A turn of the valve on the CO_2 bottle inflated the dinghy attached to his seat and he hung on to it, but he couldn't get free of the lines to climb in.

He was astonished how cold it was, so cold that the shock of immersion anaesthetised his muscles and he forgot his pressing need. But *Broke* appeared within a few minutes and someone with a boat-hook hoisted him like a flounder on to the deck. They'd already drawn a hot bath for him and they put him straight in it, clothes and all. As he sat there, and they fed him hot coffee laced with rum, relaxation of mind and muscle was at last complete.

Just before George Varley's bale-out, at 17.00, the convoy had altered course to divert it from the track on which the Condor crew had sighted it. Three hours later, following information from intercept sources that two U-boats were still shadowing, it altered course again. Extensive searches by the escort were precluded by shortage of fuel, but during the night, after strong U-boat signals had been picked up from astern, *Broke* went off on her own to act as a decoy, demonstrating her presence elsewhere with starshell, smoke and depth-charges to simulate a force of convoy size. No attack developed, so the U-boats may have been deceived.

By 3 November, bearings taken on U-boat signals showed them to be falling aft, with signal strength progressively diminishing and the convoy got through the Western Approaches without loss. Varley's was the first operational launching from a Camship, after nearly five months of convoy work. As with so many of the Fleet Air Arm launchings that preceded it, the raider was not even brought to combat and the main credit for the escape of HX 156 went to the escort. But Varley's two-hour vigil, besides driving off one Condor that was about to attack and two shadowers, deprived the U-boats of aerial reconnaissance at what proved to be a critical time.

Varley completed four North Atlantic round trips in Camships, which constituted an MSFU operational 'tour', and he was mentioned in despatches. Later, on a Tempest squadron, he won the DFC. His memory of his service with MSFU, though, remains vivid, and he especially recalls the fuss the Navy made of him when he was aboard the *Broke*. The first lieutenant was Peter Scott, the naturalist, and he gave up his cabin for Varley.

During his stay on *Broke*, however, Varley learned that had there been a U-boat scare while he was airborne, his chances of being picked up before nightfall would have been slim. One life, in that situation, meant nothing. What mattered were the ships and their cargoes.

It was normal practice, or malpractice, after a bale-out, for parachute and dinghy to be pronounced too badly damaged to be salvaged and, by agreement with Commander Couchman, the Navy kept the dinghy and Varley the parachute. Varley's girlfriend, whom he married a few weeks later, luxuriated in silk underwear for the rest of the war.

VII
Winter in the North Atlantic

By the end of November 1941, the Camships had been operating for six months and had completed sixty round trips. In the whole of that time only one hostile aircraft had been sighted and that had escaped; the biggest threat to the convoys in this period came from the U-boats. To this threat, of course, the Camships were equally vulnerable; but for three months, their luck held. Then, on 19 September and again on 2 October, Camships were torpedoed and sunk. There were no MSFU casualties in these two sinkings, but on 3 October, when the *Empire Wave* was sunk, two MSFU men were killed and another severely injured and the survivors spent fourteen days in an open boat before reaching Iceland in a distressed condition. While sharing all the hazards of the Atlantic battle, the unit seemed to be achieving little. Enthusiasm sagged and with it morale, and as winter approached the future of the unit again came under scrutiny.

The policy still remained to include at least one Camship whenever possible in every North Atlantic convoy, while on the Gibraltar run the single Camship introduced in each convoy in October was soon increased to two. Yet, with 49 pilots on the unit strength (the establishment was 50), together with 61 aircraft and 340 maintenance and administrative personnel, No. 9 Group were forecasting a barren winter, not only through the continued scarcity of targets but also through the high rate of unserviceability that must be expected due to gales, rough seas and corrosion.

Throughout that summer and autumn, the MSFU sea crews had done a magnificent job in keeping the Hurricanes serviceable on the catapults. In a total of about a hundred launchings on both sides of the Atlantic, there had not been a single incident that could be traced to faulty maintenance. But despite the spraying of all aircraft interiors with lanolin resin, and some slight spraying externally, backed up by daily inspection and treatment at sea, unserviceability on the return to the UK, making launchings impracticable at the end of the voyage, was becoming commonplace. Many pilots continued to comment on how well aircraft and catapult stood up to severe weather conditions and Davidson, first of the MSFU pilots, noted that 'although exceptionally rough and freezing weather was experienced, it affected everything very little'. But this kind of report gradually became less frequent. Mike Lyne had one period of four days during which the captain wouldn't allow anyone to go forward to the catapult and there were times when aircraft were practically submerged in heavy seas. Spray beat into closed cockpits and corroded instruments and whereas a damp aircraft had dried out in fine weather earlier in the year, now it was often impossible to take prompt remedial action. A selection of reports from returning pilots makes the worsening position clear.

> *'Inclement weather made daily inspection difficult.'*
> *'Storm caused control locking gear to break.'*
> *'Covers unmanageable in high winds.'*
> *'Airframe badly corroded.'*
> *'Weather conditions never suitable for operational work.'*
> *'Only one day on which the aircraft could have been flown off on the entire homeward trip.'*

Another description, written more recently, comes from 'Spud' Spurdle. 'I have seen the propeller forced around against the compression of a 12-cylinder motor in a gale and actually screwing up and tearing off the canvas engine-covers. Salt corrosion and dampness were an unending battle for the ground crews on the ships.'

Even the ships themselves were suffering damage which sometimes forced them to return to port and one pilot, a stocky, rugged South African of Scottish extraction named Alistair Hay, of whom more will be heard, reported that two of his men had been injured through falling from the catapult in rough weather. 'I don't think it will be possible,' he wrote, 'to maintain the aircraft if the weather experienced on this trip persists throughout the winter months.'

Other factors militating against the cause of MSFU in the North Atlantic that winter, besides the paucity of targets, were the manpower shortages stressed continually by Sholto Douglas, who wanted his pilots and maintenance crews back as soon as was reasonable, and the possible requirement for some at least of the Camships in other theatres. Convoys carrying supplies to Russia were a new and urgent requirement and the gaps in fighter cover on that route, should the Germans intervene in any strength, were alarming.

So far as the Condors were concerned, a wartime German document summarised the position as follows:

> *The continued use of the Condor on reconnaissance missions for the submarine fleet would have been to our advantage, had systematic submarine attacks on convoys been maintained. As the convoys, however, became more and more strongly escorted by destroyers and aircraft, our submarines suffered increasingly high losses and their area of operations was therefore transferred to a point on the convoy route to America outside the range of the Condors.*

The plan was that by late autumn 1941, operations should be conducted exclusively in North American waters, which provided both favourable fighting conditions and numerous targets.

By December 1941, practically all combined operations with the submarine fleet had to be discontinued for several months, no more submarines being available for operations in European waters. The Condor units were transferred to other theatres of war, some to reconnaissance units in Norway and some as transport aircraft to the Mediterranean and Eastern fronts.

British Intelligence was well aware of these changes. But the deterrent value of the Camships was appreciated. Although enemy air activity had been negligible for months, there was no guarantee that the assault might not be renewed. However, on 3 January 1942 the operation of Camships on the North Atlantic run was suspended, and no aircraft were embarked on ships loading after the 5th. Some of the Camships then began operating as pure freighters. The commitment to the Gibraltar run remained, and although future policy was regarded as uncertain, it was decided to keep MSFU and its equipment and personnel intact to await developments.

Pilots and FDOs alike, as might be expected, received this news with mixed feelings. Those with experience of the Atlantic in winter accepted it as inevitable, and those who had been torpedoed, or had sailed in convoys that had been badly mauled, welcomed a respite. But those who had not yet been to sea were bitterly disappointed, feeling that their chance would never come. However, the hiatus gave the headquarters' staff a chance to reorganise the unit and in a sense rededicate it. The formation had taken place so hurriedly, and the early training had been so sketchy, that a firm guiding hand was needed.

During his tenure as commanding officer, Moulton-Barrett had laid the foundations of the smooth operational relationships that existed at the various ports and between MSFU and the Royal and Merchant Navies; but in achieving this he had been obliged to spend most of his time away from Speke. The officers left behind did not have the background necessary to control and organise the motley collection of individual RAF and Naval men who made up MSFU, and Moulton-Barrett himself was not a practising pilot and did not appreciate the importance of a strict training programme in the operation of modern fighter aircraft. Such training programmes as his staff were able to introduce were not often fulfilled, since pilots rarely had more than two or three weeks between trips, and with seven days absorbed by home leave, a spell of bad weather could leave very little time for training.

On 26 January 1942 Moulton-Barrett was promoted to group captain and posted to a job where his flair for working with port authorities could be given full scope – station commander at the Takoradi end of the West Africa to Cairo reinforcement route. He was replaced by a man who already had a sound knowledge of the workings of MSFU and of its strengths and weaknesses – George Pinkerton. Pinkerton assembled a strong team around him and after arranging for an increase in pilot establishment he introduced a new and comprehensive syllabus of training, embracing pilots, FDOs and sea crews. The morale of the unit soon began to recover; and the sense of unit purpose was given fresh impetus when, on 3 March 1942, sailings of Camships on the North Atlantic run were resumed.

Pinkerton's problems with the unit continued at first to be mostly concerned with discipline and morale. Yet at the same time he had to impress on the crews that he was fundamentally on their side. Especially was this so in the feuding that went on between

MSFU, as a lodger unit, and the station administration staff at RAF Speke. The antics of the high-spirited MSFU men were not always appreciated by their hosts and when one of the more extrovert characters on the unit, Maxwell Charlesworth, known as Black Max, 'borrowed' the station commander's car after a party to take the girls home, the administrative staff sought a scapegoat. Pinkerton knew well enough who had done it, but he wasn't going to let on to the station commander.

The unit, not surprisingly, attracted several Canadian pilots, and one of them, Jack Sheppard, was goaded by the Merchant Navy men all the way back across the Atlantic with hints of the superiority of the Canada-based pilots, one of whom had stunted over the ship in a Hurricane when they left Halifax. 'That's what we call flying,' they said. 'Our chaps can't fly like that.'

Sheppard was a quiet, modest young man, but when he was catapulted off the Camship near Anglesey at the end of the crossing he decided to teach the Merchant Navy a lesson. The result was that he dipped a wing in the water and tore it clean off. Fortunately the wreckage floated and the crest-fallen Sheppard, sitting ignominiously on the remaining wing, had to be rescued by the men he had sought to impress. It looked a certain court martial; but Pinkerton put it to the AOC 9 Group that Sheppard had only been trying to uphold the reputation of MSFU, at a time when the rebuilding of unit morale was of paramount importance. The AOC was an understanding chap and he gave Pinkerton authority to deal with Sheppard personally. Pinkerton had a quiet word with the offender, but punishment there was none. Sheppard, he felt, had already suffered disgrace enough. Later, after leaving MSFU, Jack Sheppard won the DFC.

Although the pilots selected for MSFU were technically volunteers, it was up to their squadron commanders whether they were allowed to leave or not; and the temptation obviously was for commanders to use MSFU as a dumping ground for men whose faces didn't fit. The chap concerned, with a poor record on his squadron, might well come to MSFU and prove himself; but if he didn't measure up to Pinkerton's high standards, equal ruthlessness was applied in getting rid of him.

Pinkerton's method was to detail newcomers on a trip as reserve pilot with someone who would be likely to grab any chance of an operational launching. That way, little damage could be done. If the chap didn't settle he was soon out.

Two new pilots, both Canadians, hated each other so much that they caused an atmosphere in the unit of which Pinkerton became aware. There was a ship about to leave for Gibraltar and he gave orders that these two should go. 'It won't work,' he was warned, 'they're arch enemies, they'll never work as a team.' Pinkerton's attitude was that if they were going to stay in the unit they had better learn to get on together. 'I'm sending them on the same ship,' he insisted. The two men were embarked, and within half an hour they had such a bitter quarrel that news of it reached the captain. He ordered the top of the hatches to be cleared and sent for the two pilots and told them to fight it out. One had been a gold prospector with his father in northern Canada, and this had so toughened him that rather inevitably he gave the other a hiding. But mutual respect was won, and they became the best of friends.

The total flying hours per month for MSFU in 1941 had averaged 100 to 150, with a highest of 198 in August. By March 1942 Pinkerton, aided by a squadron leader training named Graham Austin (to whom, according to Pinkerton, 'a great deal of the subsequent success of MSFU was attributable'), the total had reached 250, and in the next two months this figure was nearly doubled. Meanwhile, on 28 March, the commitments of the unit were further increased by a decision to employ Camships on the Arctic convoys to Russia.

The most spectacular successes of the Merchant Ship Fighter Unit were about to begin.

VIII
Convoys to Russia: PQ 15

Two months after the Germans invaded Russia, on 12 August 1941, the first of the Arctic convoys sailed from Liverpool, bound for Archangel via Iceland; and from that time on, these convoys sailed at the rate of one and sometimes two a month. When Archangel became icebound, the ice-free port of Murmansk on the Kola Inlet, kept clear by the Gulf Stream, was substituted. For a long time the Germans failed to recognise the importance of these convoys and the supplies of war equipment they carried, and the first eleven convoys sailed through to Russia unmolested. It could even be that, in the interests of morale-building, too much was made of these convoys by the British propaganda services, thus focusing enemy attention on them. Churchill certainly thought this was so. But sooner or later, as Allied tanks and guns appeared in ever-increasing numbers on the Eastern front, the Germans were bound to take notice, and when they did they reacted vigorously.

For the Allies, the problem, as so often in wartime, was to reconcile political and military aims. The Arctic route to Russia was bounded on the east and south by the enemy-occupied coastline of northern Norway and to the west and north by ice. The convoys were subject to attack by surface forces over a large part of their 2,000-mile passage, to air attack for some 1,400 miles, and to U-boat attack throughout. The convoys of the winter of 1941-2 were aided not only by German inattention but also by the long hours of darkness; but from March through to September, daylight would be almost continuous and the Germans, having greatly strengthened their forces in northern Norway, were preparing to strike.

Under pressure from his chiefs of staff to reconsider the position, Churchill gave the grim opinion that 'the operation is justified if a half gets through'. He supported this with a statement that was impossible to contradict. 'The Russians are in heavy action and will expect us to run the risk.' Professional opinion remained antipathetic – the route was far too precarious in the summer months while the Germans held airfields in northern Norway – and Dudley Pound told Admiral of the Fleet Ernest J. King, C-in-C of the United States Navy: 'The whole thing is a most unsound operation with the dice loaded against us in every direction.' Yet, in the context of the war situation in the spring of 1942, with the Russians facing the main German armies almost alone, it was inevitable that the attempt should be made.

On 10 March 1942 Air Commodore John Whitworth Jones, who had succeeded Donald Stevenson at the Directorate of Fighter Operations at the Air Ministry, told the Deputy Chief of the Air Staff: 'We can provide fighter cover from British air bases for a certain part of the journey, but there is a bad gap west of Norway and past Iceland, when fighter protection cannot be provided from a shore base.' To fill this gap, in the continued absence of escort carriers, he suggested Camships.

Seven days earlier, on 3 March, the employment of Camships in the North Atlantic had been resumed and two Camships were still being allocated to each Gibraltar convoy. Yet the Admiralty's estimate of the number of Camships that needed to be allotted to the Russian convoys was no more than six, to operate at the rate of one per convoy. They saw the introduction of Camships on the Arctic route as more an attempt to provide the means to destroy shadowing aircraft, which kept out of gun range while reporting the progress of convoys, than as genuine fighter protection; and here they clearly differed from the Air Ministry. In view of the opinion so forcibly expressed to Admiral King by Dudley Pound, the modesty of the Admiralty's demands seems incomprehensible.

There was an ancillary requirement for the establishment of a small base at Archangel for the holding of a pool of three Sea Hurricanes in reserve; but this would do no more than provide servicing and replacements for the return voyage.

Arrangements were finalised at a meeting at the Air Ministry on 27 March, when the requirement was restated and agreed without query. Discussion centred around the provision of personnel and the terminal point where the reserve pool was to be located. Because of the long hours of daylight all Camships in Russian convoys were to carry two pilots. With Archangel still icebound, the first Camship would go to Murmansk; but it was expected that it would be possible to establish the pool at Archangel within six to eight weeks.

Experience with the Russians had already shown that the question of siting an RAF detachment on Russian soil would have to be handled discreetly and the Head of 30 Mission, the British Military Mission in Moscow, warned that any request to admit RAF personnel to Russia would be regarded with grave suspicion. 'All British personnel,' he said, 'are treated as spies.' The reserve pool, with its three Hurricanes, needed to be staffed by two pilots and about thirty maintenance men, but 30 Mission advised that the Russians would never accept such a figure. For the purpose of negotiation, the number of twenty-one was put forward and the word 'initially' was stressed, the implication being that this number might be reduced as trained Russian replacements became available (the Russians were already operating Hurricane IIs). The real intention, however, was that all these personnel should remain British. Eventually, on 6 April, the Russians were persuaded to agree to the figure requested.

Meanwhile HQ Fighter Command were seeking advice on protective measures that might be taken by pilots against immersion in the extreme low water temperatures they would encounter. The Medical Director-General at the Admiralty thought that no great harm was likely to be suffered from a brief immersion, say of up to fifteen minutes, even at very low temperatures. The only effective protection, he suggested, would be some form of waterproof suit, but he doubted if this would be practicable. The Air Ministry for their part consulted Sir Thomas Lewis, adviser to the Shipwreck Committee of the Medical Research Council, and he too, while recommending some sort of special suit, thought pilots should survive for fifteen minutes. But he added: 'They would suffer considerable pain and their movements would become slow and feeble.'

With this in mind the Air Ministry set in motion an investigation into the practicability of a waterproof suit; but for the next few months at least, pilots would have to sail without one. 'In view of the foregoing,' the Director of Fighter Operations told Sholto Douglas, 'it is thought that if a pilot is instructed to adjust his flying clothing to keep the cold water from his body for as long as possible, the risk he is called upon to take may be considered an acceptable one.' This evaluation, which presupposed that the period of immersion would be under fifteen minutes, was translated by the pilots into a familiar admonition: 'Please adjust your dress before leaving.'

The first Camship to accompany a Russian convoy was the *Empire Morn*, under Captain W.L. Cruickshank, with John Kendal and Deryck Faulks as pilots and Peter Mallett as FDO. Kendal and Mallett had been early recruits to MSFU, they had crossed the Atlantic together three times and got to know each other well. 'Tiny' Faulks had come in as reserve pilot for the Arctic run. Methodical and unflappable, Mallett had proved the perfect foil to the high-spirited Kendal, while Faulks was adaptable and slotted in well.

Even amongst the colourful characters of MSFU John Kendal stood out. At Ardingly he had been an indifferent scholar, but his home had been within easy cycling distance of Croydon Aerodrome and there he had developed an early fascination with flying, spending many holiday hours watching and photographing aeroplanes and chasing autographs. At eighteen he learned to fly with the RAF Volunteer Reserve and when the war came he flew Spitfires with 66 Squadron in the Battle of Britain. In a book called *Ten Fighter Boys*, published in 1942, he told of his days with 66; but of greater interest in retrospect, perhaps, are the introductory paragraphs to his section of the book. 'Shortish, he has one of those comic faces that looks as if it was made of rubber, with a large mouth and a broken nose,' said the writer; and the flexible countenance greatly enlivened a talent for mimicry. He could imitate any noise from an underground train entering and leaving a station to the ricocheting of a rifle bullet in a Western movie. As a pilot he was cheerfully aggressive and he often got shot up – and was more than once shot down – for his pains. But so far he had always managed to get his damaged aeroplane down in one piece. That, as he knew only too well, would almost certainly not be possible now.

The convoy that *Empire Morn* joined was numbered PQ 15 and it assembled at Hvalfjord, Iceland, between 16 and 25 April 1942. It was there, too, that instructions were given by the senior officer of the escort (SOE) to the Camship. Orders for launching were to come direct from the SOE, though he might at any time transfer this responsibility to the Camship. To guard against homing by hostile forces on to ships' radar transmissions,

Mallett was instructed not to use his radar unless the convoy was known to be under enemy surveillance.

There were still no escort carriers available and *Empire Morn* thus carried the only fighter protection available to the convoy once Iceland was out of range. In addition to the aircraft on the catapult she carried a crated Sea Hurricane as a reserve against an outward launching and this was to be off-loaded at Murmansk for the new Archangel Pool if no launch was made. The remaining two aircraft for the Pool, plus the maintenance party, VHF radio, and other equipment, were to follow in the next convoy.

On 26 April, with twenty-five merchant ships and a strengthened naval escort of four destroyers and four armed trawlers, plus the flak ship *Ulster Queen*, and with a force of two cruisers and two destroyers for close cover, the convoy sailed from Hvalfjord. Two days later an Iceland-bound convoy of seventeen ships, styled QP 11, set out on the return voyage from Murmansk. The aim of these more or less simultaneous sailings was to dilute the German offensive effort and at the same time take maximum advantage of the inadequate British escort forces available.

That the Germans were now fully alert to the threat these convoys offered to their dominance on the Eastern front is clear from a report published in a German newspaper eleven days before PQ 15 sailed. 'These deliveries to Murmansk play an extremely important part in the war strategy of the enemy,' said the report. After stressing the significance of recent German Navy and Air Force successes on the Arctic route, the report continued:

> *London and Washington must now realise that this route is not nearly as safe and convenient as they had believed or are repeatedly at pains to make it out to be. The eyes of our long-range reconnaissance machines do not miss a single ton of shipping which seeks to find its way to the Murmansk coast from Iceland, via Greenland, the islands of Jan Mayen and Spitzbergen, and Bear Island, to the farthest shores of Northern Norway, Finland and the Kola Peninsula…In the tundra on the most northerly flying-fields in the world we keep watch…we attack the Soviet shipping routes, dive on the harbour installations of Murmansk, interrupt the Murmansk railway afresh each day and hurl death and destruction over the Polar front. At this time of year the northern light grows longer and longer, and the sun becomes the friend of the booty-hungry bomber and dive-bomber.*

The German squadrons based on airfields in northern Norway, at Bardufoss, Tromsø, Banak and Kirkenes, were not yet anywhere near full strength and the newspaper report smacked strongly of propaganda; but the movement of packs of U-boats into the Barents Sea and massed air attacks from the Norwegian bases, were threats that were bound to develop as the summer progressed.

For the first seventy-two hours of its voyage, PQ 15 was considered to come under the protection of Iceland-based aircraft; but by 29 April the rockets on *Empire Morn*'s catapult were connected up, and on the 30th the Hurricane was ordered to immediate readiness. Two long-range reconnaissance planes, a Focke-Wulf Condor from I./KG 40, which had recently been transferred to Trondheim-Vaemes, and a Blohm and Voss 138 flying-boat from Tromsø, were sighted during the day; but both kept their distance and although aircraft and crew on the Camship remained at action stations, no instructions came from the SOE.

Again on 1 May the convoy was patrolled all day by two reconnaissance machines and for hour after hour, as the ships progressed eastwards, the threat of attack from Bardufoss and Banak became more imminent. Occasionally the circling aircraft were blotted out by snow squalls; but it was still daylight when, at 20.23, echoes from approaching aircraft animated the ships' radar. The echoes crystallised into a formation of Ju88 bombers – there seemed, in fact, to be no more than two – and while Kendal, as senior pilot, claimed the seat in the Hurricane cockpit, the sea crew made ready to launch.

The Arctic Route to Russia. When ice conditions permitted, convoys were routed north of Jan Mayen and Bear Islands.

The convoy was formed up into five columns, each column three cables apart, and *Empire Morn* was the leading ship in Column No. 5, the column on the extreme right. With the wind in the north east, Kendal would have a clear launching rim. A signal from the SOE told them to use their own discretion about launching, and with visibility good, Kendal decided to go. They were just about to fire off when the SOE signalled again that he didn't think after all that the raid warranted wasting the Hurricane. A heavy anti-aircraft barrage was forcing the raiders into cloud and the bombing was becoming increasingly inaccurate. Peter Mallett, on the bridge of *Empire Morn*, assessed it as a rather half-hearted attack, but there was nothing half-hearted about the anti-aircraft barrage, which eventually succeeded in sending one of the raiders diving into the sea. No ships were hit.

Next morning, 2 May, at 07.30, again two shadowers resumed their interminable orbiting. A Ju88 was glimpsed briefly through repeated snow squalls and with conditions unfavourable for launching it was just as well that most of the German bombers were grounded at their bases. Their numbers, however, had been increasing almost daily as the Nazis appreciated the growing importance to the Russians of this supply lifeline.

At midnight on 2/3 May there was still enough light for Peter Mallett to read a newspaper on the bridge. The radar was switched off by order, the weather was atrocious and the chances of air attack seemed remote. Half an hour later, with the weather still poor, the cloud base lifted briefly to 1,000 feet, and in a sudden clear spell between snowstorms five Heinkel 111 torpedo-bombers materialised out of the murk from the starboard quarter without any kind of warning, flattened on the water at no more than 50 feet. Each machine was seen to be carrying two torpedoes slung beneath the wing roots.

The Heinkels flew right along the starboard flank of the convoy, overtook the leaders, then turned sharply to port to develop an attack almost at right angles, just forward of the beam, their targets apparently being the leading ship in each column. From this angle, even if they missed the leading ships they had every chance of hitting a ship in the adjacent column. *Ulster Queen*, in the middle of the convoy, was unable to engage them, but every gun that could be depressed to low level was streaking its fire across the water to starboard at bridge height, putting up such a concentration around *Empire Morn* that it would have been suicide to attempt to launch the Hurricane. Captain Cruickshank, aware of this, immediately forbade it. Nothing, however, seemed to deter the opposition.

The Heinkel pilots had executed their turns to port a fraction too late, or so it seemed; anyway the Heinkel on the extreme right of the formation was squeezed out, and it broke away without launching its torpedoes, although it contributed something by plastering an escorting destroyer with machine-gun fire. It could just possibly have been a deliberate ploy, since the Heinkel on the extreme port side did much the same; but it seems unlikely, since both aircraft were carrying torpedoes. The three remaining Heinkels, still in V formation, and now seen to be painted dark green, bore down on the leading ship at low level, firing their cannon from the forward gun position as they came.

The barrage was now so intense that it seemed that no aircraft could possibly fly through it; yet the Heinkel pilots came on undeterred. No one did better at the guns than Seaman Gunner Jeckells on the starboard Oerlikon of *Empire Morn*; but the Heinkels still held on, dropping their torpedoes simultaneously at 200 yards' range. Even so it seemed to Captain Cruickshank that the pilot of the Heinkel that was attacking his own ship had had his aim deflected by the dogged persistence of Jeckells.

Standing on the monkey island on *Empire Morn*, Peter Mallett saw one of the torpedo trails hit the bows of his own ship and he cringed from the anticipated explosion. He had forgotten that torpedoes pass ahead of their wake. Then he saw another torpedo approaching amidships and heard the chief officer call for full starboard helm and increase in speed. The torpedo just missed the ship's stern.

The torpedo that passed ahead of the Camship hit the *Jutland*, the leading ship in the fourth column, immediately adjacent to *Empire Morn*. The torpedo that missed her astern hit the *Botavon*, the ship leading the third or middle column. These were the convoy commodore's and vice-commodore's ships, each of about 6,000 tons.

The ships leading the first and second columns, on the left of the convoy, combed the torpedoes as *Empire Morn* had done. But *Cape Corso*, the second ship in the first column, paid the forfeit. All three explosions occurred within seconds of each other.

After releasing their torpedoes the Heinkel pilots continued to skim the water, with the result that some ships were unable to fire at them for fear of hitting other ships. But the Heinkel that had aimed at *Empire Morn* was pouring heavy black smoke from both engines, and after a vain attempt to reach cloud it staggered and crashed into the sea. Despite the perfect timing of the attack, sandwiched between snow squalls, and lasting only two or three minutes, two more of the Heinkels were seen to fall to the convoy's guns.

Captain J.H. Smith of *Botavon*, with the commodore on board, got his entire complement of seventy-three safely away in four boats and two rafts and when he was picked up half an hour later by the destroyer *Badsworth* he found his son was the navigating officer. In *Jutland*, the only casualty was an American passenger who was asleep in his bunk. But *Cape Corso*, which had ammunition and explosives in her No. 3 Hold, blew up when she was hit and in a very few moments the whole of the after part of the ship was a blazing inferno. Of her complement of fifty-six, only six were saved.

For the Germans, in the context of wartime, three sizeable cargo ships, fully loaded with war supplies, must have seemed a fair exchange for three Heinkel torpedo-

71

bombers and their crews. If all the German pilots pressed home their attacks with such courage, there would be many more losses to come.

After picking up survivors the convoy closed its ranks and formed up again quickly, continuing on its easterly course. Later that day a bombing attack by three Ju88s was aborted by heavy snow and low cloud and with rough weather and poor visibility hampering the German effort, the convoy anchored in the Kola Inlet off Murmansk on 6 May without further loss.

After the Heinkel attack, Kendal and Faulks had taken turns to sit in the Hurricane at readiness in case of another surprise attack. But it was a practice they soon had to abandon. Even in the enclosed cockpit the temperature was down to 25 degrees Fahrenheit and the cold so penetrated their bodies that their operational efficiency would have been seriously impaired had they been launched.

It had been a grim and frustrating experience for the two Camship pilots. For most of the voyage from Iceland, German aircraft had been in sight and there had been three separate attacks, with three ships sunk by aerial torpedo and many casualties. Yet the Hurricane still sat on its catapult, pointing impotently at the horizon.

The convoy sailing in the other direction – QP 11 – had got through to Iceland unscathed, although an escorting cruiser, the *Edinburgh*, crippled in an attack by U-boats, had had to be abandoned.

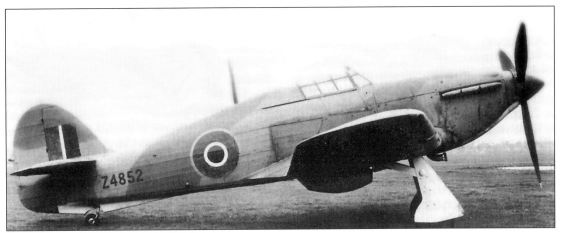

Indistinguishable on the outside from the late series Hurricane Mark I, the Sea Hurricane IA, used for Camship operations, incorporated catapult points and naval radio.

A Fairey Fulmar of the Fleet Air Arm.

To combat the Fw200 Condor Atlantic raider the Camship (Catapult Armed Merchant), Empire Tide, *was introduced. These Camships carried Hawker Hurricane Mark IAs readied for take-off on basic rocket catapult.*

The Camship Empire Tide, *1943.*

A Sea Hurricane IA, with flaps pre-selected in the take-off position, on the fo'c'sle of a Camship. The catapult was angled to starboard over the ship's bows partly to prevent the rocket blast engulfing the bridge but also to lower the risk of the pilot being run down by the ship should he hit the water after launch.

Preparing for a practice launch at Speke.

Sea Hurricane IA is launched from a rocket catapult during training at Speke in 1941.

76

'The most frightening experience of all': lifting the Hurricane on to the catapult.

Sea Hurricane Mark IAs, with MSFU code letters are ferried by barge to a Camship anchored in the Mersey.

A spectacular launching on the Clyde.

Bernard Jope and his crew after their successful attack on the Empress of Britain, *October 1940.*

German photograph of a Ju88.

A Focke-Wulf Condor, showing the fore and aft dorsal gun positions and the ventral gondola.

Edgar Petersen, commander of Kampgeswarder 40, seated at the controls of a Focke-Wulf Condor.

A Condor's tail: keeping the score.

John Kendal in the cockpit of a Hurricane.

Heavy weather on a Camship in mid-Atlantic

A Heinkel 115 floatplane.

A Heinkel 111 drops the first of its two torpedoes.

PQ 18 under air attack, September 1942.

The Empire Stevenson *blows up.*

IX

Two in One Day: PQ 16 and QP 12

After discharging her cargo alongside the wall at Murmansk, *Empire Morn* lay at anchor in the Kola Inlet for the next fortnight awaiting the assembly of a return convoy. The crated Hurricane earmarked for Archangel was off-loaded and taken to nearby Vaenga Airfield, but lack of cranes prevented the disembarkation of the Hurricane on the catapult and it remained on its perch, such servicing as was possible being carried out on board. Meanwhile a period of bright, sunny weather brought German dive-bombers over in strength.

On 12 May, at 18.00 hours, twelve Ju88s based at Kirkenes launched a dive-bombing attack on a cluster of ships a little further up the inlet from *Empire Morn*. 'The arrival of the raiders,' noted Peter Mallett, 'was well known throughout the surrounding district as their vapour trails were visible for some minutes before the actual attack.' Russian fighters took off from Vaenga in large numbers and made desperate attempts to gain sufficient height for combat – although they were unsuccessful on this occasion, the sky was a mêlée of dog-fights in the days that followed. Several ships were damaged and one stick of bombs from a Ju87 narrowly missed *Empire Morn*. Later that day, ironical cheers greeted a BBC news broadcast which claimed that 'this convoy is now resting safely in a Russian port'; but then the weather changed to cold and overcast and aerial activity decreased.

All the arguments that had been put forward by the British chiefs of staff and especially by Admiral Tovey, C-in-C Home Fleet, to stress the vulnerability of Arctic convoys in the summer months still held good; but so too did the political motivation which had overruled these objections. Thus it was that the largest Russian convoy yet assembled, PQ 16, gathered in Iceland at the same time as PQ 15, renumbered QP 12 for the return run, prepared to leave Murmansk. Once again, and for the same reasons, the sailing of the two convoys were to be roughly simultaneous, timed so that they met somewhere between Jan Mayen Island and Bear Island, about half-way.

Thirty-five merchant vessels were allocated to PQ 16, and they were carrying a total cargo of 125,000 tons. Among the most important items were 201 aircraft, 468 tanks and 3,277 vehicles. Other vessels in the convoy were carrying two spare Sea Hurricanes for the Archangel Pool, together with pilots, maintenance party, W/T vehicles and general equipment. The senior pilot, Flight Lieutenant Roy Lane, had fought with Dickie Turley-George in the Battle of Britain and was a close friend; he was aboard the *Empire Baffin*. To spread the risk the other pilot, Deryck Lamb, was aboard the *Lowther Castle*. The close escort for this large convoy (by Arctic standards) consisted of no more than five destroyers, five corvettes, four trawlers, one minesweeper and an anti-aircraft ship; but a strong cruiser force was to provide close cover west of Bear Island against possible interference from the pocket battleships *Lützow* and *Scheer*, based at Narvik, while the Home Fleet was cruising north-east of Iceland to cover any sortie by the *Tirpitz* from Trondheim.

Like its predecessor, PQ 16 was allotted a single Camship, the 7,457-ton *Empire Lawrence* (Captain H.S. Darkins). In addition to the Hurricat she was carrying 5,000 tons of military stores. Armed with one 4-inch gun, one 12-pounder, four Oerlikons, two twin Hotchkiss and four P.A.C. rockets, her total complement, including naval gunners, MSFU men and radar ratings, was sixty-eight. She was destined to have the most eventful voyage of all the Camships.

The senior pilot was the South African Al Hay already mentioned, short in stature, intensely physical, and always ready for a rough and tumble. From under beetling eyebrows his eyesight was reputed to be the best on the unit. Like all the pilots on the Russian run he had been specially selected by George Pinkerton. His FDO, Leo Powell, had been a telegraphist in the same ship as Peter Mallett when the war started.

They had got their commissions together and joined MSFU together; but Powell was the older by several years. Hay's reserve pilot, Bruce Macpherson, was a Canadian.

The convoy conferences for both convoys took place on the afternoon of 20 May. At these conferences the two Camships were instructed not to use their radar unit until the respective SOEs gave permission. The SOEs would also issue instructions for launching.

QP 12, consisting of fifteen merchant ships, with a naval escort of six destroyers, four trawlers, one minesweeper, and the anti-aircraft ship *Ulster Queen* (with the SOE on board), and with an umbrella of assorted Russian fighters, sailed from Murmansk at 16.00 on Thursday 21 May. Meanwhile PQ 16 was forming up outside Hvalfjord.

In the westbound convoy, *Empire Morn* was leading the extreme starboard column. In the eastbound convoy, *Empire Lawrence* was leading the extreme port column. Both Kendal on *Empire Morn* and Hay on *Empire Lawrence* were thus well placed for launching.

QP 12's escort of Russian fighters did not persist beyond ten o'clock on Friday morning, 22 May, and the rockets on *Empire Morn*'s catapult were then connected up. But for the next two days the weather was overcast, dominated by snow squalls and low cloud, grounding the German reconnaissance machines and ruling out any chance of a launching even if they appeared.

Profiting from this bad weather to the east, PQ 16 proceeded without incident until Saturday the 23rd, when it began to run into heavy fog. During the morning an aircraft, assumed to be an enemy reconnaissance machine, was heard overhead, but nothing was seen of it from sea level.

On Sunday 24 May visibility began to improve, especially for the eastbound convoy and during the morning a Condor was sighted a long way ahead. Its radio reports back to base were intercepted by the convoy, but it kept well out of combat range. There were no further sightings by either convoy that day; but the progress of PQ 16, at least, was known to the enemy.

By midnight on that Sunday night the two convoys were less than 500 miles apart and closing rapidly. And at 03.00 on the 25th, as PQ 16 passed south-east of Jan Mayen Island, a Condor began circling at a radius of ten miles. Visible only intermittently because of a glutinous mist, and dodging in and out of cloud wherever possible, it gave the eastbound *Empire Lawrence* no chance to launch its Hurricane. Two and a half hours later, at 05.45, a flying-boat was spotted on the horizon by the westbound *Empire Morn*, and soon it began circling at a distance of about twelve miles. 'Tiny' Faulks, who had the midnight to 06.00 watch, identified it easily enough from its three engines and high wing as a BV138. 'We won't launch for this,' ruled the SOE, 'they'll only put up another one. We'll see first what they're up to.'

The Germans would certainly know, from their daily intrusions over Murmansk, that the westbound convoy had sailed, so there was little hope of evasion. To give the covering naval forces the best chance of offering protection, course was maintained according to plan.

Thus while PQ 16, although still on the fringes of the danger zone, moved closer hour by hour towards its centre, QP 12 still lay well within range of the German air bases and would remain so for many hours.

The forces that were poised to strike against the two convoys were:

KG 30 (Junkers 88 bombers) based at Banak; I. and II./KG 26 (Heinkel 111 torpedo-bombers) based at Bardufoss and Banak; Coastal *Gruppen* 406 and 906 (Heinkel 115 seaplanes and Blohm and Voss 138 flying-boats) based at Tromsø and Stavanger; I./KG 40 (Focke-Wulf Condors) based at Trondheim-Vaernes. There were also three long-distance Ju88 reconnaissance squadrons, a weather reconnaissance squadron, and two *Gruppen* of Messerschmitt 109s.

At 06.00 that morning in *Empire Morn*, 'Tiny' Faulks was relieved by John Kendal; with the weather still improving, and an attack likely after several days of inactivity, Captain Cruickshank gave instructions for MSFU personnel to be at five minutes' readiness. As Kendal warmed up the Hurricane and the gun crews went to their stations, Faulks joined Mallett on the bridge.

A second reconnaissance aircraft, this time a Condor, joined the BV138 at 07.00, and after the flying-boat had fired two red recognition flares the Condor began circling in an opposite direction, anti-clockwise. Visibility was only moderate, but with the convoy now about halfway between Jan Mayen and Bear Islands, and within about 400 miles of Banak, there was every prospect of a major attack developing.

At 07.45 Captain Cruickshank received a message from *Ulster Queen* amending his previous instructions. If he thought of shooting off the Hurricane, signalled the SOE, he was to use his own discretion but to endeavour to choose the right moment. Soon afterwards this instruction was rescinded, the SOE reverting to his original opinion that a launching should be delayed until further enemy aircraft appeared on the scene.

All preparations, though, were made for a possible launching. Kendal strapped himself into the cockpit and Faulks, going forward, stationed himself in the firing hut and connected the safety link, after satisfying himself that the catapult was clear. The Hurricane was warmed up again and switched off, and Faulks had the clamps and safety-bars removed from the trolley, leaving only the retaining pins in position.

At 08.30 a Ju88 appeared and was joined soon after by another. That made four enemy aircraft circling the convoy, with the two Ju88s apparently looking for a chance to dive-bomb. When no more aircraft appeared, the consensus of opinion in *Empire Morn* was that if these aircraft could be driven off, a break in the continuity of enemy surveillance might be achieved.

The decision to launch, on this Arctic run especially, was bound to be a gamble. But it had always been held that 'present fears were worse than horrible imaginings'. *Empire Morn* had now been at sea, on the outward and return voyages, for fifteen days, and within another twenty-four hours or so would be virtually clear of German air intervention. Prodded by Captain Cruickshank, the SOE agreed that the time to launch was now.

Mallett spoke to Kendal on the voice radio and asked his opinion – Kendal was enthusiastic. Here at last was his chance. 'We'll wait for a situation where the enemy aircraft are either ahead or astern,' said Mallett. 'That'll give them less chance of seeing the flash from the rockets. We'll try to give you maximum chance of achieving surprise.'

At 08.50 Mallett noticed that one of the Ju88s had flown into a rain cloud directly ahead, while the other three aircraft were lurking astern. It seemed an opportune moment. The cloud was ten-tenths at 1,500 feet, but visibility was eight to ten miles and the conditions were reasonable.

Empire Morn was still leading the extreme starboard column, and as Cruickshank increased speed to 12 knots, Faulks signalled to Kendal to start up the Hurricane engine. The routine signals were exchanged, and after a last look round to make sure that everything was clear, Faulks gave Kendal the OK.

Kendal opened the throttle, locked the throttle nut, raised his right hand, and then cut it down as the final signal. Faulks counted up to three and then made the switch. Nothing happened.

Exhibiting the red flag, and making sure that both Kendal and Cruickshank had seen it, Faulks examined the safety link. He found the connection slightly loose at one end. He tightened it, ensured that the points were making contact, and repeated the drill. This time the rockets fired.

There was very little wind, but the launching was a good one, and the Hurricane sank hardly at all as Kendal overran the catapult rail and shot clear of the bows. The blast of the rockets, however, hit the gunshield of the Oerlikon on the port wing of the bridge so violently that it dislocated the aiming mechanism.

As Kendal climbed away and selected flaps up, Mallett, on the bridge, saw the BV138 on the port quarter, several miles distant, but heading in the same direction and maintaining a steady course. The pilot had evidently not seen the launching. Mallett called Kendal on the R/T. 'Vector nine o'clock. Angels one.'

Turning to port and climbing, Kendal sighted the flying-boat and soared after it. Within half a minute both aircraft vanished into a belt of rain cloud.

Realising that Kendal was highly unlikely to find the BV138 in cloud, Mallett advised him to 'return to Control'. He wanted to send him after one of the Ju88s or the Condor. But he got no reply. He had no idea where Kendal was and with the use of radar now sanctioned he asked his operator to get him a fix on the Hurricane.

Kendal's transmitter was giving trouble but he could hear Mallett well enough. He had already abandoned the chase of the BV138 and begun stalking an alternative prey. Suddenly Mallett saw the Hurricane swoop down out of the cloud astern of the convoy and begin a long pursuit of one of the Ju88s.

The German pilot, shocked and dismayed at the sight of a Hurricane in these latitudes, used all the boost he could muster. Charging up the starboard side of the convoy, he gave the crew of *Empire Morn* a grandstand view. But he could not shake off Kendal. Approaching first from the port and then the starboard quarters, Kendal fired two long bursts at 200 yards' range in a perfectly judged attack. Each burst was heard clearly on the Camship as Kendal first overtook and then overshot. It looked as though the German gunners had been silenced, as there was no return fire.

For a moment the Ju88 appeared to stagger as the pilot tried to maintain height. Then black smoke began to pour from both engines. One engine cut out completely, and in *Empire Morn* they could hear the other one misfiring. Faulks, back on the bridge, and watching the combat through binoculars, saw bombs and other gear falling away from the fuselage as the crew jettisoned everything they could and the pilot made a last bid to regain control. The plane continued to lose height and speed, and finally, still streaming black smoke, it plummeted into the water several miles away on the starboard bow.

The Hurricane, by this time well ahead of the convoy, was suddenly obscured by another rain squall and Mallett called Kendal. 'How are things, John?' He was hoping to vector him on to another target. 'I've got no more ammunition. I expended it all on the Ju88. But I think he's down.' 'He's down all right.'

Soon afterwards the Hurricane appeared again through the clouds, and Mallett told Kendal to orbit and await instructions. Communication was still no more than intermittent due to the fault in Kendal's transmitter, but Mallett established, by asking him to rock his aircraft, that Kendal was receiving him loud and clear.

Nothing more had been seen of the BV138 since Kendal chased it into cloud, and the Condor and the other Ju88, too, had rapidly made off. With the skies clear of aircraft, the Hurricat had done its job. 'See what happened to the one you shot down,' suggested Faulks.

Kendal acknowledged this signal and made off in the direction of the fleecy residual smoke that still clung to the sea. Soon he was lost to view in another rain squall, and for a time nothing more was heard from him. Kendal had in fact spotted some aircraft wreckage, with a rubber dinghy close by. So far as he could see, there was no one in the dinghy.

As the minutes passed and there was no word from Kendal, and nothing showed up on the radar, the men on the bridge of *Empire Morn* grew anxious. But they were scarcely more anxious than Kendal himself. He had lost contact with the convoy and in worsening visibility he could not re-locate it. At length he spotted one of the outlying vessels and fired off recognition signals, and Mallett, seeing the Hurricane on the horizon, gave him a vector.

Kendal reported what he had seen and, rightly or wrongly, the assumption was made that the Ju88 crew had gone down with the plane. Kendal, after relating how he had lost the convoy, told Mallett how relieved he was to find it again. 'Congratulations,' called Mallett, 'from Captain Cruickshank and his crew.'

The time was now approaching for Kendal to bale out. It had been arranged earlier that the destroyer *Boadicea* would do the pick-up and she had taken up position ahead of the convoy. But she was steaming straight into the patch of misty rain cloud in which Kendal had temporarily lost his bearings. Warning Kendal of this, Mallett advised him to select one of the escort vessels astern.

Mallett got no reply to this message. But by flying east over the convoy and orbiting the destroyer *Badsworth*, on the starboard quarter, Kendal showed he had received it. Meanwhile Mallett signalled the change of plan to all escorts.

By flying a left-hand circuit, and rocking his wings as he did so, Kendal confirmed his intention to bale out rather than ditch. Maintaining his heading until he was well astern of *Badsworth*, he turned so as to overtake her, gaining height meanwhile and preparing for the bale-out.

Even astern of the convoy the cloud base was down to 700 feet, and as Kendal climbed to his bale-out altitude the Hurricane disappeared again into the overcast. Faulks estimated its rate of climb as 1,000 feet per minute. For perhaps another thirty seconds the roar of the Hurricane's engine reached them as Kendal continued to climb. Faulks estimated that he must have reached about 1,200 feet. It was at this point that Faulks, his pilot's ear attuned to every nuance, heard the Hurricane's airscrew change into fully fine pitch.

Soon afterwards the men on the bridge of *Empire Morn*, listening intently, heard the Hurricane's engine cut out abruptly as Kendal closed the throttle. Then there was silence.

At any moment the Hurricane would come hurtling through the cloud, followed by Kendal on his parachute. Within a few seconds, with a thousand pairs of eyes watching for it, the Hurricane plunged through the overcast, falling in a true perpendicular and splashing headlong into the sea.

Immediately in the wake of the Hurricane came Kendal. But as he dropped out of the cloud, a tiny, puppet-like figure, he was still cartwheeling, his parachute not yet open.

Fifty feet above the water the parachute canopy began to flutter, and the somersaulting figure checked slightly, still swinging. But the canopy was still only half open when, seconds later, and close to the Hurricane, the somersaulting figure hit the sea. The plane sank immediately. But the yellow canopy, billowing strongly, floated on the water.

Racing to the spot, *Badsworth* lowered a boat. From *Empire Morn* the boat was seen to heave-to alongside the canopy, and at 10.04 Kendal was picked up. The boat then returned to *Badsworth*.

At 10.10 *Badsworth* signalled *Empire Morn* by lamp. The pilot had been picked up, but he had sustained serious injuries.

Ten minutes later came the news that Kendal was dead. The distinction of being the first MSFU pilot to shoot down an enemy plane was one he had not lived to enjoy. At 14.00, 221 miles east of Jan Mayen Island, with the crew of *Empire Morn* formed up in two ranks facing *Badsworth*, John Kendal was buried at sea.

> *From the sudden cutting of the engine* [says Faulks] *and the vertical dive of the aircraft, it is my belief that Kendal endeavoured to abandon the Hurricane by the 'jack-in-the-box' method, and for some reason which will never be known he did not, or was not able to, pull the parachute ripcord until he had descended too far for the parachute to effectively prevent him from hitting the water. He had not complained of being wounded.*

Faulks ended his official report as follows: 'As a result of his attack on the Ju88 the remaining enemy aircraft scattered and no more were sighted subsequently by the convoy, although we were well within range for the next twenty-four hours.'

QP 12 got through to Iceland without loss and Captain Cruickshank was convinced that Kendal's launching and combat had been instrumental in saving the convoy from attack. He also believed that but for Kendal the eastbound convoy, which they were expecting to pass soon after midday, would have been attacked earlier than it was. In the event, when at 13.00 *Boadicea* signalled that a suspicious-looking vessel was in sight and it turned out to be the vanguard of PQ 16, this convoy too was still intact.

Throughout that morning, mist and cloud still surrounded the eastbound PQ 16, and even at 13.00, when the two convoys first sighted each other in the distance, visibility was poor. But by 16.00, when the two convoys had long since passed out of each other's vision, the cloud base lifted to such an extent that Al Hay climbed into the cockpit of the Hurricane on *Empire Lawrence* and a state of instant readiness was reported by Captain Darkins to the senior officer of the escort.

Following Kendal's combat, enemy air activity seemed to have ceased, and the orders on both convoys were for all radar equipment to be switched off. Thus it was that at 18.45, when six Ju88s appeared from an easterly direction in two formations of three, flying at about 6,000 feet on a course that would take them right over the convoy, no warning of any kind was given. Al Hay was still in the Hurricane cockpit, but it was already too late to launch, and very soon the Ju88s began unloading their bombs. An intense barrage from the convoy and its escort kept the bombers at a reasonable height and harassed the crews into dropping their bombs indiscriminately; and meanwhile a close watch was kept for the synchronised torpedo attack from low level that had to be expected.

Radar restrictions were now lifted and almost immediately the display picked up a number of blips approaching from dead ahead at a distance of fifteen miles. These would be the torpedo-bombers. A minute later the leading aircraft was spotted from the bridge of *Empire Lawrence*, flying at 100 feet above sea level, directly towards the convoy. As it came into sharper focus, four more aircraft were picked out, one after the other, following their leader in line astern at widely spaced intervals. The leading aircraft was now less than ten miles distant, and the escort vessels opened fire.

The Hurricats were much better suited to breaking up torpedo than bombing attacks, and Hay immediately urged that conditions were right for interception. Captain Darkins signalled the SOE for permission to launch and the reply came back: 'Prepare to take off.'

The number of enemy aircraft converging on the convoy was growing, with torpedo-bombers approaching at low level and waves of bombers on the starboard side coming in at high level five or six at a time. The sole air defence against these attacks was Al Hay and his Hurricane.

Empire Lawrence was already head to wind and as Hay gave the signal to go the switches were made and the Hurricane bolted in a sheet of flame down the catapult rail. As soon as he was airborne Hay picked out the low-level formation dead ahead and closed them rapidly, recognising them as Heinkel 111s. As before they were painted a dark green camouflage to resemble the sea and they were all carrying two torpedoes. As soon as they saw the Hurricane they closed up into V formation and turned away sharply to starboard. Hay followed.

The last plane on the starboard side, No. 4 in the formation, straggled slightly, and Hay saw his chance. With a small height advantage, he dived on the straggler from the starboard quarter and fired two 3-second bursts, the second from about 250 yards, closing right in. He saw the starboard engine erupt in a red flash, then watched fragments of airframe fall into the sea. Yet amazingly the German pilot somehow regained his place in the formation, and all five aircraft returned his fire from their dorsal guns.

Breaking away to the north and gaining height, Hay began another attack from the starboard quarter, selecting No. 2 in the formation as his target this time, confident that No. 4 could not last. Facing heavy return fire, he got in a 5-second burst from 250 yards' range and saw numerous strikes on No. 2 abaft the cockpit. But even before he lifted his thumb from the firing button, his windscreen began smearing up and he knew his glycol tank had been hit. Temporarily blinded, he broke away again to the north. As he did so an explosive missile penetrated his cockpit and detonated against his seat. A white puff of smoke, and a searing pain in the thigh, told him he had been hit.

Confused and still half-blinded, he nevertheless saw a stray aircraft flash into his sights as he turned away. He fired the rest of his ammunition into it, then broke off and headed back towards the convoy. His engine was overheating through lack of coolant, and he called up Leo Powell and told him he had a bullet in his leg, had run out of ammunition, and was about to bale out.

Crossing to the starboard side of the convoy, he climbed to 3,000 feet, then noticed yet another section of Ju88s, sporting a duck-egg blue camouflage, coming in on that side from the west. Swinging back towards the north, where there was now less enemy action, he flew up the middle of the convoy to show himself to friend and foe alike, watching the enemy formations that he had temporarily dispersed gaining height and trying to re-group. The torpedo attack, at least, had been completely broken up, and even many of the aircraft at a higher level had been spreadeagled. Circling ahead of the leading ships, he flew back down the centre of the convoy only to be fired at continually by two American ships positioned astern. Escaping to the port side of the convoy, he waited until he was abeam of *Empire Lawrence*, jettisoned his hood and side panel (a recent modification had catered for the jettisoning of the hood), throttled back, lowered his flaps, and dived over the side. He cleared the aircraft without mishap and descended in comfort under a billowing canopy.

His troubles started when he entered the water. Trying to inflate his dinghy, he found it had been punctured by a bullet from one of the Heinkels. Fortunately the destroyer *Volunteer* saw his predicament and although under violent bombing attack stopped and picked him up. He had been in the water six minutes.

For more than two hours, during and after Hay's launching and bale-out, the convoy was attacked by bomb and torpedo. But Hay's fierce assault on the Heinkels had upset the planned co-ordination, and the rest of the attack, although protracted, was haphazard and desultory. There were many near misses, but not a single vessel was hit.

The gunnery officer in *Volunteer* saw the first Heinkel that Hay attacked go down, as did many others and it was confirmed as destroyed. Hay was also credited with one Heinkel damaged. But more important than anything else was the rebuffing of the initial torpedo attack. All too often it was the swift low-level stab by the first section of torpedo-bombers that decimated convoys and forced individual vessels off course, breaking up the concentration of defensive fire. The attack on PQ 16 on 25 May never recovered its symmetry and this must surely have been the reason why, for that day at least, the convoy escaped scot-free.

Six hours after Hay's bale-out, Bear Island was sighted from *Empire Lawrence* fine on the port bow. Soon afterwards the convoy had to alter course to starboard to avoid encroaching ice. German reconnaissance planes were heard circling, but a heavy mist rising from the ice gave the convoy protection. Then the time came for the escorting cruisers to steam off west to join QP 12, leaving the close escort to shepherd the convoy the last 500 miles to Murmansk.

It was now 26 May and all day the convoy was subjected to heavy air attack, the bombers venturing in lower now the cruiser force had gone. Thirty bombers in the morning, fifty-five in the afternoon, and another strong force in the evening, dropped a large number of bombs, keeping up the offensive until 23.00. Two ships suffered near-misses which forced them to drop back for a time, but both caught up and only one ship was lost, the crew taking to the boats. The major credit for this immunity must go to the skill displayed by the masters in manoeuvring their vessels and to the determination of the gunners. But again the convoy owed much to Al Hay. Not a single torpedo-bomber showed up all day.

The most determined bombing attack came on the 27th, in a final attempt by the *Luftwaffe* to inflict severe damage before the convoy escaped. About sixty mixed He111s and Ju88s came over, and some of them singled out the Camship *Empire Lawrence*, which suffered near misses. But the ship was not making water and all went well until, in a further raid that afternoon, three Ju88s flying in V formation made straight for the Camship. They approached at about 4,000 feet, then dived at an angle of 45 degrees down to 1,000 feet before releasing their bombs. The gun crews opened up with all guns, but two bombs whistled over the bridge and exploded in No. 2 Hatch.

As the bombs hit the ship there was a terrific explosion and all electricity failed. One of the bombs penetrated the hatch and went out through the port side before bursting, leaving a large hole in the ship's side, and the No. 2 Hatch beams and derricks were blown across to the port side, smashing the gun box. Captain Darkins ordered the second officer, a man named Hulse, to lower the boats and prepare to abandon ship and as Hulse left the bridge he heard the captain ring 'stop' on the engine telegraphs.

There were two lifeboats, one on each side, and both of these were lowered clear of the water – there was too much way on the ship to lower them into the sea. Hulse then went to help lower the jolly-boat in case it should be required.

As the ship lost way most of the crew began climbing into the port lifeboat, which was eventually lowered into the water and cast off. Captain Darkins and the chief wireless operator then threw the confidential books overboard in a weighted box before going to the galley, accompanied by the FDO, Leo Powell, to burn the secret papers. They had completed their task and were about to leave when there was a shout that the ship was being dive-bombed again. Only eight minutes had elapsed since the first attack. Hulse and two of the remaining crew were still in the starboard alley-way and they threw themselves flat on the deck as the planes screamed down, but Darkins, Powell and the wireless operator were trapped. There was another deafening explosion, the magazines blew up, and Hulse felt the deck splitting beneath him. The ship broke in two and sank in fifteen seconds, but most of those who were still on the deck, among them reserve pilot Bruce Macpherson and second officer Hulse, managed to get into the water.

The force of the explosion blew the starboard lifeboat from alongside and turned it upside down, but two or three men were still clinging to it. As Hulse jumped towards them he saw splashes from machine-gun bullets roughening the water, but he was not hit. Far worse was the situation on the other side, where the port lifeboat, in which most of the crew had escaped and got clear of the ship, had had its bow and stern ripped off by a bomb which had exploded between the lifeboat and the ship's side. Several of the men in this boat were killed, and one man, the third engineer, was wounded by machine-gun fire. After swimming about for a quarter of an hour, Hulse managed to board a raft that had floated off the ship, and soon afterwards he saw the trawler *Lady Madeline* picking up survivors from the damaged port lifeboat. The trawler then lowered a jolly-boat, which searched amongst the wreckage. At least thirty survivors were still in the sea, which was intensely cold, and some were on the point of losing the will to resist when they were picked up by the destroyer *Hyderabad*.

One of the last men to be rescued was the Canadian Bruce Macpherson, of whom it was afterwards said that 'by his example and courage he saved the lives of several survivors who were inclined to give up the struggle'. He and the rest of the MSFU men had had a remarkable escape. But Captain Darkins, Leo Powell, eleven crew and three gunners were lost.

The German torpedo-bombers, too, were back in business, and it was they who did most of the damage in this attack, sinking three ships, among them *Lowther Castle*, which was carrying MSFU pilot Deryck Lamb. Roy Lane, the other pilot destined for the Archangel Pool, wrote afterwards: 'I was on the *Empire Baffin*, between the *Empire Lawrence* and the *Lowther Castle*, and I saw both ships go down. Actually we dodged the torpedo that hit the *Lowther Castle*, which I personally thought was a cunning move. However, Lamb does not agree.'

More than 100 enemy aircraft were employed against the convoy that day, but the only other sinking was achieved by a U-boat. 'Owing to the absence of fighter opposition,' wrote Bruce Macpherson afterwards, 'the attacks were made from all angles and no use was made of the sun.' It was fortunate for the convoy that the high-level bombing was inaccurate. The success of the torpedo crews, though, underlined the folly of sparing only one Camship for these Arctic convoys.

Although in the next few days the convoy was bombed by small formations many times, the scale of attack fell away to nothing as the Kola Inlet drew near. On Thursday the 28th two light Russian cruisers came out to meet them, and in the next few days the Red Air Force – including among their number a flight of twenty Hurricane IIs – appeared overhead, though they did not attempt a standing patrol.

At last, on the afternoon of 30 May, the convoy entered the Kola Inlet. Reduced in numbers from thirty-five ships to twenty-eight, battered and tired, but, in the words of Commander R. Onslow, senior officer of the escort, still keeping perfect station, PQ 16 approached the end of its journey. Of her 125,000 tons of cargo, 32,000, or just over a quarter, had been lost. The sinkings had borne especially heavily on the ships carrying the most important items, yet the final figures disclose a substantial credit balance:

	Loaded	**Lost**	**Delivered**
Vehicles	3,277	770	2,507
Tanks	468	147	321
Aircraft	201	77	124

This took no account of German losses in aircraft and crews.

For MSFU the balance sheet was strangely symmetrical: the pilot lost from one convoy, and the FDO safe; the FDO lost from the other convoy, and the pilot safe. Yet for MSFU, too, the accounts were very much in credit. Two certain victories for the loss of two Hurricanes might sound like stalemate, but many other aircraft had been driven off or damaged, and the saving of merchant shipping, although not calculable, had undoubtedly been real and significant. With greater enthusiasm from the Admiralty, much more might have been achieved.

Up to this point the justification of MSFU had rested on its deterrent effect. Now it had something positive to show for the long months of patient endeavour. Taken together the two combats fulfilled the highest hopes of the men who had sponsored and fostered the Hurricats.

> *An eloquent last word came from Mr N.S. Hulse, second officer of* Empire Lawrence. *I would like to pay special tribute to our captain – H.S. Darkins. He was a fearless and extremely good leader… He remained on the bridge throughout the numerous attacks. His cool and courageous bearing was an inspiration to all, and his skilful handling of the ship gave the crew confidence. He lost his life in the execution of his duty, his last act being to burn the confidential papers in the galley fire. All the crew and particularly the gunners behaved magnificently throughout, firing the guns and keeping them supplied with ammunition without the slightest sign of fear or panic.*

To this tribute, written at the time, Hulse added a percipient comment. 'I do not think that a single Camship is much use in an attack of that scale. There should be a large number of Camships in these convoys…'

More weight, perhaps, might have been attached to the opinion of the SOE, Commander Onslow, who urged that many more Camships, or an escort carrier, be included in the next convoy. But the lesson had still not been learned. Indeed the tendency was to reduce the commitments of MSFU, rather than to increase them.

X

Convoy HG
and the 36th Escort Group

In the Atlantic, as already related, the Focke-Wulf Condors had largely abandoned their individual bombing role and were concentrating on co-operation with U-boats; proving especially damaging to Allied convoys operating to and from Gibraltar. For the first time since the war began, Admiral Dönitz was getting the kind of aerial reconnaissance that his U-boat force needed; this again was especially true of the packs now operating in the Bay of Biscay, well within range of the Condors.

By keeping their distance, eschewing offensive tactics and taking advantage of cloud cover, the Condors proved a tantalising target, pursuing their surveillance role with impunity. For a short period towards the end of 1941, HMS *Audacity*, a captured German merchant ship converted into an escort carrier – she had a small flight deck and carried six Grumman Martlet fighters – enjoyed considerable success, both as a destroyer of Condors and in spotting and attacking U-boats from the air. But in December 1941 she was torpedoed while helping to protect convoy HG 76 (homeward-bound from Gibraltar), and that left the Camships as the sole air protection travelling as part of the Gibraltar convoys.

By this time, however, the U-boat packs preying on these convoys had a new enemy to contend with – the 36th Escort Group, based at Liverpool, and commanded by a regular officer whose aggressive methods were to revise all notions of convoy escort work and earn him the reputation of contributing more than any other man to victory in the Battle of the Atlantic. This was the legendary U-boat killer Captain F.J. Walker – 'Johnnie' Walker, or Walker RN. Coming on the scene with his Escort Group in

November 1941, he was attached at once to the Gibraltar convoys. The delivery of convoy HG 76, despite the loss of *Audacity* – had Walker had his way she would not have been placed on the exposed starboard flank of the convoy – was acknowledged as a great victory.

The Group acted as escort to several more Gibraltar convoys, outward and homeward, in the ensuing six months, never fearing to seek out their prey, and convoy losses fell accordingly. But the successes were not achieved without damage and loss to the vessels of the Group. By the time convoy HG 84, consisting of eighteen merchantmen, left Gibraltar on 9 June 1942, wear and tear and enemy action had reduced Walker's available escort vessels from nine to four. The rump consisted of the sloop *Stork* (captained by Walker), and the corvettes *Gardenia*, *Convolvulus* and *Marigold*. It was a measure of the Admiralty's confidence in Walker that the convoy was allowed to sail with such a weakened escort.

> *The Group's career* [writes Terence Robertson in *Walker RN*] *had been short, eventful and successful. Whenever the enemy approached in number they had been counter-attacked and forced to retire while the Group sailed home with trophies and prisoners. In between they had their full share of patient, monotonous slogging waiting for an enemy who rarely appeared but might easily launch surprise attacks at the most unlikely times. This had taken its toll of the Group's strength and they needed action to restore their morale.*

In the leading ship of the centre column, the *Pelavo*, was Commodore H.T. Hudson RNR, the convoy commodore. Astern of the convoy was the rescue ship *Copeland*, responsible for picking up survivors if any ship was sunk. Leading the port outer column, on the flank furthest away from the coastline, was the Camship *Empire Moon*. For her pilots, after a stay of three months in the fleshpots of Gibraltar, where they had been attached to the Pool, the need for action was hardly less pressing.

At the convoy conference on the Rock before sailing, the Merchant Navy captains had had some pointed-things to say about the strength of their escort; a sloop and three corvettes hardly seemed adequate protection for crossing an area known to be more infested with U-boats than any other. But having sailed, they took what comfort they could from the sight of *Stork*, patrolling ahead of the convoy by day and astern by night, changing places with *Convolvulus*, and of *Marigold* on the starboard beam and *Gardenia* to port.

The pilots on *Empire Moon* were both young men appointed to a commission on joining MSFU. Pilot Officer A. Vernon 'Sandy' Sanders, slight, slim, and of ruddy complexion, with clipped moustache, was a Rhodesian. Pilot Officer J.A. Sabourin, or 'Smoothie Sab' as he was quickly dubbed because of his ability to organise his own and everyone else's comforts, had had his own private flat in Gibraltar and had shared it with Sanders; it had become a sort of unofficial MSFU Mess. Sub-Lieutenant Don Perrett, the FDO, fair and crinkly-haired, was also a character in his own right. He had taken part in the evacuation at Dunkirk with the Royal Navy and was credited with a description of that mass retreat that was later to become legendary: 'My dear chap, the noise...and the people!'

The convoy was to be joined by three more merchant ships off Lisbon; and at 13.00 on

12 June, when the rendezvous was made, they brought trouble with them. Most of the way from Lisbon they had been followed by a Condor and, with no means of shaking it off, they could not avoid leading it on to the main convoy. The intruder was picked up on *Empire Moon*'s radar at a distance of fourteen miles; but it was on the far side of the convoy and was not at first sighted from the Camship. Meanwhile the alarm was given by flag signals from *Pelavo* and action stations were immediately sounded. Sanders mounted the ladder to the cockpit and the engine was started up.

The intruder had still not been sighted and identified from the Camship when *Stork* came alongside and Walker, believing as always that attack was the best defence, demanded to know why the Hurricane had not been launched. He addressed his remarks to the one man in naval uniform, Don Perrett, which caused some embarrassment, since the decision to launch did not lie with him. The explanation that the aircraft had not been seen from the Camship and therefore could not be identified may or may not have satisfied Walker; but from this incident, and from what followed, it seems that the role and operation of Camships were still imperfectly understood. A few minutes later, when a visual was at last obtained from *Empire Moon* and the aircraft was identified as a Condor, *Stork* lay directly across the bows of the Camship and it would have been extremely difficult to launch the Hurricane. To save everyone's faces, however, the Condor crew made off towards land at the first sight of the Camship, having got all the information they wanted.

Walker knew that his probable course and speed would now be plotted at Dönitz's headquarters and in every U-boat within call. He continued on a northerly course until midnight and then, having seen nothing of the enemy for ten hours, he turned the convoy due west, away from land and straight out into the Atlantic and kept on that heading for the next five hours. Meanwhile, throughout the hours of darkness, all ships' radars were switched off, so that there could be no homing by search receivers. It was a manoeuvre that might at least give the Condors something to think about when they tried to relocate the convoy next day.

At 05.15 on 13 June Walker altered from a westerly heading to north-west, still increasing his distance from the enemy bases but making progress at the same time across the Bay. Low cloud and poor visibility hampered the Condor crews throughout that day and no aircraft were seen by the convoy, neither were any plotted on the radar, which was switched on during daylight hours. For the moment, at least, the enemy predators had been shaken off.

Sooner or later, however, the rediscovery of the convoy by enemy reconnaissance planes, or by U-boats in transit, was almost inevitable; and next day, 14 June, at 13.30, the alarm was given by flag from *Pelavo*: 'Suspicious aircraft in sight.' In *Stork*, Walker's opinion, as before, was that the swift destruction of this single aircraft, before its crew could pass comprehensive information about the convoy back to its base, might seriously hamper enemy attempts at surveillance. But first the aircraft had to be positively identified.

It was five minutes before Don Perrett got a plot from his radar operator, and this showed a single aircraft on a relative bearing of 175 degrees, distance sixteen miles.

Soon afterwards the echo was lost. Meanwhile 'Sandy' Sanders had reached the cockpit and the Hurricane was being prepared for launching. The intruder was picked up again on the radar at fourteen miles, but then it retreated, the echo being lost again between sixteen and eighteen miles.

After evading the enemy for forty-eight hours, Walker was impatient to see the intruder destroyed and he asked for the launching of the Hurricane, being careful this time to direct his request to *Empire Moon*'s captain. At 13.40, when the intruder was next seen from the Camship, both by radar and visually, it was identified as a Condor.

In the Hurricane cockpit, Sanders found as he fastened his seat harness that the straps of his parachute harness had slipped and were much too loose. It was too late to adjust them now. The Condor, as he learned from Perrett, was coming in towards the stern of the convoy at a distance of ten miles and a height of 1,200 feet, and if he was to launch at all he must do so now. A layer of cloud thickening to ten-tenths between 2,000 and 3,000 feet, with some scattered lower patches, gave the Condor crew several possible avenues of escape; but just to drive the intruder off might be sufficient.

The ship's heading was 342 degrees magnetic; and with a light north-north-east wind and a slight swell, conditions were perfect for launching. At 13.41 Sanders was catapulted off and as soon as he had the Hurricane under control he took in the sea conditions and resolved that when the time came it would be safer, with his loose parachute harness, to ditch rather than bale out. Meanwhile Perrett had established R/T contact with Sanders, and the vectors he gave him – 180 degrees and then 160 degrees – lined the Hurricane up nicely. After about two minutes on a course of 160 degrees Sanders spotted the Condor ahead and to port. 'Tally-ho!'

The Condor crew, too, had seen the Hurricane and the German pilot had turned east and climbed to 1,500 feet, aiming for the nearest patch of cloud. Sanders, using full hotted up boost of 12 lbs, had achieved a speed of 260 mph and was approaching within a mile of the Condor. Then he lost sight of it as it turned to starboard and disappeared into a bank of cloud.

Copying the turn to starboard, and exaggerating it, Sanders reached the other side of the cloud, then turned to port to close in on the spot where he expected the Condor to emerge. At 600 yards he saw the Condor again and immediately began a beam attack from the starboard side.

The Condor pilot, evidently anticipating this, turned straight into Sanders' approach and prevented him from developing his beam attack into an attack from the quarter. At the same time his manoeuvre enabled the gunner in the top turret to open fire point-blank at the Hurricane. Before he could open fire himself, Sanders saw tracer passing directly over his head. He replied at once with his eight machine-guns, opening up at 300 yards and closing to a hundred, but he was being fired at himself all the time and he could not tell whether his own fire was effective.

Passing above and behind the Condor, Sanders found himself hurtling in and out of cloud patches below the base of the layer. After turning and climbing he caught sight of the Condor again, 500 yards ahead and to starboard, climbing for the cloud layer. Swinging straight in, he opened fire at 250 yards and closed this time to fifty yards. The Condor pilot again turned into the direction of attack, but Sanders got in a two-second burst and saw his tracer straddling the fuselage. Passing close behind and below as he pressed home his attack, he was severely jolted by the Condor's slipstream. His last impression of the Condor, as he passed underneath it, was of its pale duck-egg blue and green camouflage, almost exactly the same as he had seen on many a Coastal Command Hudson. Then it disappeared into the cloud layer.

Throughout the combat, R/T silence had been maintained; but now Sanders asked Perrett for a vector. He had plenty of fuel and ammunition left, there must be clear patches in the cloud and if he could get a vector on the Condor he was determined to chase it. But it had not only disappeared into cloud; it had vanished from the radar screens as well. Presumably it was making for home.

Climbing through cloud until he had the open sky above him, Sanders had a final look around, then reported back to Perrett and asked for a vector to return to the convoy. Instructed at first to orbit, he was then sent off on a sub-hunt, following up a contact report by one of the escort. From 500 feet he searched the area thoroughly but found nothing. Eventually he had to report that he was running short of fuel.

In *Empire Moon* a signal was then received from Walker: 'Instruct the pilot to bale out near me when ready.' Perrett passed these instructions on to Sanders, but Sanders had no intention of obeying them. The shoulder straps of his parachute harness were still too slack to be safe and he could not tighten them while sitting in the cockpit flying the aircraft. So his resolve to ditch was unchanged. Calling Perrett, he announced that he was going to 'pancake'. The time was 15.15.

There was another factor influencing Sanders' decision. His two previous experiences of aircraft crashes, one in a Harvard while training back home in Salisbury and another more recently in a Tiger Moth, had given him confidence in getting away with crash-landings and despite what the book said about ditching the Hurricane he had no great qualms on that score.

Flying low over the senior escort vessel, doing right-hand orbits and rocking his wings, Sanders waited for the signal flag to be flown that would give him the go-ahead. It was some time before his manoeuvres were understood and the flag was hoisted, and then, with *Stork* making no apparent attempt to steam into wind, he decided on a cross-wind landing, ahead of *Stork* and with the aim of hitting the water in a depression of the slight swell.

The next thing was to get rid of his helmet, inflate his lifejacket, and slide back the cockpit hood. The first two were accomplished easily enough. But when he tried to open the hood he couldn't move it. It was jammed.

Visions of being trapped in the cockpit as the Hurricane sank drove him into panic. Exerting all his strength he beat at the hood with his fists in a frenzy, trying to free it. But something had fouled the guide rails, and he couldn't shift it.

During his three-months' stay in Gibraltar, Sanders had not been made aware of the modification to the Hurricane whereby, in addition to the usual sliding back of the Perspex cockpit hood, an alternative release mechanism allowed the whole hood to be jettisoned. The Hurricane he was flying had been so modified, so the means of salvation was at hand. But he was totally ignorant of it.

He beat at both sides of the hood with his elbows until they were swollen and discoloured, and at last he succeeded in getting some movement, though not enough to make room for escape. Despite his slight build, the strength of desperation now came into play and he drove the hood back inch by inch with his blackened elbows, against whatever snag was causing it to jam. Eventually he banged it back far enough to give himself room to squeeze through. But he was unable to lock it. If it pitched forward with the deceleration of ditching he might never get it open again.

He pulled the lever to jettison the side panel and was relieved when the panel fell away. Then he tightened the straps of his seat harness, put the flaps down sixty degrees to ensure a low stalling speed, and throttled back to 80 mph. Skimming along a few feet above the water, he noticed that the surface looked much rougher than it had done from higher up. His left arm, braced against the reflector sight, cut out his view of the airspeed indicator, but he guessed his speed was down to about 70 mph when he hit the water.

As the Hurricane, true to form, turned straight over on its back, Sanders looked up to see a paler shade of green above him than in the water around him. Pulling the safety release of his harness, he kicked himself clear of the cockpit and quickly bobbed to the surface. There he found that he couldn't have been more than a few feet under water as the Hurricane, although inverted, was still floating. For forty-five seconds he clung to the mainplane. Then the Hurricane sank.

He pulled out the dinghy from the seat portion of his parachute and turned on the CO_2 bottle, which quickly blew the dinghy into shape. He noticed as he climbed in that the dinghy was leaking; but within three or four minutes he was picked up by a sea boat from *Stork*.

> *The Navy made me very welcome and looked after me well* [wrote Sanders later], *but I was soon to put my own exploits into the background, as within an hour of the Stork picking me up a submarine was sighted on the surface and I was having another new experience, chasing and attacking a sub, involving the dropping of scores of depth-charges. Later that night we rejoined the convoy and I got my first taste of being attacked by subs.*

It may well be that the attack on the convoy would have developed that night anyway, even if Sanders had been successful in shooting down the Condor, since as many as eight U-boats were believed to be in the area in the days that followed. But the Condor crew lived to make their report and this may well have assisted the U-boat commanders.

The commodore's ship, *Pelavo*, was the first to go, at four minutes past one on the morning of the 15th, vanishing in a cloud of smoke, flames and spray. The blast from the exploding torpedo blew Commodore Hudson up through the canvas awnings stretched over his bridge and out into the night. He was never seen again. Two more ships were torpedoed almost simultaneously, and all three sank within minutes.

Soon after 04.00 Walker hit back from *Stork* with a pattern of ten depth-charges that sank one of the U-boats; but within another half-hour two more ships had been sent to the bottom.

> *The SS* Thurso, *in the middle of the convoy* [writes Terence Robertson in *Walker RN*] *literally exploded into fragments and for a moment seemed to disintegrate into a white, blazing ball of fire. Darkness had time to close in tightly again before the SS* City of Oxford *shuddered to a standstill under the impact of an internal explosion caused when a torpedo pierced her hull and detonated inside a cargo hold. She sank while the ships following her were altering course round her heavily listing hulk.*

For Sanders, watching from the bridge of *Stork*, it was an unforgettable night of mingled excitement and horror. First he saw the stricken merchant ships, then the bobbing little red lights of the life jackets of the men in the sea. Next came the tension of pursuit as Walker hunted down the U-boats, followed by the trauma of two further sinkings. As every ship in the convoy began firing star-shells or illuminant rockets, often wildly and indiscriminately, the chaos became total. Walker, who had sent *Marigold* astern to help *Copeland* pick up survivors after the first attack, raged inwardly; but if this dispersal of his slender forces was a mistake, it paid off in the limiting of casualties, 172 survivors being picked up from the five ships.

Walker's aggressive tactics continued to pay dividends in the days that followed, when a second U-boat was confirmed as sunk. The pack of U-boats that had been assembled was certainly intended to massacre convoy HG 84, yet no more attacks were pressed home to a conclusion. 'The fact that only two attacks developed on this very weakly escorted convoy in spite of the number of U-boats hunting it,' summarised the C-in-C Western Approaches, 'reflects great credit on the Senior Officer of the 36th Escort Group and on his ships.' Walker had expected criticism. Instead he got congratulations.

This was not one of the convoys that were greatly helped by the Camships, yet the contribution of *Empire Moon*'s Hurricane may not have been without significance. After the Condor that came up with the main convoy on 12 June had vanished on sighting the Hurricane on its catapult, the convoy had been unmolested for forty-eight hours – a considerable respite. The driving off of the second Condor, too, with the damage it almost certainly suffered, may have left the U-boat commanders temporarily short of precise information. But the major credit must obviously go to 'Johnnie' Walker. An Admiralty communiqué issued in 1950, long after the events it eulogised, put it like this:

> *Captain Walker, more than any other, won the Battle of the Atlantic. His methods had amazing success and more than any other factor gave the Royal Navy supremacy. It is only now that we have learned the full impact he had on the enemy. No tribute could be too high for the work he carried out.*

Captain Walker himself did not live to hear this tribute. Selected to take command of a carrier task force in the Pacific, with promotion to Flag rank, he died suddenly in July 1944 as a result of overstrain directly attributable to his wartime service with the 36th Escort Group.

XI

PQ 17: Why the Hurricat Stayed on its Perch

One day in June 1942, Dickie Turley-George was called into George Pinkerton's office at Speke. 'I've got a trip for you,' said Pinkerton.

Turley-George had just spent a ten-day leave period flying with No. 602 Squadron under Paddy Finucane, keeping abreast of Fighter Command tactics and getting in some fighter sweeps over France. Returning to Speke, he heard that some American trips were in the offing and he had every reason to think he might get one. He had done two trips to Canada, and he thought it must be about his turn.

'A trip to America?'

'No. To Russia.'

'Christ! I don't want to go there!'

His old friend Roy Lane was already out there, in charge of the Pool, but to join him, he decided, would be carrying friendship too far.

'What about one of the new chaps? Shouldn't one of them go?'

'I'm not sending any of the new chaps to Russia,' said Pinkerton. 'We can't get volunteers for this job any more and these chaps have been drafted here out of the hat. Some of them are pretty disgruntled. I've got to give them something to interest them. They're not ready for the Russian convoys, and they'll be getting the American trips from now on.'

'Well, I think that's bloody unfair.'

No one could take offence at the good-natured Turley-George. He proceeded to elaborate his views. 'This is just like the story of the prodigal son. I always thought that was bloody unfair too.'

Pinkerton had a relationship with his pilots which allowed them considerable licence. They even threw parties and entertained their girlfriends in his house. But he retained their respect. 'I'm a wing commander,' he reminded Turley-George, 'and I'm not asking you, it's an order.'

'Oh well, if you put it like that…' Turley-George was thus appointed first pilot on the Camship *Empire Tide*, the only Camship allocated to Convoy PQ 17.

Towards the end of May 1942, after the passage of PQ 16, the attention of the German naval staff inevitably focused on the need to prevent the continual flow of Allied supplies to Russia. Already efforts had been made; but more than two-thirds of the supplies carried by PQ 16 had got through, and this was a proportion that dismayed the Nazi hierarchy. Discussions were therefore held on how best to intercept and destroy the next convoy, which was expected by the Germans, from past experience, to sail on or about 21 June.

For many months Hitler had lived in continual dread of an Allied invasion of Norway, threatening his northern flank; and to meet this wholly imagined threat, powerful naval forces had been moved to the Norwegian fjords. The battleship *Tirpitz* and the cruiser *Hipper* were at Trondheim, the pocket battleships *Scheer* and *Lützow* were at Narvik. Now, with the threat of Allied invasion believed to be diminished, and with oil supplies for the moment adequate, provisional assent was given by the Naval War Staff for preparations to begin for surface attack on the next Allied convoy to Russia by Battle Groups I and II. But Hitler was determined not to expose these ships to any serious risk of being brought to battle and the final decision rested with him.

On the Allied side, too, final decisions were not allowed to rest with the men on the spot. Commander J.E. Broome, commanding the First Escort Group, the group entrusted with the close escort of the convoy, learned this from an Admiralty signal addressed to Admiral Tovey and copied to him. The significant passage read '…as Admiralty may be in possession of fuller and earlier information of movements of enemy surface forces than our [escort] forces will be and as you may not wish to break W/T silence it appears necessary for Admiralty to control movements of convoy as far as this may be influenced by movements of enemy surface forces.' This meant that if the German Battle Groups looked like interfering, the Chief of Naval Staff at the Admiralty – not the First Escort Group, nor the C-in-C Home Fleet, who was to provide the Battle Fleet Covering Force, nor Rear Admiral L.H.K. Hamilton, commanding the Cruiser Covering Force – would decide the tactics to be employed.

On the face of it this sounded like good sense. So too did the orders given to the master of *Empire Tide*, Captain F.W. Harvey, to Dickie Turley-George and his reserve pilot, Charles Fenwick, and to their FDO, Johnny Macdonald, when the convoy conference was held at Hvalfjord, Iceland on 27 June 1942. Broome told Harvey at the conference that he would suggest the best time for the Hurricane to be launched; and when they were having a drink after the conference, Broome took the opportunity of confirming this with Turley-George. 'I'll tell you when to fire off,' he said.

Turley-George demurred. 'Well, sir, I don't agree with that. I know when the conditions are right for launching and that's the way it's always been.' In this Turley-George was mistaken, at least so far as the Arctic convoys were concerned. On both PQ 15 and PQ 16 the decision to launch had rested with the SOE.

'It may have always been that way,' said Broome, 'but on this convoy, I'm the commander of the close escort and I'm responsible for the safety of the convoy. You are one of my weapons, and I want to use you at the most opportune time.'

'I agree with that, of course. But the point is this. If you give me an instruction to take off and I don't think the conditions are right, then I must reserve the right not to go.'

'That's your privilege. But you will not shoot off – and I wish Captain Harvey to hear this – unless I give personal instructions for you to go. Carry on normally in every other way, and be ready to get into the cockpit if an attack develops. But I'll give you the order to go.'

Since *Empire Tide*'s Sea Hurricane was the only fighter aircraft available to Broome and the only aircraft of any kind travelling with the convoy, it is not surprising that he should insist on personal control of its use. Once it had been launched, the only remaining air deterrent, if it could be called such, was a dummy aircraft which the Navy had made out of old packing-cases and which was to be hoisted on the Camship's catapult as a sort of scarecrow. What the two Russian officers who were allocated to *Empire Tide* for interpreter duties thought of this they were too polite to say.

Later that day, 27 June 1942, PQ 17 sailed from Hvalfjord. There were thirty-seven merchant ships, three rescue ships and two tankers; but two of the merchant ships and one of the tankers sustained hull damage soon after sailing and were forced to turn back. Broome's close escort group – with Broome himself in the destroyer *Keppel* – consisted of four destroyers and four corvettes, reinforced by two Home Fleet destroyers, two anti-aircraft ships, three minesweepers, four armed trawlers and two submarines. The cruiser covering force under Rear Admiral Hamilton, keeping to the north of PQ 17, consisted of four cruisers and three destroyers; and the Home Fleet force, which had already sailed from Scapa Flow, comprised the battleship *Duke of York*, the American battleship *Washington*, the aircraft carrier *Victorious*, two cruisers and fourteen destroyers.

Broome placed *Empire Tide* inside the convoy in position sixty-three – the third ship in the sixth column – in order to protect her from U-boat attack; but he promised to move her out to the wing of the convoy approaching the air danger zone.

Orders were that radar was not to be switched on until the convoy was definitely known to have been located by the enemy; and similarly, radio silence was to be strictly observed. But indications of the probable departure of another big convoy reached the Germans through their agents at Reykjavik and through their radio monitoring service.

In *Empire Tide*, Sub-Lieutenant Macdonald had nothing to report in his log for the first four days; and by the evening of 30 June a third of the distance to Archangel had been safely run. The convoy was now steering north-east to pass to the north of Bear Island, increasing the distance from the nearest German airfields to 400 miles and more; but the Germans were well aware of the Allied practice of co-ordinating the sailings of eastbound and westbound convoys and when QP 13 was sighted at 16.50 on 30 June, the imminent approach of PQ 17 was confidently expected.

On the morning of 1 July, as PQ 17 continued north-east with barrage balloons flying, many of the close escort vessels that surrounded it refuelled from the one remaining tanker. Then came the first enemy sightings of the convoy, by U-boat and by Blohm and Voss flying-boat. By two o'clock that afternoon, *Empire Tide's* radar was operating continuously. Meanwhile Commander Broome was steering a course that was an inevitable compromise between conflicting orders – to put a greater distance between the convoy and the North Cape on the one hand and to keep the convoy moving eastwards whatever damage it might suffer on the other.

From this point on, shadowing aircraft were a permanent feature of the convoy's progress, disturbing the peace with the metallic whine of their motors and keeping tantalisingly out of gun range. One BV138, orbiting until the frustrated gunners got dizzy, was eventually signalled pointedly by lamp: 'For Christ's sake go round the other way.'

Empire Tide's noon position on 2 July was 73.12 north, 01.30 west, still more than 400 miles north-west of Banak. During the afternoon they passed the westbound convoy, QP 13. The cloud base was down to 500 feet, but two more BV138s were sighted. So far Broome had not moved the Camship from her position inside the convoy. Then at 16.25 two more aircraft were picked up on *Empire Tide's* radar at a distance of fifteen miles. When they emerged from the cloud they were identified as Heinkel 115 floatplanes, and each was carrying one torpedo. Eight of these Heinkels had taken off from Tromosø, but not all of them had found the convoy. They were slow and vulnerable machines, they were many hundreds of miles from home, and although they made several dummy attacks they kept their distance. In the face of heavy gunfire they eventually dropped their torpedoes at long range, apparently aiming at two of the outer escort vessels. At 16.40 the leading Heinkel, piloted by the squadron commander, Captain Herbert Vater, caught fire, alighted, and sank. But the crew scrambled into their dinghy, and one of the other Heinkels, piloted by *Oberleutnant* Burmester, immediately alighted alongside and picked them up, an operation with which the convoy did not interfere.

All this was watched patiently – and with one eye on *Keppel* – from the Camship, where it was thought that the Heinkels might be trying to lure the Hurricane off. Eventually Macdonald noted in his log, with some relief: 'No "suggestion" to take off was received from the Senior Officer of the Escort.'

The rescue floatplane, despite its load, continued to circle the convoy until 19.15 hours, when it set course for base, leaving the BV138s to continue the patrol. By 19.45 the convoy was enveloped in thick fog; but when the fog cleared shortly before midnight, a single BV138 was still keeping up the interminable patrol.

On the following afternoon, 3 July, at 16.30, the convoy and its cruiser covering force made visual contact for the first time. Estimating that the convoy had strayed twenty miles south of its planned route – twenty miles nearer the German airfields – Admiral Hamilton sent a Walrus amphibian from the cruiser force with a message suggesting that Broome alter course to the north. Broome altered 30 degrees, but on a second sighting at 22.15 Hamilton again sent the Walrus with a similar message; this time Broome altered course reluctantly, since every alteration to the north added time to the voyage and he believed he was already steering to pass fifty miles north of Bear Island as ordered. Meanwhile he received the following signal from the Admiralty:

1 Visual reconnaissance confirmed by photographs of Trondheim reports no heavy units present.

2 The Admiralty appreciate that:

    (a) A move by enemy heavy units to the northward is in progress.

    (b) This threatens the convoy but there are no indications of immediate danger.

    (c) Weather to be favourable for the convoy to continue eastward.

3 Admiralty is therefore taking no action at present but is awaiting developments.

Unknown to the Admiralty, or to Convoy PQ 17 and its various escorts, *Tirpitz, Scheer* and *Hipper* with six destroyers had arrived in Altenfjord, south of the North Cape, earlier that day, 3 July; and they remained there all day on the 4th awaiting aerial reconnaissance of British fleet movements. The British Home Fleet, in fact, was off Spitzbergen, too far north to prevent the German warships from falling on the convoy; but the presence of the aircraft carrier *Victorious* was known and feared by the Germans. In addition, two of the cruisers of Hamilton's force had been wrongly reported by German reconnaissance as battleships and in view of Hitler's personal orders that his ships were not to operate if there was any risk involved, they remained for the moment in port.

Fourth July was American Independence Day; and for PQ 17, which had a strong American contingent, it began promisingly enough. Although the dawning of this 166th anniversary was no more than metaphorical – since daylight was continuous – the catalyst of hot sun and cold ice produced a protective fog into which the ships of PQ 17 gratefully vanished. Yet somehow, at 04.52, two Heinkel 115s, unseen by most of the convoy, dropped through a hole in the fog and torpedoed the US freighter *Christopher Newport*. A radar plot had been picked up six minutes earlier on *Empire Tide*, but it had faded. 'We were flying a wide search,' writes *Luftwaffe* pilot Rolf Pohler, 'partly above the clouds and partly through fog near the water surface, when our wing captain suddenly hit upon the convoy.' This was Captain Eberhard Peukert, and he and Pohler were the only men to find the ships. 'We attacked immediately and launched a torpedo, hitting one vessel.' The *Christopher Newport* immediately dropped astern, but forty-seven survivors were picked up by one of the rescue vessels. Soon afterwards one of the two submarines in the escort sent her crippled hulk to the bottom.

Somehow, despite the fog, column leaders kept their distance and ships in column kept their station; this was revealed when, all too soon, the fog dispersed and the convoy was silhouetted in bright sunshine against a glass-calm sea. A BV138 then reappeared so promptly that Johnny Macdonald, on *Empire Tide*, thought it must have rested on the water astern of the convoy to conserve fuel until the fog cleared.

The invulnerability of the circling flying-boat to the convoy's guns, and its insect-like persistence, were maddening to Jack Broome. 'At times it was very tempting to catapult our precious Hurricane,' he has since written, 'then sit back and watch the fun. But our fighter was not recoverable and could be used only once; instinctively, I held on to it for future counter-attack.'[2]

By midday the convoy was passing immediately north of the nearest German airfield at Banak. The sun was still shining, visibility was phenomenal and the main air attack must surely come soon. From this point on, the range from the Norwegian airfields, now about 400 miles, would be opening every hour. After travelling more than half-way to its destination the convoy had lost only one ship. Where was the *Luftwaffe*?

During mid-afternoon the convoy passed close to the occasional fog-bank, while to the north the icebergs formed a wraith-like background to Hamilton's zig-zagging cruisers. Then at 16.41 the shadowing BV138 was reinforced by a single Ju88 whose mission was soon disclosed: the homing signals its crew were transmitting, to some unseen force of unknown strength, were intercepted by the convoy.

Empire Tide had still not been moved from her position in an inside column. This might hamper a launching; but it would not necessarily prevent it.

At 18.30 five Heinkel 115s were seen orbiting the convoy outside gun range, very low down on the water. 'This time we saw the whole convoy presenting itself through a cloudless sky at a distance of 35-40 kilometres,' writes Rolf Pohler. One of the American destroyers accompanying the cruiser force, the *Wainwright*, happened at that moment to be refuelling from PQ 17's one remaining tanker; and as the Heinkels prepared to attack, *Wainwright* immediately cast off from the tanker and sped round the convoy, driving off the Heinkel pilots with fierce and accurate anti-aircraft fire, far more concentrated than anything the close escort destroyers could produce. The Ju88 crew gave the Heinkels what support they could by dropping two bombs that fell between *Wainwright* and *Keppel*; but the lumbering floatplanes could not find a way through the escort defences and their crews had been ordered not to commit their aircraft in unfavourable conditions. One torpedo was launched, but it exploded harmlessly outside the convoy perimeter.

To the men of the convoy it seemed an untypically timid display, and indeed in *Empire Tide* it was not even realised that a torpedo attack had been attempted.

Within minutes of this fiasco, however, a much more characteristic attack developed, this time by twenty-five Heinkel 111s of I./KG 26, led by the senior squadron commander, Captain Bernot Eicke. Seen first on the horizon dead astern, they veered to the right before heading straight for the convoy in line abreast at 100 feet. Turley-George was already in the cockpit, engine running and clear to go, and Johnny Macdonald, watching the attack from the bridge through binoculars, warned him of the large formation of Heinkels that was coming in low down from the starboard quarter. The first officer of *Empire Tide* was standing by at the firing hut, and Captain Harvey was preparing to pull *Empire Tide* out of the column for the shoot off. But with no

---

[2] *Convoy is to Scatter* (William Kimber, 1972).

suggestion to launch from *Keppel*, Harvey signalled to Macdonald, who called Turley-George on the R/T. 'You'd better close down, Dickie. These Heinkels are getting very close and Captain Harvey won't shoot off without the OK from Commander Broome.'

This was the moment Turley-George had been waiting for ever since leaving Hvalfjord, indeed ever since joining MSFU. It was the first big attack on the convoy, and it had come comparatively late. Every nautical mile they covered made the task of the *Luftwaffe* more difficult, and if they could exact swift retribution on these Heinkels it might prove decisive. Turley-George was confident that, given a quick decision, he could get off and storm into the enemy formation before they could make their attack and thus at least prevent them from having it all their own way. But now, with the Heinkels nearing the convoy, a terrific barrage was being put up and many of the gunners were firing so wildly that streams of tracers were pouring across the bows of the Camship. 'It's impossible to shoot off from the position we're in,' ruled Captain Harvey; and Turley-George and Macdonald could only agree. Already one of the gunners on *Empire Tide* had been severely wounded by a bullet from an American machine-gun.

Meanwhile attention was centred on one particular Heinkel in which the pilot was pressing his attack right home. *Keppel*, under full helm, avoided one torpedo by inches, but in the course of the combined attack three ships were hit. 'The leader of the formation,' wrote the convoy commodore afterwards, 'never wavered but came in at about twenty feet in the face of a terrific barrage, hit his target, only to crash ahead of the convoy…he must have been riddled with every kind of projectile; a very brave man.' This was in fact not Eicke but Lieutenant Konrad Hennemann, and the ship he hit was the 4,941-ton freighter *Navarius*. Eicke was meanwhile scoring a hit on the US freighter *William Hopper*.

Turley-George, jumping out of the Hurricane cockpit, watched the crippled Heinkel fly over *Empire Tide*, both engines on fire but steady as a rock. He caught a glimpse of the ship immediately to port shuddering as the torpedo struck, then watched the Heinkel turn over on its back and plough straight in.

As the surviving Heinkels left the convoy, still keeping low on the water, the two freighters could be seen abandoned and down by the stern. The third crippled ship was a Russian tanker. The freighters had to be sunk by gunfire, but the tanker, although badly holed, signalled her ability to keep up with the convoy. Four German airmen rescued from their dinghy – not from Hennemann's plane – said they had been briefed before take-off that they would not be fired at because the convoy was in thick fog.

As soon as the Heinkels withdrew, the shadowing BV138 resumed its vigil. There was no sign of the Ju88 which had homed the Heinkels on to the convoy; like them it had apparently headed for base.

It occurred to Commander Broome that this might be the moment to strike at the remaining shadower, which had almost certainly played a part in homing the strike forces. He therefore signalled Captain Harvey: 'Suggest your pilot takes off and tries to shoot down the spotter aircraft.'

Psychologically it was not perhaps the best moment to order Turley-George into the air. He was still fuming at missing what he saw as the opportunity of a lifetime. 'However bad I may be at shooting,' he said recently, 'I had plenty of time to get round to the arse end of that convoy. These Heinkel chaps were flying low and were laden with torpedoes. They were close together and they couldn't have done much manoeuvring. If I'd made a head-on attack, I would at least have broken up the formation, even if I didn't shoot anything down.'

When he got the message that he was to try to shoot down the BV138, he couldn't see the point of it. To knock down a spotter aircraft when the Germans knew exactly where the convoy was and would in any case only put up a replacement hardly seemed adequate compensation for the loss of their only Hurricane, not to mention a personal ducking. Nevertheless he ran to the ladder, climbed it, got into the cockpit and started up the engine. 'You may be sure,' he says, 'that one of those blokes in the BV138 was looking out with binoculars and would have seen us start up. Anyway they headed at once for a big bank of cloud and flew round and round underneath it. Had I taken off, they'd have gone into that bank of cloud and stayed there for a couple of hours, by which time I'd have run out of fuel. So I called Johnny Macdonald and told him I wasn't going.'

Recalling his suggestion to launch, Commander Broome later wrote that the Camship 'immediately hoisted the aeroplane flag, and although the Hurricane was not seen airborne, it was seen with engine running, waiting for a favourable opportunity.' Then, after a note explaining what Camship Hurricanes were and how they functioned, he added: 'It was a pity this one never got off its perch.'

To Turley-George this sounded like a criticism, and in his quiet way he resented it. He believes that Broome was so engrossed with his other responsibilities at the time of the torpedo attack – *Keppel* herself, it will be remembered, narrowly escaped destruction – that he had no time to think about the Hurricane until the action was over, then sought to repair the omission. With the prospect of further torpedo attacks to come, Turley-George was surely right not to risk wasting the Hurricane. Broome himself, on an earlier occasion, had taken the same view.

It is one of the minor tragedies of PQ 17 that this whole controversy was to prove academic. Three hours later, deceived by false reports of the sighting of German warships heading for the convoy and motivated by what seemed the imminent threat of annihilation for both convoy and escort by superior surface forces, Admiral Sir Dudley Pound, from the remoteness of Whitehall, sent two fateful signals. The first ordered the convoy to disperse and proceed individually to Russian ports. The second ordered an even more drastic manoeuvre: 'Convoy is to scatter.'

Both Hamilton and Broome took this latter signal to indicate that an attack by the *Tirpitz* was imminent. It was the only possible justification for such an order. Broome's instructions clearly laid down that in the event of such an attack it was his duty to shadow the enemy and seize any favourable opportunity of attacking him, and he therefore concentrated his close escort forces with the cruisers as fast as he could to meet the expected assault. Meanwhile the captains of the merchant vessels, still in good heart up to that point, but now appalled and incredulous, scattered in all directions in compliance with their orders, proceeding alone and unprotected on their perilous way.

Hindsight suggests that, if the choice had lain with Hamilton and Broome, their reaction might reasonably have been to launch Turley-George on a long-range reconnaissance patrol, to see what really did lurk out of sight over the horizon. But the final decision, as had been made plain, lay with Dudley Pound, and his orders were clear.

The story of the slaughter that followed has been told many times. In the event the German battle squadrons did not emerge from Altenfjord until the following day, 5 July, and even then they returned the same evening, after no more than a minor sortie. Great as was the anxiety at the Admiralty at the threat these ships presented, it was no greater than Adolf Hitler's at the thought of their destruction. The annihilation of PQ 17 was left to the *Luftwaffe* and the U-boats.

For the next six days the scattered vessels were bombed and torpedoed until all but eleven had been sunk. Of the total of twenty-four ships destroyed, eight were sunk by air attack and nine by U-boats, while the remaining seven were 'shared'.

What of the surviving eleven? For days they hid in sheltered bays along the coast of Novaya Zemlya, waiting for an escort to take them through the White Sea to Archangel. One of the surviving eleven was the Camship *Empire Tide*.

Two days after the order to scatter, Captain Harvey had been heading south down the Novaya Zemlya coast, having seen numerous other vessels torpedoed and dive-bombed and having rescued 148 survivors, when he had come abreast of another freighter several miles to starboard. Suddenly there was an explosion and the accompanying ship started to list. 'Christ, submarines,' said Harvey. 'Dickie, get in the cockpit.' One of the submarines surfaced between the stricken ship and *Empire Tide*, and Harvey turned north and increased to maximum speed. 'If they get close enough to attack,' he told Turley-George, 'take off and shoot at them.'

Surprisingly, no one seems to have thought before this of launching Hurricats in an anti-submarine role, although Vernon Sanders, after his combat, had done a sub-hunt for Walker and the 36th Escort Group; but for Turley-George it was an exciting prospect. He planned to launch, have a good squirt at the submarines, force them to submerge, and keep them down while *Empire Tide* escaped. He would then land somewhere on Novaya Zemlya, or possibly bale out near the ship if that seemed preferable. But as he warmed up the engine of the Hurricane and waited for the order to launch, the submarines turned away abruptly to the south, and they did not reappear. Once again it had been the deterrent effect that had counted.

Nosing into a small bay later that day for shelter, Captain Harvey started soundings but nevertheless ran aground, although the chart showed 17 fathoms. As soon as he refloated he continued north until he found a larger bay, where he anchored. Soon afterwards a number of small boats approached from the shore. He had come upon a small settlement of Russian scientists at Mali Karmakul, on Novaya Zemlya.

Harvey decided that they must invite the welcoming party on board. 'Every officer will produce a bottle of booze,' he ordered. There was no spare food, but this only concentrated the effect of the drink and it was a somewhat befuddled group of scientists who returned late that night to the shore. 'Come and have dinner with us tomorrow,' was their parting invitation.

The ship's officers, together with Turley-George, Fenwick, Macdonald and the two Russian interpreters, were duly entertained next evening by the officials of the settlement, the dinner party numbering about twenty. During the meal they drank to Churchill, to Stalin, and to Roosevelt, and when the Russians drank their vodka straight down, Turley-George did the same. Tears rolled down his cheeks and he thought he would choke, but he gobbled in some food and was soon ready for the next toast. The Royal Navy, the Red Navy, the United States Navy, the Royal Air Force – all had to be toasted in gulps of vodka. When they got up from the table after the meal, Turley-George realised that he must take a breather, and he excused himself and went outside.

The huts of the settlement were built on stilts because of the winter snows and when he staggered out of the room the cold air hit him and he fell down the steps like a rag doll. As he staggered back afterwards he overheard one of the Russians say: 'Now we can get down to some serious drinking.' Changing course quickly into the corridor, he started looking for a bedroom. Opening a door at random, he found a darkened room with curtains drawn, in one corner of which he could vaguely discern a huge bed. He took off his shoes and battle-dress top and passed out on the bed.

He had hardly got his head down, as it seemed to him, when one of the Russian interpreters opened the door. 'I'll be with you in a minute,' slurred Turley-George. 'No, no,' said the Russian, 'you're sleeping with my friend's wife.'

Turley-George turned to find that he did indeed have a companion. 'We do not do this sort of thing in Russia,' said the interpreter, 'especially when we are a guest.'

'Honestly…' For once Turley-George was at a loss. Then he saw an angry-looking chap lurking about outside the door. The husband. 'He wishes to duel with you,' said the interpreter. The Russians kept it up for some time, until at last Turley-George realised he was having his leg pulled. Then it was back to the party.

After the traumas of the North Cape, the fortnight they spent at Mali Karmakul was pleasant indeed. A Catalina flying-boat came to collect the wounded gunner, and at length they joined a convoy of five ships with naval and air escort (Russian) and headed for the White Sea, reaching Archangel shortly before midnight on 24 July. Their passage from Iceland had taken exactly four weeks.

XII
Archangel and the North Cape

The MSFU servicing party started work at Keg Ostrov airfield, Archangel, on 30 June, having travelled by train from Murmansk. The three crated Hurricanes, one from PQ 15 and two from PQ 16, were also sent on by rail. The crates, badly buckled in transit, had been further distorted through being dragged up from the landing jetty at Keg Ostrov without being put on rollers to protect the floors; but fortunately the contents were undamaged. As the rest of the equipment and stores did not arrive for several days, however, work was slow at first; then, as the unpacking, checking and listing of material proceeded, six cases and a quantity of ammunition were found to be missing – an irritant with which the British in Russia continually had to contend.

Keg Ostrov airfield was on an island one and a quarter miles west of Archangel, in the middle of the Dvina river. In winter, transport was possible over the ice; but there was no communication with Archangel in summer except by ferry. There were no runways and the grass surface, although good in dry weather, deteriorated rapidly after rain. Since in the previous year No. 151 Wing, the RAF Hurricane Wing that had operated in North Russia, had recorded that the snow started in mid-September, it seemed that the duration of MSFU operations in this theatre might be limited.

At first Flight Lieutenant Roy Lane, in charge of the party, found the Russians none too helpful. They seemed to harbour some residual resentment from past brushes with the Allies, but Lane was determined to win them over. 'I hope to convince them,' he wrote in a letter to Pinkerton, 'that MSFU is a different matter.' He and his party soon had the three Hurricanes assembled and flight-tested and the VHF radio station erected, and their energy and expertise evidently impressed the Russians; anyway Lane was soon writing in different vein of Russian co-operation in the lending of tools and the making of spare parts to replace the missing stores.

No sooner were the three Hurricanes ready then, on 24 July, *Empire Tide* arrived along with the remnant of PQ 17. For Lane and his party, after the hours they had put in, it was disappointing to see the Hurricat still on the catapult. Off-loaded on to a barge, it was towed to Keg Island, where it was disembarked and given a thorough inspection. Meanwhile there were compensations. There was no accommodation available on the island, and Turley-George, Fenwick, Macdonald and their sea crew joined Lane and Lamb at the Intourist Hotel in the town.

Archangel was still under regular aerial bombardment and although the buildings in the main street were substantially built, behind them the town was a maze of wooden structures, and fires were frequent. More than once, during their rest time at the hotel, the MSFU men were called upon to help extinguish fires. Lane and Turley-George, discussing the raids, realised that the Germans came over in the greatest strength in the short period of near-darkness and that during these periods the Red Air Force rarely interfered. If the Russian pilots were short of night-flying experience, as seemed obvious, the four RAF pilots sitting in the Intourist Hotel were not and here it seemed was a chance to give some practical help. Next day Lane offered to fly a standing patrol over Archangel nightly during these periods. The Red Air Force commander reacted favourably, but when Lane asked for one of his Hurricane Mark IIs to get in some practice, his attitude changed. 'You can't fly my Hurricane IIs. If you want to keep a standing patrol you must use your own Hurricanes.' Since Lane's machines were all Sea Hurricanes, specially adapted for catapult work, and sent to Archangel for that purpose, he dare not risk losing them. The only thing to do was forget the whole thing.

With no news of a further incoming convoy, Lane could do little more than keep his party in flying practice, holding one machine in reserve for the next Camship, picketed at dispersal and flown only rarely. By arrangement with the Red Air Force, who in other respects continued to co-operate, one of the Hurricane packing cases was moved to dispersal and converted into an office and store, while the other two cases were used to erect offices and stores in and near the hangar allocated to MSFU. Meanwhile on 14 August the Hurricane from *Empire Tide*, having been thoroughly overhauled and air-tested, was taken back to the quayside and reloaded on the Camship.

On pilot-to-pilot level the Russians were relaxed and friendly, and they showed a keen interest in the performance of the Hurricats and in the way the RAF men handled them. Inevitably, though, there were periods when the MSFU men found time on their hands. Wherever they went in Archangel they were confronted by huge pictures of Lenin and one night in the International Club they spotted a statuette of Lenin, fifteen inches high, standing on a pedestal on a table half-way down the big room that the Russians used as a cinema and dance hall. 'We've got to get that as a mascot,' said Lane. 'Right,' said Turley-George. 'But it's a bit bloody dicey. They love old Lenin.' Nevertheless the idea simmered, until one evening towards the end of August, with Turley-George expecting to leave on a westbound convoy some time in September, Lane put the question. 'How about going and getting Lenin?' There was a dance on at the Club, and this seemed to present an opportunity.

They paid their kopeks to go into the dance, which was well attended, and after a good look round they strolled across the room and stood in front of the statuette. 'I think the best thing,' said Lane, 'is to lift it while they're dancing. When they're sitting round between dances they're looking straight at it across the floor. You're taller than me so I'll keep watch and when I think there's no one looking I'll give you the word. Lift it off the pedestal and hide it behind your back.' 'That's all right – but how are we going to get it out?' Turley-George was wearing battle-dress, but Lane was dressed in his best blue. 'I'll undo my tunic,' said Lane. 'Shove it up the back of my tunic.'

As Turley-George stood there waiting, the dance-floor filled with a confusing whirl of people. Suddenly he heard Lane whisper 'Right – now!' Turley-George grabbed the statuette and pushed it somewhat clumsily under Lane's tunic. 'What do we do now?' 'We'll just have to walk out like this.' Step by step, their bodies just touching, like some music-hall double-act, they strutted triumphantly out, eyes turned left towards the dance floor, grinning like dummies at the dancers. The chap on the door gave them a quizzical look, but he bade them good night and a moment later they were in the street.

'We can't walk back to the hotel like this,' said Turley-George.

'Of course we can't. Put it down your battle-dress trousers!'

'Christ – I've got to carry it, have I?'

'You're the tall one.'

So down Turley-George's trouser leg it went. Putting his hand in his pocket, he held on to it by the neck. It made him limp, but that, in the Archangel of 1942, was not conspicuous.

They hid the statuette in the wardrobe of the hotel. When the time came, on 9 September, for *Empire Tide*'s MSFU crew to re-embark, Turley-George packed it in the bottom of a hold-all and covered it with an assortment of soiled shirts, underwear and pyjamas, throwing in an old toilet bag for good measure on top. He had got to the quayside at Archangel and reached the gang-plank when he was stopped by two security guards. 'Ship's crew,' he said nonchalantly. 'OK,' said one of the guards; but he motioned to him to open the hold-all. Turley-George tried to look bland, a pose at which his escapades gave him frequent practice, but someone on deck shouted: 'He only wants you to open your bag.' Is that all, thought Turley-George despairingly. 'Tell him it's not necessary,' he said. 'Well, if it's not necessary,' countered the seaman, with infuriating logic, 'what's the objection?'

With a shrug of the shoulders, Turley-George opened the bag. The old dirty clothes trick repelled the guard and with the statuette lying snugly in the bottom of the hold-all, Turley-George climbed aboard.

For PQ 17, the *Luftwaffe* had amassed more than 250 bombers, torpedo-bombers and reconnaissance planes in northern Norway, and their success against this convoy had been spectacular. Impressive as it was, however, the Germans had been inclined to exaggerate it and they had claimed the complete destruction of the convoy. Even more significant, they had drawn the wrong conclusions from it. Overlooking the fact that PQ 17 had scattered because of a wrongly-inferred surface threat, Dönitz was misled into recommending that aircraft rather than U-boats or surface vessels should be used against the Arctic convoys in the summer months. Thus the main offensive against the next convoy, PQ 18, would be mounted from the air. Would the *Luftwaffe* be equal to it?

Even in summer the German Air Force in northern Norway endured hardships and privations that were more than the equal of anything the MSFU men were asked to face. The almost permanent daylight allowed operations to be mounted round the clock, giving no respite. Living conditions were primitive, fresh meat and vegetables were scarce, recreation was almost non-existent, leave infrequent.

> *Banak, the airfield from which we operated* [wrote one Ju88 pilot, Captain Ernest Holtschmidt], *was fifty-five miles south of the North Cape, at the end of Porsanger Fjord, and surrounded by mountains. Tatting off in a bumpy south wind was a tricky business; moreover, the weather, during the hours we were airborne, often changed completely, and we would return to find the vertical cliffs of the fjords blanketed in cloud. As all the fjords looked alike, it was easy to find oneself in a blind alley where many aircraft crashed.*[3]

A worse enemy than the unpredictable weather and the conditions on land was the Arctic Ocean. Even in the attacks on PQ 17 the losses had been considerable, and the chances of rescue were slight. 'I shall not forget circling over ditched crews,' says Holtschmidt, 'sending fixes back to base and knowing after half an hour that it was useless to wait any longer: no one would be alive.' Yet there is no doubt that for the German crews PQ 17 was a great morale booster. Says Holtschmidt:

> *We knew the importance of our missions. Operations usually followed much the same pattern. Our reconnaissance aircraft, which maintained regular patrols, would report a concentration of ships at Reykjavik, and from that moment the harbour would be constantly watched. As soon as the convoy sailed, every squadron in Norway would be alerted. When it came within range of the first formation, near Narvik, they took off and bombed. Next day it would enter our area, and from then on we were responsible until it reached its destination.*[4]

In winter the ice barrier to the north kept the convoys well within range. But as the barrier receded, the distance to be covered before an interception could be made increased. Liaison with the German Navy was good and sighting reports from U-boats were indispensable, but in bad weather convoys could still be hard to find. Intelligence and sighting reports were not always accurate and the most notorious error came shortly after PQ 17. A false alarm on 1 August of a new and mammoth ship concentration at Hvalfjord, followed three days later by another report that the fjord was empty, deceived the Germans into thinking that another big convoy was on the way. 'For two weeks every reconnaissance squadron of *Luftflotte 5* was kept busy searching every corner of the Arctic Circle,' writes Cajus Becker in *The Luftwaffe War Diaries.* 'The result was completely nil…The convoy appeared to have evaporated into thin air. Only on the 17th, after 140 sorties lasting 1,600 hours and costing nearly a quarter of a million gallons of high octane fuel, was the two weeks' search finally broken off.'

---

[3] *Royal Air Force Review*, January 1952.
[4] Published by Macdonald in 1966.

In fact, there was no attempt to sail an Arctic convoy that month. British naval forces were preoccupied with Operation *Pedestal*, the August convoy aimed at relieving beleaguered Malta; and in addition, many voices were raised against attempting to run a further convoy through the Barents Sea before winter. But solemn promises of urgent aid to Russia had been made, and at the end of that month Churchill returned from a visit to Stalin with renewed determination to 'aid Russia to the very limits of our power'. PQ 18 was therefore set in motion.

XIII
PQ 18: The Germans Miscalculate

'Well gentlemen, I have not had the pleasure of doing this highly amusing little trip before, but I can tell you we're going to succeed.'

The jocular phrases with which Rear Admiral R.L. Burnett, 'Uncle Bob' to his subordinates when out of earshot, introduced himself as commander of the fighting escort for the latest fleet of merchant ships to brave the Arctic route to Russia may not in retrospect seem particularly well chosen. But they gave the crews who were listening to them a badly needed boost. They knew what had happened to PQ 17. The consecutive numbering of these Russian convoys inevitably meant that the announcement of the imminent departure of PQ 18 somersaulted more than a few stomachs.

On 2 September 1942 the British section of the convoy headed north from Loch Ewe through the Minches in perfect weather. Off the west coast of Iceland they were joined by an American contingent and the convoy set course north east for Jan Mayen Island and Spitzbergen. There were forty merchant ships in all.

This was the biggest convoy yet to sail to North Russia, and it was given the strongest escort. Admiral Tovey's objections to taking heavy ships into the Barents Sea, far from their bases and exposed to heavy concentrations of U-boats and aircraft, with little hope of bringing enemy naval units to action, meant that the Home Fleet would again restrict themselves to long-range cover north-west of Jan Mayen and west of Spitzbergen. But a fighting escort of eighteen destroyers, with Bob Burnett directing operations from the cruiser *Scylla*, would this time supplement the normal ocean escort.

Two squadrons of Hampden torpedo-bombers had been flown to Russia to strike at enemy surface units if they appeared and a squadron of Catalina flying-boats, also based in Russia, would provide long-range reconnaissance. Most important of all, the first of the new 'Woolworth' escort carriers, as they were known, adapted merchantmen provided under American lease-lend, would accompany the convoy into the Barents Sea. This was the *Avenger*, and she carried on her flight deck twelve Sea Hurricanes, together with three Swordfish biplanes for reconnaissance.

With such powerful protection, the presence of the single expendable Hurricane on the foredeck of the only Camship in the convoy, the *Empire Morn*, seemed almost an irrelevance. Indeed, so long as *Avenger* stayed with the convoy, Flying Officer A.H. 'Jackie' Burr, twenty-three-year-old senior RAF pilot on the Camship, had orders not to launch.

The time would come, though, when the bulk of this strong naval escort, having fought PQ 18 through to a point 300 miles east of Bear Island, would transfer its allegiance to QP 14, the homeward-bound convoy that, as usual, had started out simultaneously from Archangel. Among the ships to turn on to reciprocal would be *Avenger*. At that point Jackie Burr and his stand-by pilot, twenty-one-year-old New Zealander John Davies, would become the convoy's sole air protection. In June the Admiralty had proposed that two Camships should accompany PQ 18, but the idea seems to have been dropped.

After losing her fighter escort, PQ 18 would make further east until it moved to the limit of range of concentrated air attack from northern Norway. But when it reached a position due north of Kanin Point, it would be forced to turn south for the run down into the White Sea and Archangel. As it approached Kanin Point, with several hundred miles still to go to Archangel, it would come, for a few climactic hours, within more practical range of the *Luftwaffe*.

For Jackie Burr and John Davies, and for their fighter direction officers, Canadian John Carrique and Yorkshireman Norman Gostelow (formerly with George Varley), this final period was their justification. To afford the absolute minimum of air protection at this vulnerable point, all the hazards of the North Cape route were being accepted.

Jackie Burr, tall and fresh-complexioned, with dark eyes that were full of expression, had been born in Isleworth, Middlesex. His clipped, rather high-pitched voice and his slight reticence of manner, provided the perfect foil to Davies' Antipodean exuberance.

The captain of *Empire Morn* was a Geordie who had made the trip before. Blue-eyed and grizzled, he had enough troubles of his own and his attitude to the Hurricat and its personnel was hostile. Burr and his team did their best to avoid friction; but the underlying antagonism would certainly have erupted but for the single human emotion that united them all. Fear. Not a man aboard *Empire Morn*, or any other ship of PQ 18, was ashamed to admit that he was scared. Indeed he would have prefixed that word with another less polite one of four letters.

German air reconnaissance located the convoy as early as 8 September off Iceland, but because of low cloud and poor visibility they lost it for the next few days. When they picked it up again, on the morning of the 12th, it had reached a point to the north of Jan Mayen and was steering north-east for Spitzbergen. The sighting report came from a BV138, which patrolled the convoy at a safe distance, evading the Hurricanes that took off from *Avenger* by slipping into cloud.

The Hurricanes might have destroyed the flying-boat had they been faster and better armed. Ironically, Mark IIC Hurricanes, armed with cannon, were in fact present in the convoy; but they were in crates in the merchant vessels, earmarked for delivery to the Red Air Force.

The circling BV138 called up the U-boats, but they did not have it all their own way.

Swordfish from *Avenger* took off and harried them, and that night a U-boat was sunk by a destroyer. Eight more U-boats were probing the convoy's defences and the depth-charging kept off-duty personnel awake all night.

For the Germans, the news that the convoy was accompanied by an aircraft carrier came as a shock. This, for the strike squadrons at Banak, Bardufoss and Kirkenes, was something new. But by 13 September, as the convoy began to pass through the macabre flotsam spilled from the deck cargo of PQ 17, the *Luftwaffe* was ready. Meanwhile the U-boats began to apply maximum pressure and that morning two ships were torpedoed and sunk.

The convoy was keeping as far north as land and ice barriers would allow. But that afternoon, 150 miles north-west of Bear Island and 450 miles from the nearest German airfields, the mass air attacks began.

The first aircraft to appear over the convoy were the Ju88s of KG 30. Twenty-eight Heinkel torpedo-bombers of I./KG 26, led by a new squadron commander, Major Werner Klümper, had been timed to arrive simultaneously, but they had missed the rendezvous in light drizzle and overflew the target. As the Ju88s began their dive-bombing attack the Hurricanes on *Avenger* took off in pursuit. Meanwhile the Heinkels were approaching their point of no return. Heading back to the east, they came up almost at once with the convoy.

The squadron plan had been to attack in two waves of fourteen aircraft each. The priority target, on Göring's orders – for reasons of prestige he wanted to be able to claim a major air victory – was *Avenger*, but at first the German crews could see no sign of her. A third wave of Heinkels, from III./KG 26 under Captain Klaus Nocken, was following up Major Klümper's two waves.

At three o'clock that afternoon, with *Avenger*'s Hurricanes on the deck refuelling, forty-two Heinkels, carrying two torpedoes apiece, attacked the convoy from the port quarter at low level. Despite a fierce curtain of fire which threw up great gouts of water ahead of the Heinkels, forcing them up to 150 feet, they kept up their line-abreast attack.

This was the dreaded 'Golden Comb' technique, adding up in theory to eighty-four torpedoes converging on the convoy, forming the ever-lengthening fangs of a giant comb. The only defence was to line up the ships fore and aft in parallel with the direction of the protruding teeth. The convoy commodore, Rear Admiral E.K. Boddam-Whethem RNR, was quick to order an emergency turn and the columns nearest to the attack escaped. The Heinkels faced a murderous barrage and many of them were hit, forcing the crews to jettison their torpedoes and break off. But the remainder held on with marvellous courage, not releasing their missiles until they were within a thousand yards of the port column. Two ships in the middle of the convoy, and six of the seven in the two starboard columns, were sunk. One of them, the *Empire Stevenson*, loaded with explosives, blew up, spattering adjacent ships with debris and belching a vast column of fire and smoke to cloud level and beyond.

The whole attack lasted only eight minutes. There were hundreds of survivors from the other vessels, but none from *Empire Stevenson*. The British claimed five Heinkels destroyed, but according to German records they all got back to their bases. Every single aircraft, however, had been hit and at least six of them had to be written off.

For the Allies, though, the attack had been calamitous; with the losses from U-boats, a quarter of the convoy had been destroyed in a single day. The following day, with the sky cloudless and visibility unlimited, further destruction seemed certain. But two things contributed, for the time being at least, to the convoy's survival. First, Commander Colthurst, captain of *Avenger*, changed his tactics, holding his fighters back until the mass attacks developed. Second, Göring's orders that *Avenger* should be the priority target were reiterated, to the extent that every available crew was briefed to attack her. The Hurricanes were ready for them; and for the Germans this day was as catastrophic as the previous day had been triumphant. Of twenty-two Heinkels that took off under Major Klümper from Bardufoss, five were lost over the convoy and a further nine were written off on their return. What the Heinkel crews had to fly through is illustrated by the fact that three of *Avenger*'s Hurricanes were shot down by ships in the convoy. (All three pilots were saved.)

The German losses were not confined to the Heinkel 111s; the Ju88s and He115s suffered severely too. 'My own wing [Heinkel 115s],' writes Rolf Pohler, 'lost during the attack against PQ 18, out of eight, five planes, three of them with their whole crews.' Only one of these total losses was over the convoy: two crashed into the mountains in foggy coastal weather on their way home. Pohler speaks of the tactical mistake that was made in aiming the attacks principally at the escort carrier.

After the traumas of 13 September, only two more ships were lost while *Avenger* and the fighting destroyer escort remained. But on the 16th, with the convoy 400 miles north-west of Kanin Point and still heading east, the cruiser *Scylla* and the carrier *Avenger* left with the main body of the escort to join QP 14. The merchant seamen, less versed in the paradoxes of wartime operations than the servicemen, demanded to know 'Why now?'

PQ 18 was left with one flak-ship (*Ulster Queen*), three destroyers, three minesweepers, four trawlers and the Camship. Next day the escort was reinforced by four Russian destroyers; but the fifty-one warships, long range and close escort, that had made up the most heavily defended of all Russian convoys had largely evaporated.

Later that day the convoy turned due south for Kanin Point and the entrance to the White Sea – a change of course that was at once reported by German air patrols, who had already reported the departure of the main escort. The last chance for the depleted German strike squadrons was approaching.

Both U-boats and aircraft had meanwhile been concentrating their attention on the homeward-bound convoy, QP 14. But all day on 17 September, despite poor visibility, the Germans kept PQ 18 under surveillance and with the weather improving it seemed likely that the 18th would be the crucial day.

It began predictably with a Focke-Wulf Condor and a Ju88 circling the convoy, which was steering south at 9 knots. Position, course and speed being known to the Germans, there was nothing to be gained by launching the Hurricane.

The sky was overcast, with solid banks of cloud at 2,000 feet thickening to ten-tenths at 4,000, ideal for dive-bombing. All the ships were ordered to fly their protective balloons. Visibility was at least ten miles and by mid-morning Kanin Point, bleak, barren and uninhabited, was clearly visible on the port bow.

The convoy was formed into eight columns, most columns containing only three ships. *Empire Morn* was the last ship in the fourth column from the right. Steering a southerly course, with a south-easterly breeze, the Camship would have to alter course very little to launch the Hurricane into wind. But the pilot would have to pick his way through a barrage of balloons after launching. Neither Johnny Davies, who was on watch until 08.00 hours, nor Jackie Burr, replacing him until midday, worried unduly about this. The sport of balloon dodging was one that both men had practised, albeit illegally.

At 10.15 the *Ulster Queen*, keeping radar guard, reported that enemy aircraft were massing in the vicinity. While Burr went forward from the bridge to the foredeck to take his seat in the cockpit, Davies, deputed to fire the rockets, made for the firing hut, leaving Carrique and Gostelow on the bridge with the captain.

The sailing of QP 14 while PQ 18 was still at sea had stretched German resources to the limit, especially as they had lost a total of thirty-four aircraft in the earlier attacks. So anxious was Göring to sink *Avenger* that he had kept on attacking her. But PQ 18 now seemed to be at his mercy.

The plan as usual was for synchronised attacks by bomb and torpedo, greatly complicating the ships' avoiding action. But operating as the aircraft were near the limit of range, much depended on accurate timing. Neither bombers nor torpedo-carriers could afford to loiter in the target area.

First to appear on the scene was a squadron of Ju88s. Flying in just below the cloud base, they bombed and dive-bombed the convoy from 4,000 feet down to a thousand. Fire from the Russian destroyers helped to drive them off and none of the ships was hit. Everything was made ready to launch *Empire Morn*'s Hurricane, but the dive-bombers showed themselves only briefly before regaining cloud and Carrique and Gostelow preferred to wait for the torpedo-bombers that they knew must come.

Sure enough at exactly 11.00 hours twelve Heinkel 111s, flying too low to show up on *Ulster Queen*'s radar, were apprehensively picked out approaching from the north, skimming the water, developing their threat from astern. The responsibility for launching had been left to the MSFU men on the Camship, with the captain retaining the power of veto. 'Now's the time to launch!' said Carrique. The captain immediately protested that the ship wasn't clear ahead.

Certainly Burr would have to negotiate the balloons of other ships immediately after launching. But he was prepared for that. What neither he nor Davies nor Carrique nor Gostelow were prepared for was the captain's assertion of his right of veto.

Fortunately for PQ 18 the determination of the first wave of Heinkel pilots did not match that of their comrades five days earlier. Morale, not surprisingly, had taken a tumble. Facing a barrage which, although formidable enough, bore no comparison with that of the fighting escort, and with no air opposition of any kind, they dropped their torpedoes early and never achieved the awesome symmetry of the Golden Comb. Thus only one of the twenty-four torpedoes reached its mark. All the other ships found time to turn parallel with the attack and avoid being hit. The captain's reluctance to launch was thus vindicated, however fortuitously. Burr and the Hurricane lived to fight another day, or, more probably, the same day.

As the torpedo attack faded, Burr noticed that his electrics had failed. With bombs still falling from stragglers amongst the Ju88s, the sea crew calmly checked the fuses and then, locating the trouble, changed the battery. Once again Burr was ready to go.

John Davies, standing at the firing hut, could hardly contain his frustration. Burr's time was up: it was 11.50. Come on, it's my turn, he wanted to say. They normally allowed themselves a few minutes for the changeover. But with enemy aircraft still about, it would be madness to attempt to switch pilots now.

Another formation of He111s, having worked their way round behind the convoy to the north and east, beyond visibility distance, chose this moment to attack from that quarter in an effort to achieve surprise. Skimming in across the water at thirty-five feet, they had already closed to within five miles of the convoy. 'We're going to shoot you off now!' Burr knew attack was imminent. But his view astern was blocked by the Camship's bridge. 'What are they?' 'About fifteen Heinkel 111s.'

There was no dispute with the captain this time. The hand signals were made, Burr opened the throttle before cutting his hand down and the noise level multiplied tenfold as Davies operated the lever that fired the rockets. Tongues of flaming cordite licked the foredeck, carpeting Nos 1 and 2 Holds and ricocheting off the bridge front structure on the port side, and the impact and sibilance were so stunning that Carrique, sheltering on the right-hand wing of the bridge from the heat and blow-back, was deafened.

'I can't hear a damn thing,' he shouted to Gostelow. 'You'll have to take over.' Gostelow grabbed the microphone as the Hurricane spurted clear of the catapult rail. The trolley on which it was mounted was halted by the buffers at the end of the rail and the Hurricane, bereft of its launching impetus, sagged visibly as Burr fought for flying speed. 'Stop these bastards firing at me!'

The startling glare of the rockets may have deceived some of the convoy gunners into thinking *Empire Morn* was being dive-bombed and that the Hurricane was the agent of destruction. But in any case they had already shown themselves to be understandably trigger-happy. An American ship on the port beam and a Russian destroyer on the port bow, both started blasting away with Bofors and Oerlikon. 'OK Jack, I'll do that.'

Gostelow had no idea how to go about it. He was only trying to reassure Burr. Then *Empire Morn*'s own gunners, volunteers from the Army, supplied the answer. On the same principle as that adopted by their allies, they shot first at the culprits and prepared to ask questions afterwards.

Careering on across the convoy, swerving violently to avoid balloons and balloon cables and somehow dodging the flak, Burr climbed rapidly to 700 feet and swung round towards the port quarter of the convoy in response to Gostelow's directions.

'Tally-ho!' He could see the fifteen Heinkels now, black and forbidding, stretched out in rigid line abreast, flattened on the water at fifty feet, less than three miles from the convoy. It was the Golden Comb technique all over again. He could tell at a glance that their flying discipline was altogether different from the Heinkel attack of earlier that morning. They were holding their course and position with a geometry that was chilling to watch.

Somewhere in the middle of that formation must be the leader. Some angle of attack must be best to avoid the formation's combined fire-power. But even as these thoughts came to him he dismissed them. He had to get straight in there and break up the formation, regardless of the odds and the only way to do that was by instant and impetuous head-on attack.

Diving at the Heinkels with all the pugnacity and desperation that his fears for the convoy inspired, he sprayed the centre section of the formation from 300 yards down to 150, then found himself hurtling towards one particular Heinkel. Firing all the way, he saw his bullets spattering the nose of what proved to be the fourth Heinkel from the left.

He realised that he was expending his ammunition with prodigal abandon. But the swiftness and virulence of his attack utterly distorted the exquisite parallels of the formation. Amongst the escort vessels a cheer went up as one of the Heinkel pilots, convinced that his adversary was determined on a collision course, wrenched at his controls so violently to avoid him that he flew straight into the sea.

Ignoring the curtain of fire that was now being put down by the destroyers, Burr turned above and behind the fourth Heinkel and saw white smoke pouring from its starboard engine. Coming in this time on the starboard side he closed to 250 yards and exhausted the last of his ammunition in a beam attack. White smoke was pouring from both engines of the Heinkel as he broke off.

'I've got one of them!'

'Good work.'

'Did you see it go down?'

'No. We're far too busy dodging torpedoes. Are you OK?'

'Yes. But I'm out of ammunition.'

As he came up astern of *Empire Morn* Burr watched the Heinkel he had attacked limp across the convoy before crashing into the sea between columns five and six. Two other Heinkels had been hit, either by the escort or in Burr's attack, one so badly that it had little hope of reaching its base.

'Enemy aircraft coming in at four o'clock!' called Gostelow.

'How many of them?'

'About ten.'

'I'll try and worry them.'

Breaking away to starboard, Burr showed himself to the section that was attacking from that side and made a spirited dummy attack. As soon as he did so the German planes dropped their torpedoes and sheered off. 'Orbit convoy,' called Gostelow.

Already Burr had the satisfaction of knowing that most of the Heinkel pilots, losing their poise in the heat of the combat, had released their torpedoes at too great a range to be sure of success. Now he could see for himself that not a single torpedo had struck home.

The vessel torpedoed in the previous attack had been bombed by Ju88s while Burr was chasing the Heinkels and a direct hit had finished her off. She was the only casualty.

Burr's duty was to stay with the convoy for as long as he could assist in its defence. Then would come the bale-out. But another possibility occurred to him. Did he have enough fuel to reach Keg Ostrov, the airfield he had been told about at Archangel? At 12.10, when he had been in the air for twenty minutes, he asked for his distance from Archangel and was given a figure of 200 miles.

All he had with him in the air was a copy of a small-scale Russian map of the run down to Archangel which Davies had traced from an original back at Loch Ewe. Apart from an airfield at Panoi on the White Sea which Intelligence sources had categorised as a swamp, he knew of no alternative. 'I've got sixty gallons left,' he told Gostelow. 'Shall I try and land or stick around?' Gostelow felt that only the pilot could make the decision. 'Do as you please.' Burr's answer lay in the Ju88s that were still circling the convoy. 'I'll stick around.'

The prospects of saving the Hurricane and of a comparison between the risks of the bale-out and an attempt to reach Archangel, were matters that were also being considered on *Empire Morn*. The problem was passed to John Davies, who had returned to the bridge and his reaction was immediate: give Jackie Burr the best information we have and leave it to him.

'I could make this piece of land on the port side,' suggested Burr. They were just rounding Kanin Point. 'Yes,' agreed Davies, 'but I don't think there's an airfield there.'

At 12.25 Burr dived at a gaggle of Ju88s that were approaching from the starboard side and they made off, leaving the convoy unmolested apart from a single shadower. He had been airborne now for thirty-eight minutes and his chances of reaching Archangel were slim.

'Are you going to bale out, Jack?'

'Too bloody cold. I'll try and save the aircraft.'

'Good idea.'

'What's the course for Archangel? 180 degrees isn't it?'

'170 degrees magnetic.'

Just as Burr was setting course, Davies called him with a correction. He had forgotten to convert the nautical miles of the Admiralty chart into statute miles. Archangel was not 200 miles away at all. It was 230. To his dismay he could get no answer.

That additional thirty miles must surely put Archangel out of reach. But Burr was now committed. When Davies at last raised him, all Burr could do was hope his fuel gauge was under-reading.

He was navigating with the aid of an improvised schoolboy map. His endurance was critical. He dare not fly at his most economical height – about 10,000 feet – in case the winds, which were south-east at sea level, changed direction and velocity with altitude. He knew of no high ground along his proposed track, so he kept below 2,000 feet. Soon he flew into a fog bank.

Somehow he made a landfall at the entrance to the Dvina river and pinpointed his position, grinning at the extravagant hues with which Davies had coloured the tracing. If his fuel held out he might make it.

Noted on the tracing was the fact that the pier and the town of Archangel were prohibited areas. He would have to avoid them. One RAF Hampden crew had already paid the price for ignoring this warning.

Although a signal had been sent to the Russians, the MSFU detachment at Keg Ostrov had not been alerted to the imminent arrival of the convoy and no radio watch was being kept.

Approaching Archangel Burr could see no sign of an airfield in the position marked on his tracing. Searching for it, over a heavily-defended and much-bombed town, held obvious perils.

Suddenly, on an island in the river to the west of Archangel, he saw a grass airfield. There was a dip in the centre, and patches of water and mud. With his fuel gauges now stuck at zero, he fired the recognition signal hopefully.

The map was wrong. Without realising it, he had found Keg Ostrov. Fearing that even now the control tower might fire a red to warn him against landing, he did a brief right-hand circuit. Aiming to miss the worst of the mud, he landed hurriedly but safely into wind and bumped to a stop. He had four gallons left in his tanks – a margin of less than six minutes.

There were no more torpedo attacks on the convoy, and although it was harried by bombers far into the White Sea, no more ships were hit. The final German onslaught on PQ 18 had been repelled, and 'Uncle Bob' Burnett's 'highly amusing little trip' was over.

There had been distressing losses; but of the forty merchant vessels that had set out to carry munitions to the hard-pressed Russian armies, twenty-seven had got through. 'For the Russians,' writes Cajus Becker in *The Luftwaffe War Diaries*, 'their cargoes represented hundreds of modern tanks and aircraft, thousands of road vehicles, and a mass of other war and industrial materials – enough to equip a whole new army for the front.'

XIV
V for Victor: The Stolen Hurricane

Two days after Jackie Burr's great flight, on 20 September 1942, the Admiralty signalled their decision to discontinue using Camships on the Russian convoys in the winter months. From the beginning of 1943, auxiliary carriers were to accompany all Russian convoys and the detachment at Keg Ostrov was to be recalled forthwith. On receipt of this news the Air Section of No. 30 Mission asked Air Ministry for instructions on the disposal of the aircraft and equipment that would become redundant, suggesting that the Hurricanes and radio equipment be returned to the United Kingdom and the remaining equipment and stores be handed over to the Russians. The Air Ministry agreed, and Party 'A', the RAF port detachment at Archangel, were instructed to load all spare machines and equipment on to the recently arrived Camship *Empire Morn*.

On board *Empire Morn*, intended for the Pool at Keg Ostrov was a crated Hurricane – V.6881, soon to become famous as V for Victor – which would now have to be returned from whence it came. But in order to facilitate the discharge of other cargoes it was necessary to off-load it on to the quayside, to be reloaded after the discharge had been completed. The crate was clearly marked RAF Equipment Officer, Bakharitsa, and Flight Lieutenant A.G. Heath, the officer thus addressed, gave prompt instructions to the Russian port authorities that it was not to be removed. These instructions, it seems, aroused the interest of the Russians; here, they may have thought, was some updated version of the Hurricane which they were not being allowed to see. Anyway within forty-eight hours the crate, with V for Victor inside it, disappeared.

It was a sizeable crate by any standards, and Heath and his senior assistant, Sergeant Mills, after doing some sleuthing, followed up a chance remark made by an Army driver who had seen a crate resembling the missing one in a railway siding behind Bakharitsa. A spot-check confirmed that it was still there and before the Russians could spirit it away, Heath and Mills posted a guard on it. Meanwhile another officer of Party 'A', Flight Lieutenant Wiltshire, called at the offices of the Department for Foreign Trade (*Narkomvneshtorg*, or NKVT), where he saw a Major Rogulov. It took him two hours to convince Rogulov that the crate was intended for the RAF, Rogulov continually maintaining that it must have been sent for the Russians. Eventually Rogulov gave the assurance Wiltshire was asking for – that he would see that the crate was not removed.

The PQ convoys had been delivering Hurricane IIs to Russia for many months, and Red Air Force pilots were flying them daily at Archangel. The Russians had no interest in the obsolescent Hurricane I and indeed had expressly asked that this type should not be sent to them. But the evident determination of the RAF port authorities to repossess this newly-delivered crate only deepened Russian suspicion. Heath and Mills, satisfied with the assurance obtained from Rogulov, seem at this stage to have relaxed their vigilance; anyway on 13 October the crate disappeared again. This time the Russians took the precaution of loading it on to a truck and carrying it off into the interior before the RAF could intervene. All that Heath and Wiltshire were able to discover were the number of the truck and its probable destination – Yaroslavl, on the railway running south from Archangel to Moscow, 500 miles from Archangel and 150 short of Moscow.

The Senior RAF Officer North Russia was a wing commander of maturity and humour named Tom Harpham. Forty-seven years old, he had served in the ranks of the London Irish Rifles for three years in the First World War before transferring briefly to the RFC, being recalled to the RAF in October 1939. On 17 October 1942 he reported the theft of the Hurricane to 30 Mission, ending his signal 'endeavouring to trace – suggest you endeavour to trace'. The officers of 30 Mission, already smarting under numerous acts of circumvention in which the Russians, inspired perhaps by their own suspicions, had indulged, moved quickly into action, and the senior equipment officer of the Mission, Squadron Leader R.H. Mason, obtained from Engineer-Major Kovalioff, of the Department of External Relations in Moscow, an assurance that the crate would be returned with the least possible delay. A further complication was the fact that the river Dvina might soon be iced up. Kovalioff was requested to notify 30 Mission immediately the crate was traced, giving its location, so that it could be transported by rail, via Murmansk if need be, for onward shipment to Britain.

Despite the promises of Kovalioff and others, another fortnight passed and there was still no sign of the crate. On 30 October Harpham sent a reminder to 30 Mission. The Hurricane had not yet been returned, he told them. And the plot had thickened. It seemed likely that the plane had been assembled by the Russians, as they were now saying that it was no longer crated. They were asking for fresh particulars and serial numbers – typical of the procrastination and evasion at which they had already proved so adept. Harpham was convinced that they had no intention of returning the aircraft if they could possibly avoid it and he didn't want to continue the battle unless he could be sure of determined support from 30 Mission. He concluded his signal to Moscow: 'Are we to insist on its return?'

Repossession of the missing Hurricane, in this atmosphere of Oriental intrigue, had now become a question of 'face'. The Mission's reaction was brief and immediate: 'Yes, ad infinitum.'

Three more weeks passed and Harpham was still unable to get any satisfactory answer from the Russians in Archangel. V for Victor, it seemed, was irretrievably lost in the interior. Meanwhile what was expected to be the last east-west convoy – QP 15 – was about to sail, taking the redundant MSFU Hurricanes (less V for Victor) and their equipment on the *Empire Tristram*, and the personnel on the *Ulster Queen*. (Among the passengers on *Ulster Queen* was Jackie Burr, replaced as pilot on *Empire Morn* by Roy Lane.)

On 20 November Group Captain W.G. Cheshire, air attaché in Moscow, wrote a strongly-worded note to the head of the Department of External Relations in Moscow reiterating the details of the Hurricane's disappearance and referring to Engineer-Major Kovalioff's promise to expedite its return. But in their anxiety to find out if they were being tricked the Russians had not only assembled the Hurricane, they had also flown it. Now, satisfied that their suspicions were unfounded, they cut their losses and flew the machine back to Keg Ostrov. But in their irritation they did not pass this piece of information to the British, who, with no one left at the MSFU Pool to note the Hurricane's arrival, remained in ignorance of it. It was not until 7 December, when Cheshire finally succeeded in getting a meeting in Moscow with another Engineer-Major named Ryabchenko, that the information that the Hurricane had been found and flown back to Archangel sixteen days earlier was extracted.

Cheshire went back to his office in the British Embassy and signalled the news to Harpham. 'You are to contact Colonel Popov,' he added, 'to confirm this.' Colonel Popov was head of NKVT in Archangel. 'If no more ships available at Archangel on which this can be loaded (due to freezing of Dvina) the Hurricane is to be sent to Murmansk at Russian expense. Signal action taken.'

Next day Harpham sent his deputy to Keg Ostrov, where the Hurricane was duly inspected and found to be intact. That same day, however, QP 15 sailed. And all efforts to get a meeting with Colonel Popov proved abortive. Employing familiar tactics, he was 'too busy to see anyone'. So on 10 December a letter was sent to him which, after reviewing past events, continued:

> *As there is at present no British ship either in Archangel or Molotovsk on which this aircraft could be loaded for onward shipment to Great Britain, it is requested that you will make arrangements for it to be transferred to Murmansk, crated, and loaded on to the first available British ship.*
>
> *I am instructed that this move should be carried out at the expense of the Soviet Government.*
>
> *Please inform me when the aircraft reaches Murmansk the name of the ship on which it has been loaded, and the date of loading.*

The British had taken their stand. The Russians had removed a crated aircraft from the quayside clearly addressed to the British, despite assurances to the contrary, and despatched it to the interior, where they had assembled and flown it. It was now up to them, having flown it back to Keg Ostrov, to dismantle and re-crate it and transport it to the only operable port, Murmansk and there load it on to a British ship. The entire expense must be borne by the Russians. If this smacked of rubbing the Russians' noses in it, the British no doubt thought this would make a nice change. Absolute firmness, it had become clear, was the only thing the Russians understood, and the stand was fully supported by air attaché Cheshire in a letter of 11 December to NKVT Moscow.

For the Russians too the Hurricane had become more than a mere pawn on the political chequer-board. They were now equally determined to keep it in Russia. Next day, 12 December, the intervention of a third party, who knew nothing of the history of the matter and was therefore entirely innocent of the convolutions of 'face' that were involved, breathed a note of sanity into the confrontation, a note, which, for the British at least, was both inopportune and unwelcome. This was a Mr Dalgleish, the representative of the British Ministry of War Transport at Archangel. Acting independently, Dalgleish recommended to the Admiralty that the Hurricane be handed over unconditionally to the Russians, giving a number of excellent reasons. This was the text of his signal:

> *Have been requested by RAF to load a Sea Hurricane now to Archangel ex a Camship back to UK. This will involve Russians crating plane and forwarding it to Murmansk. RAF inform us that Russians could usefully use this plane here. Could you contact Air Ministry and get their agreement to leave plane with Russians. It seems unnecessary to expose such a useful war weapon to the dangers of another sea passage especially when fighter planes are short here.*

There were faults no doubt in this logic, but in any case it was anathema to 30 Mission, and poor Mr Dalgleish, with no idea of the vital war issues at stake, found himself under bitter attack. His reaction was to put another pertinent point: surely it would be much easier to build another Sea Hurricane in the UK.

Such an anti-climax to the battle for V for Victor, wrote Harpham, could not be tolerated under any circumstances and the big guns of 30 Mission were called up. On 15 December they complained to the Air Ministry that Dalgleish's signal had been sent without prior consultation with either the RAF in Archangel or with 30 Mission. 'Quite apart from interference of Ministry of War Transport (Russia) in question involving disposal of RAF equipment,' they began testily, 'proposal to leave Hurricane in Russia is unacceptable.' They enumerated their reasons as follows:

> *1. Russians have on several occasions appropriated equipment addressed to RAF and other British services.*
> *2. This Hurricane had been dismantled and packed by RAF Archangel and was awaiting loading when it was spirited away by Soviet authorities into the middle of Russia; these authorities were fully aware that Hurricane was not meant for them.*
> *3. After much argument erected Hurricane returned to Archangel, this being almost first occasion when equipment intercepted by Russians had been returned by them.*
> *4. If we allow Russians to retain Hurricane we shall only encourage them in further acts of piracy.*

> *This is type of Hurricane which Soviet Mission have specifically asked you not to send to Russia. In view of foregoing most strongly recommend that as long as Ministry of War Transport can*

provide necessary shipping space without sacrificing cargo from Russia the Sea Hurricane should be returned to UK.

The small error in sub-para 2, made no doubt in good faith – the Hurricane had never in fact been erected at Archangel – did nothing to temper the Air Ministry's sense of outrage and their reply was unequivocal. 'Support your views entirely and agree aircraft should be shipped back to UK.'

Meanwhile, on 13 December, the elusive Colonel Popov had at last made himself available for interview. Present at the meeting, on the British side, were Wing Commander Harpham, Flight Lieutenant Wiltshire and Sergeant R.P. Hunter (interpreter); and on the Russian side, Colonel Popov and Major Rogulov, of NKVT, and a female interpreter. Colonel Popov opened the meeting by saying that he had just received an instruction from Moscow to hand over to the RAF the Hurricane now at Keg Ostrov, and would Harpham detail a representative to receive and sign for it.

This, for the aggrieved RAF, must have sounded like progress; but it wasn't enough. 'I've been instructed,' said Harpham, 'to ask you to dismantle and crate the Hurricane as it was when it was taken away. As you have unpacked, erected and flown it, it's your obligation to pack it for shipment.'

'But it's ready for flight,' protested Popov. He suggested that an RAF pilot fly it to Murmansk.

'We haven't got a pilot available.'

'Neither have we.'

'I'm not asking you to find one. I'm asking for the plane to be dismantled and repacked.'

'That can't be done. We have no facilities available.'

'Couldn't the Russian erection party at Molotovsk be approached to do the work?'

'That's impossible. They belong to another organisation.'

When in a tight corner, even the inflexibility of Communist bureaucracy, it seemed, could be invoked as a screen. 'My instructions from Moscow,' continued Popov, 'are to tell you that we have no facilities to do anything more in the matter.' Harpham countered with equal obstinacy. Would Colonel Popov, through his organisation, kindly take steps, by approaching the appropriate authority, to get the aircraft dismantled and crated?

'I can't do that,' said Popov. 'It's not my responsibility!'

'Whose responsibility is it?'

'The Red Army's.'

'Would you then please approach the Red Army, and ask them to dismantle and crate it?'

'I can't do that without instructions from Moscow.'

'Then could you signal Moscow for the necessary authority?'

Popov replied that it was Harpham who must take the matter up with Moscow. The whole thing was the fault of the British, because they had allowed the aircraft to be taken. (It was the householder who should be in the dock after a break-in, Popov was suggesting, not the burglar.) Suspecting that Popov had his tongue in his cheek, Harpham fell back on the undertaking given by Rogulov, and this gave Wiltshire a chance to remind Rogulov of their meeting and of how it had taken him two hours to convince Rogulov that the crate was intended for the RAF. He could not possibly have forgotten it. Thus cornered, Rogulov agreed that he had thoroughly understood the position. But he had not handed the crate over to the Russians. Taking his cue from Popov, he blamed the Red Army. It was they who had taken it, and it was their responsibility.

Popov now moved to close the meeting. He could do nothing more to help. Harpham should contact 30 Mission in Moscow and ask them to make representations to the appropriate authority to get instructions sent for the work to be done.

'Will you signal your organisation in Moscow and request them to co-operate with the Mission?' asked Harpham. Popov agreed to do this, and the meeting broke up.

For the rest of that month (December 1942), V for Victor remained sealed and guarded at Keg Ostrov awaiting dismantling. But behind the scenes, on a political level, progress was made. The buck was duly passed, on the Russian side, to the Red Army, and on 30 December Harpham was invited to meet Engineer-Captain Zorin, of the Red Army Air Force, at Keg Ostrov. Zorin had been given the job of arranging the dismantling of the Hurricane.

To Harpham the aircraft seemed in a normal, serviceable condition, and Zorin promised to start work on the dismantling next day. Harpham arranged with Zorin that either he himself or Wiltshire would inspect the work daily until the job was done. The dismantled sections would then be transported to the quayside at Bakharitsa, where NKVT would pack them and arrange onward transit to the UK. Harpham also arranged for daily checks to be made by the RAF during the packing.

Dismantling actually began on 2 January 1943 and was completed in two days; but there progress ended in an argument over who was to supply the crate. The Red Army Air Force said they hadn't got one and 30 Mission, on being appealed to, said it was the responsibility of the NKVT. Popov rejected this and said the crate would have to be obtained from the Red Naval Air Force by 30 Mission; he thought they had one at their base at nearby Yagodnik, but it was up to the British to arrange it.

On 4 January Group Captain Cheshire arrived in Archangel from Moscow and gazed at the now celebrated V for Victor for the first time. Disappointing as he must have found it as a spectacle in its dismantled state, he was able to confirm that all the pieces were there. He succeeded in arranging, through one Kominsky of the Russian Naval Staff, that the base at Yagodnik would hand over a Hurricane packing case to NKVT on demand. Fortified by this assurance, he returned in better humour to Moscow.

Euphoria, however, did not last long. The next signal from Archangel to Moscow began: 'Intolerable situation likely to arise here shortly.' Representatives of NKVT had gone to Yagodnik on 10 January to collect the crate, but they hadn't been able to find one and had returned empty-handed. Kominsky, on being given this news, said he 'thought there were two cases there, but apparently he had been misinformed'. He would be unable, he added, to help further.

In the same signal, 30 Mission were told that the Russians had treated V for Victor with anti-corrosive grease, but that the grease had been heated before being administered and there was no telling what damage might have been done. Whether this mistake was genuine or deliberate was not clear.

The Russians, calculating that sooner or later the British would get exasperated and would abandon the useless pieces of a rusted and obsolete Hurricane to their fate, were no doubt enjoying the joke. The Russian tactics all along had been to give a certain amount of ground under pressure only to adopt a stand even more frustrating than before, but the British still refused to give way. On 18 January, in an interview with Popov, Harpham rejected a suggestion that the aircraft be shipped to the UK uncrated. Next day Popov, after sending for Harpham, told him that the Chief of the Port of Archangel, a man named Dekoi (suspicions immediately aroused, noted Harpham), had been instructed to make a crate and Harpham was to negotiate with him direct.

On 30 January Harpham met Dekoi and stressed the importance of speed; there was still a chance of shipment from Archangel if the crate could be produced quickly. Reporting all this to Moscow, Harpham advised: 'Do not miss our next thrilling instalment.'

The next instalment came nine days later, in a signal from Harpham to Cheshire that was entitled, in Agatha Christie fashion, *The Case of the Missing Hurricane*, the pun being intended. The crate, said Harpham, had been excellently constructed and the Hurricane was now packed inside ready for shipment. Whether by accident or by design, however, the delay had exhausted the period in which it might have been possible to ship from Archangel. A tractor would be required to move the crate to the railway and that meant further delay. 'Have asked Russians to load on railway trucks for early transit to Murmansk, stressing importance that it must not be lost again,' wrote Harpham, who sensed further skulduggery. 'What will happen to mystery aircraft when handed back to Russians for transport to phantom port? He concluded. 'Watch out for next gi-normous episode.'

On 2 February the Russians drew up a document reproduced below, the meticulous phrasing of which seemed to indicate good intentions:

> *This statement has been drawn up to the effect of the packing of the Merlin Hurricane V. 6881 belonging to the British Government. The Hurricane is to be sent to England via Murmansk. The packing of the Hurricane being requested by the British Mission has been done under the supervision of the representatives of the British Mission, Flight Lieutenant Clark and Wing Commander Harpham.* [Flight Lieutenant Wiltshire had been relieved by Flight Lieutenant D.S. Clark.] *The wooden case made by the Bakharista Port Office is considered to be strong enough and the whole work has been done perfectly well. The packing being over, the case containing the Hurricane has been loaded in the Bakharista Port for conveyance by rail, the number of the truck being 988/24.*

The Russians, it seemed, while anxious to cover themselves against possible damage *en route*, were saying goodbye to the Hurricane with good grace.

Four days later, on 6 February, the train left Archangel on the long and circuitous route round the indentation of the White Sea, bound via Belomorsk and Kandalaksha for

Murmansk. It was a journey, as the British knew from experience, that was subject to continual interference from a combination of German bombs and Russian bureaucrats and could take anything from three days to a fortnight. Harpham signalled the plane's departure thus:

> *1 Hurricane V.6881 despatched 17.00 hours 6 February Train 1605 from Archangel to Murmansk in truck 889/240 for onward transmission to England.* [The discrepancy in the truck numbers was not explained.]
>
> *2 Crate painted light blue marked BAK/2/U/V.6881 addressed O.C. M.S.F.U. Speke, England.* [BAK/2/U was a pun which it was not thought the Russians would interpret.]
>
> *3 Crate also marked in Russian 'Murmansk for despatch to England'.*

The rest of the signal asked the addressee (RAF Murmansk) to acknowledge safe arrival and expedite shipment, and to signal particulars to Air Ministry, repeated to MSFU Speke, 30 Mission and Party 'A', when the case was safely loaded for transit to the UK. It also listed the contents of the crate.

Within a day or so of the train's departure from Archangel, Harpham received an invoice from the port authorities for loading the crate on to the train. He returned it to them, pointing out that all expenses connected with the re-positioning of the Hurricane alongside a British ship for transit to the UK were the liability of the Russian Government. He heard nothing further from the port authorities; but nor did he hear anything of the train's progress towards Murmansk. On 14 February, after eight days, he signalled RAF Murmansk, repeated to 30 Mission: 'If Hurricane not yet arrived take immediate steps through Narkomvneshtorg to locate. Report result.'

Unknown to Harpham, the train had already reached Murmansk. But the crate containing the Hurricane had not. The man at the Murmansk end was Squadron Leader Kitching. He had met the train and had thus been on the spot to make enquiries, of officials and passengers alike. By the exercise of some personal charm on a female passenger, who had no notion of the political undertones, he elicited the vital fact that the crate had been off-loaded *en route* at Belomorsk. Since Belomorsk was the rail junction for Leningrad, 350 miles to the south, Kitching feared the worst.

Aware that she had spilt some pretty significant beans, the passenger clammed up and, according to Kitching, went from that moment in fear of her life. Unable to get any further information, official or unofficial, Kitching notified the railway authorities and the NKVT that the crate containing the Hurricane had not arrived. Meanwhile he signalled what he had learned from the passenger to Harpham.

After establishing that Belomorsk was in territory under the control of Dekoi, the Chief of Archangel Port – a piece of good fortune he could hardly believe – Harpham saw him on the morning of 18 February and persuaded him to contact Belomorsk to instruct them that the Hurricane crate was to be found and sent on to Murmansk as soon as possible. 'Keep worrying Port Authority and NKVT your end,' Harpham advised Kitching. Next day the Hurricane arrived at Murmansk.

At last, on 26 February 1943, after five months of wrangling, RAF Murmansk were able to signal Air Ministry, repeated to MSFU Speke, 30 Mission, and Party 'A', that case No. Bak/2/U/Victor. 6881 consigned to MSFU Speke had been shipped on the *Empire Portia*. 30 Mission, Air Attaché Moscow and Party 'A' had won their victory.

But in war there are no winners, only losers. Later that morning came the perfect denouement. Soon after sailing, *Empire Portia* was attacked by enemy dive-bombers, and a direct hit on No. 2 Hatch passed right through her main and twin decks and pierced her side. Her principal cargo was timber and that night she was still burning.

There were no casualties to personnel; but next day RAF Murmansk signalled all interested parties: 'Am informed Hurricane V.6881 was victim of enemy action of Kola Inlet.'

Anchoring in a safe position, *Empire Portia* underwent temporary repairs and was passed as seaworthy for the return voyage five weeks later. But she sailed without one item at least of her original cargo, carefully packed in a blue-painted, back-to-you crate. As Harpham noted without comment in his diary of events: 'Exit VICTOR.'

XV
The Man who Couldn't Swim

In May 1942, with the introduction of Camships on the Arctic convoys, MSFU reached its operation peak with a total of twenty-nine Camships in operation on three different routes. Up to that time, Camships had made 104 round trips to various destinations and there had been 118 launchings at the end of voyages, with no launching mishaps. But in July it was decided to withdraw Camships from the North Atlantic run and close the Pool at Dartmouth. Eight Camships were promptly taken out of service and by the end of the summer the unit's commitment had been reduced to the manning of thirteen ships. Eight of these thirteen were earmarked for the Gibraltar run and five for Russia. Then in September the Camships were withdrawn from the Arctic run, at any rate for the winter, a decision which was only partly offset by the news that MSFU pilots were to be trained in deck landings so that in future operations on this run they could land on the decks of accompanying escort carriers. Training began in October at selected Fleet Air Arm stations.

As a result of these decisions, a new establishment was worked out for MSFU, based on a total of eight ship detachments plus a pool of two ship detachments in reserve at Gibraltar. This was translated, in terms of personnel, into 38 pilots, 10 fighter direction officers and 182 airmen. 14 Sea Hurricanes were retained to supply the Camships, and 10 Hurricane Is were kept at Speke for training. But what the unit lost in quantity it was intended to make up for in quality and various improvements were made or planned in the course of that summer.

As early as 18 March 1942 the Admiralty had asked for a replacement for the Sea Hurricane and in June the idea of the Seafire was put forward. Trials of the aircraft were carried out at Farnborough, at Speke, and on the Clyde and it proved an ideal type for catapult launching. But it was never used operationally, partly because of transportation difficulties to and from the ports of embarkation and partly because of priority demands from elsewhere. As an alternative, it was decided to update the Sea Hurricane Mark IA by fitting it with Mark IIC wings, arrester hooks and a modified form of cockpit heating which could be used while on the catapult at sea. As the Mark IIC wings were equipped with cannon, the expectation was that the modified Hurricat would prove a much more effective weapon. But there was no chance of its introduction before the spring of 1943.

More time was now available, however, for the training of pilots and crews, and following the loss of John Kendal, schooling in bale-out procedure was much more thorough. Synthetic training in parachute jumping, culminating in a live drop into a lake at Tatton Park, after a ten-day period at the Parachute Training School at Ringway, was arranged for all pilots. Meanwhile the special waterproof suits that had been in preparation at the RAE Physiological Laboratory at Farnborough were supplied to the unit. After minor adjustments suggested by the pilots the suit proved satisfactory, causing no problems in live jumps at Ringway and no discomfort during long periods of readiness on board ship.

Throughout this period, Sholto Douglas had continued agitating to get his pilots back as soon as possible; a tour with MSFU took about a year to complete and then the pilots were entitled to go on rest. One method of hastening their return to the squadrons was to rule that the MSFU tour was non-operational and that after the regulation four round-trip voyages pilots could return at once to a front-line squadron. Pinkerton demurred, pointing out the strain of long stand-by periods during which imminent sea attack as well as the chance of air action had to be faced and Air Vice-Marshal J. Whitworth Jones, by this time A.O.C. 9 Group, backed him up. 'It has been argued,' he wrote, 'that the long period of sea voyage beyond the enemy threat imposes on MSFU pilots a rest rather than a strain. No one would claim that a return sea voyage to Murmansk with its attendant sea and air hazards was a rest cure!' He added that with the impending invasion of North Africa, action on the Gibraltar run was likely to increase. He won his point.

The hey-day of the Focke-Wulf Condors in the North Atlantic had been the latter half of 1940 and the early months of 1941, when, as Edgar Petersen himself remarked, 'You could hardly miss.' With the strengthening of convoy defences and the introduction of the Hurricats, they had limited their playground to the area the Allied convoys had to cross on the route between Britain and Gibraltar. With the approach of the winter of 1942, the sole justification for the continued existence of MSFU was the defence of these convoys.

It was inevitable that the Hurricat pilots should be individualists. They would not have lasted long in the job unless they had liked working on their own. With the lustre of the Battle of Britain that so many brought with them, a talent for flamboyance was to be expected. But the senior of the two pilots in the Camship accompanying a convoy of sixty-five merchant vessels northwards from Gibraltar on 1 November 1942 exhibited none of the eccentricities of the archetype fighter boy. Apprenticed before the war to the aircraft industry, with an ambition to graduate one day to test flying, he had fought in the Battle of Britain and afterwards as a sergeant pilot, and the ribbon of the Distinguished Flying Medal was sewn on his tunic. Now commissioned, he was one of a hard core of professional flyers on MSFU who outnumbered the exhibitionists and the only concession he made to them was to wear his peaked cap at a rakish angle. Tall, slim, and of friendly disposition, he had come up the hard way and knew it. He kept cool in the heat of action, knew his own mind, and had things done his way. His name was Flying Officer Norman Taylor and he was twenty-two.

At 09.55 that morning, with the convoy 250 miles from the Spanish coast off Cape Finisterre and 700 miles west of the Condor airfields at Bordeaux, in perfect weather, the convoy commodore hoisted the general signal that an air attack was expected. Captain R.G. Hammett, master of the Camship *Empire Heath*, at once warned his crew.

Standing on the monkey island above the bridge with his FDO, Sub-Lieutenant S.L. 'Ginger' Ward, Taylor scanned the horizon for a sight of the intruder. It could be friend, it could be foe. Nothing was seen for the next hour, during which Taylor took over from reserve pilot P.D. 'Paddy' O'Sullivan. Then there was a sudden shout from Taylor. 'Christ – it's a Condor.'

He was pointing into the distance, ahead and to the right, where an aircraft was crossing in front of the convoy from starboard to port, landwards to seawards, too low to be picked up by radar. Taylor estimated the distance as eight to ten miles. Ward, like Taylor, soon recognised the distinctive silhouette, the sleek cigar-shaped body, the four protruding engine nacelles, the shapely dihedral of the wings. Allied bombers of that size looked thicker and fatter and more cumbersome. They lacked the sinister elegance of the Condor. He shouted the news down to Captain Hammett on the bridge. 'It's a Condor all right.'

'Action stations!' As the alarm bells sounded Taylor scrambled down the vertical ladder to the wing of the bridge, ran down the next ladder to the deck, then crossed to the port side and hurried forward to the ladder that led up to the catapult platform. From there he climbed on to the wing of the Hurricane and into the cockpit, where he had already planted his parachute and flying helmet on taking over from O'Sullivan. The alarm bells meanwhile brought O'Sullivan out of his cabin and he raced after Taylor to the firing hut. The sea crew had already plugged in the starter motor, and after Taylor had settled himself in the cockpit and strapped himself in, the Merlin burst into life.

The corporal in charge of the sea crew removed the safety locking pins from the catapult trolley and took them forward to O'Sullivan. 'Catapult ready for firing!' But while this familiar procedure was being enacted, Ginger Ward was facing a dilemma.

What were the Condor pilot's intentions? Was he merely stalking the convoy, or did he mean to attack? After crossing low on the horizon in front of them, the Condor began circling in an anti-clockwise direction, keeping to a distance of eight to ten miles, running down the convoy on the port side on an opposite but parallel course. When it reached the port quarter it curved to the south-east as though continuing its orbit astern.

Captain Hammett had delegated the responsibility for the decision to launch to Ginger Ward. And Ward was uncertain what to do. In many ways he was of a similar mental stamp to Taylor: cool, calculating, organised, logical. He had shown these qualities in good measure during four days spent in Spanish gaols at Huelva at the end of the outward voyage. Arrested by Spanish police for a supposed landing-permit irregularity, he had subsequently written a report on conditions and attitudes in southern Spain under Franco which were a model of concise observation. But this flair for Intelligence appreciation now had to be translated into action.

He knew that the Hurricane, for all its well-deserved reputation for robustness, was not really a fast aeroplane. It had the edge on the Condor for speed, perhaps, but the margin was modest. To launch the Hurricane when interception was uncertain would be a prodigal act. But to launch it too late might mean the unnecessary loss of a ship. This was his dilemma.

Another problem was that if he hesitated too long the Merlin engine would overheat. There was only one answer to that. Crossing his arms in front of his face, palms open, he gave O'Sullivan the wash-out signal. O'Sullivan relayed this to Taylor, who switched off.

The convoy was arranged in eleven columns, six ships to a column, presenting a broad front but a narrow beam, reducing the vulnerability to U-boat attack. Leading the centre column was the commodore, in the biggest ship in the convoy. At the rear of the eleventh column – at the stern extremity on the starboard or landward side – was the second largest ship, the Camship *Empire Heath*.

The Condor continued its orbit in the rear of the convoy, holding to the same radius low on the horizon. As it passed astern of the Camship it began another gentle turn to port, as though to continue its orbit.

Suddenly the Condor pilot tightened his turn. He had seen what he was looking for – one of the largest ships in the convoy, carelessly placed on the flank and at the rear. That was how it must have seemed to him. Nothing could have been more inviting.

Empire Heath, her protective role not yet appreciated on the Condor, had been singled out for attack. Ward ordered the Hurricane back to full readiness on the R/T, and the engine was restarted.

Of the three principals in the action, Taylor, O'Sullivan and Ward, only Ward, from his spotting point on the monkey island, could see the Condor. It was up to him to time the launching accurately so as to give Taylor the best chance of making an interception and with the Camship itself under attack, he had to keep his nerve. He told Captain Hammett he was proposing to launch the Hurricane, and the helm was put over to starboard. With the wind fifty degrees on the starboard bow, the turn caused no interference with other vessels and gave Taylor a clear run.

A glance over his shoulder and Ward saw that the Condor was now only five miles astern. At the steel cabin in the bows, O'Sullivan was holding up his blue flag to indicate that everything was ready for launching.

'Take cover!' The alarm bells sounded again, this time to warn the ship's crew of the impending heat and blast from the rockets that would fire the Hurricane. 'Buck from Ginger.' Taylor and Ward had agreed to use abbreviated radio procedure, prefaced by these simple nicknames for call-signs. 'He's coming in about four miles astern. We reckon to launch you now.'

Ward gave O'Sullivan the visual signal and O'Sullivan, facing aft, and deafened by the engine noise, acknowledged the signal and rotated his own flag to warn Taylor. Opening the throttle, Taylor raised his right hand aloft to show he was ready. He could still see nothing of the rapidly approaching Condor, but he could see the rise and fall of the bows as the ship pitched and plunged on the swell. Sea conditions were lively, and it might be fatal to launch on a downward scend. Urgent as the launching had now become, Taylor waited until the bows began to lift on the next upward scend, then cut his hand down.

Retreating into the protection of the firing hut, O'Sullivan grabbed at the firing lever and tried to jerk it across. It wouldn't move. For a fraction of a second he hesitated. Then he remembered that he had to pull the lever out first, against a spring-loaded plunger, before turning it through forty-five degrees. The delay was so small that he actually caught the crest of the scend.

Locking the throttle wide open, forcing his skull hard back against the head-rest, Taylor braced himself for the shock as the rockets ignited behind him, tearing the morning apart with their dazzling brightness and their ear-shattering displacement of air. In the firing hut, under the sweep of the starboard wing of the Hurricane, O'Sullivan ducked instinctively as the machine fizzed overhead. From the monkey island Ward, aware that he had left the launching to the ultimate moment and perhaps beyond, watched the Hurricane stagger with sickening uncertainty as it hurtled off the trolley at the end of the rail.

For Taylor, in the cockpit, the moment of truth had come; but he could feel the exhilarating power of the Merlin and knew it would pull him clear. As soon as he was airborne he selected flaps up, closed the cockpit hood and switched on IFF and R/T. But when he called Ward he found that the R/T frequency was blotted out, apparently by jamming from the Condor.

Even now that he was airborne Taylor could see nothing of the Condor. The sun was so brilliant that it was reflecting strongly off the sea, spoiling his vision. He began a wide turn to port which brought him back towards the Camship like a boomerang, aiming to fly low over the top.

'Buck from Ginger. Bandit bearing seven o'clock, very low, Vector 220.' But Ward's voice was badly distorted by the jamming, and Taylor couldn't hear him.

'Where is he?'

'Bandit bearing seven o'clock,' repeated Ward. 'Seven o'clock. Is this understood?'

'Understand seven o'clock. Is this OK?'

'That is correct. Heading seven o'clock, below you.'

Taylor still wasn't absolutely sure that he'd heard Ward aright. Then, on the monkey island of *Empire Heath*, he saw a little cluster of figures, each one waving and pointing to the south-west.

The Condor pilot, half-blinded by the pyrotechnic display from the Camship as the Hurricane was catapulted off, soon saw his error. Or it may be that up to now he thought he had not been seen. So good was the discipline in the convoy that there had not been the usual wasteful expenditure of ammunition on an aircraft well out of range. But directly the Hurricane sprinted from its moorings, the Condor pilot banked steeply to port before making off in a south-westerly direction fifty feet above the water.

Opening up again to full throttle, Taylor completed his S-turn and raced off in the direction indicated by the pointing fingers. But the passage of the convoy had impaired visibility and the Condor pilot knew his job. Still flattened on the water, he altered course from south-west to south, flying straight into the sun.

For fully two minutes Taylor continued at full throttle on a south-westerly course.

It was beginning to look like a fruitless chase. But knowing the reputation of Condor pilots for expert flying, he guessed what his adversary's tactics might be and squinted hopefully up sun.

'I see him! I see him!' Only the Condor's size had given its position away. Against the background the pilot had chosen, a smaller aircraft might have escaped.

The Condor was about six miles away, just about at the limit of visibility in the conditions and Taylor kept his Merlin at full throttle, aiming to get into a favourable sun position. Flying 300 feet above the sea, at an indicated air speed of 250 miles an hour, he found he was gaining rapidly on the Condor, and he throttled back so as not to overshoot.

The German pilot was flying so low that he almost seemed to be following the contours of the swell. He changed course now perceptibly to the south-south-east, and Taylor thought he might be working his way round towards his base at Bordeaux. But Taylor still found himself staring into the sun. Then, as he closed to 500 yards, the Condor suddenly increased speed and began to draw away.

Keeping his height advantage, but still blinded by the dazzle off the sea, Taylor opened his throttle again and aimed a one-second burst ahead of the Condor to try to force the pilot off his course. Somehow he had to improve his position relative to the sun. The Condor pilot knew his business and held on. Meanwhile, to keep the Hurricane at a distance, the German gunners were putting up a curtain of fire for Taylor to fly through.

Neither the Condor, because of its low flying, nor the Hurricane, because of its small size, was showing up on Ward's radar; and with the radio channel still blocked by interference, no one in the convoy knew how the chase was going. Taylor decided to pull the boost override to close the distance. It was rough treatment, he knew, which the Merlin would only stand for a limited time. Then came the inevitable thought that it wouldn't be needed again and he used the full emergency 12 lbs of boost.

The effect was alarming, a film of glycol spreading stickily across the inside of his windscreen. Throttling back immediately to 9 lbs boost, he cleared his windscreen hastily and continued the chase.

The glycol leak stopped, and the revised throttle and boost settings proved adequate. He was closing now on the starboard quarter, flying through a sleeting blizzard of fire that seemed to be coming from the forward upper turret of the Condor and from a beam gun on the starboard side. Firing up at their target, the Condor gunners were searching for the right elevation, and Taylor saw their first bursts splash into the sea ahead of him. But the gunner in the forward upper turret soon adjusted his aim. Still dazzled by the sun on the water, but determined to go in for the kill, Taylor meanwhile took note of the dull sea-grey camouflage, the compactness of design, the position of the gun mountings and the marked dihedral of the wings.

Closing in to 150 yards and meeting continuous return fire, Taylor ruddered across the stern of the Condor from starboard to port, delivered a four-second burst from his eight machine-guns as he slid over and dropped back to 250 yards to confuse the German gunners. This did not save him from an accurate burst from the forward upper turret that riddled his port wing; but in the clatter and judder of his own guns he noticed nothing. Neither did he know whether or not he himself had scored any hits.

The Condor was still hugging the water and Taylor retained his height advantage.

Approaching this time from the port quarter, he was caught unawares as the Condor pilot, seeing a layer of cloud at 1,200 feet, decided to make for it. But as the Condor climbed it had to pass through Taylor's sights, briefly exposing the whole dorsal area.

'He's pulled up in front of me. I think I've got him.' Holding his height steady at 300 feet, and closing to 200 yards, Taylor fired a three-second burst, using slight deflection, and watched his tracer pouring into the most vulnerable section of the aircraft – the cockpit. The Condor, however, rose rapidly, passing through his sights in a moment. It went on climbing strongly, with Taylor in hot pursuit, until it reached a height of 900 feet.

Taylor, with his fixed guns, was at a disadvantage as he fought to line up astern of the Condor. The German gunners, with their free guns, had the edge on him, and they kept up a withering fire. Another 300 feet and the Condor would be safe.

The German pilot now abruptly changed his mind. That was how it seemed to Taylor. Deciding perhaps that the cloud was not quite so opaque as it had appeared from below, he thrust his control column forward and made for sea level, presumably trusting to his skill at low flying to frustrate the British pilot until either his fuel or his ammunition or his patience ran out. The manoeuvre again took Taylor by surprise, so much so that he was unable to follow up immediately as the Condor shallow-dived towards the sea.

The manoeuvre, it seemed to Taylor, was brilliantly executed. He was even more impressed as the Condor pilot kept up his dive almost to sea level. Indeed he began to wonder how he would ever pull out.

He watched astounded as the Condor, staggering helplessly at the bottom of the dive, hit the sea without completing the expected recovery. For a moment the huge bird-like machine was completely obliterated by the splash. When the foaming waterspout had subsided, and the turgid water had settled, nothing was visible of the Condor but the tail.

'He's down! He's gone down!'

Almost certainly the pilot had been mortally hit, either in the first exchanges of fire at sea level or as he made for the sanctuary of cloud. Tugging back on the elevators in his last despairing moments, he had reached 900 feet before collapsing over the control column. What had at first seemed like a brilliant piece of flying had been the last throw of a dying man.

Taylor made two wide orbits of the wreckage, trying to see if anyone had got out, but there was no sign of movement. Meanwhile he called Ginger Ward again on the radio. He was forty-three miles from the convoy, however, and although Ward heard him calling, he did not hear Ward's reply. After a last look at the patch of disturbed water, illuminated bright green now by the fluorescent sea-markers automatically released by the Condor, Taylor turned until he had his back to the sun. Soon afterwards, climbing through the cloud to 2,000 feet, he picked up Ward on the radio and was given a course to steer.

When he sighted the convoy he began a fast run at low level over the top, punctuated by a succession of slow rolls to announce his victory. As he did so, virtually the entire ship's company of *Empire Heath* assembled on the deck and cheered, while every ship in the convoy sounded its siren in salute.

Rumours that there was another Condor in the area encouraged Taylor to stay airborne for as long as he could. But as he was executing his third slow roll he noticed that his port wing was perforated with bullet-holes.

'Good God, Ginger! I've been hit in the port wing – right through the bull's-eye of the roundel!' On the monkey island of *Empire Heath*, Ward repeated this to O'Sullivan. 'Tell him not to do any more slow rolls,' said O'Sullivan. Ward passed on the message and asked Taylor to orbit the convoy. With no sign of a second Condor, the next order must be for Taylor to bale out.

O'Sullivan grabbed the microphone and began questioning Taylor urgently: he was thinking of Kendal, who had failed to survive his bale-out. 'Before anything happens to you, Norman,' he asked brutally, 'you'd better give me all the details of the combat you can.' Information on tactics, performance, armament and return fire might be invaluable for future interceptions. Taylor gave precise details while he was orbiting and Ward checked that the starboard escort vessel, a corvette, was standing by for the pick up. Then he ordered Taylor to bale out.

Taylor was aiming to drift down just ahead of the corvette. He removed his helmet, then jettisoned the hood and the emergency panel, leaving the way clear for his exit. After unbuckling his seat-belt, he trimmed the Hurricane slightly tail heavy so that it didn't nose forward prematurely when he left his seat, then worked his feet to the right of the control stick. Resting them on the ledge formed by the jettisoning of the panel, he throttled back, crouched down, and half dived and half pushed himself head first out of the cockpit, falling neatly past the trailing edge of the starboard wing. As soon as he saw he was clear of the tail he pulled the ripcord of his parachute and almost immediately felt the welcome jerk as the canopy opened.

Looking up he saw the Hurricane continue in a gentle climb for perhaps five seconds. Then the port wing dropped and the aeroplane glided down in a graceful, reluctant curve, finally splashing lightly and daintily into the sea.

Taylor had survived launching, chase, combat, and bale-out. All he had to do now was survive descent and immersion. But his contortions while worming his way out of the cockpit had twisted his parachute harness behind him and when his weight came on the parachute the right-hand strap of the harness cut savagely into his neck and shoulder on that side. Throughout his descent, which lasted ninety seconds, he was unable to straighten himself up or manipulate the shroud-lines, with the result that he hit the sea on his back.

Unknown to Ward and O'Sullivan, or indeed to anyone else in the convoy, Norman Taylor was a non-swimmer. He had not told anyone this when volunteering for MSFU, for the simple reason that no one had asked him.

A half-turn now on his quick-release box, followed by a sharp tap, and his harness mercifully collapsed, releasing him from his agony. He kicked off his flying boots and pulled the air bottle to inflate his lifejacket. But for some reason, perhaps connected with the manner of his descent, the seal did not break.

There was enough buoyancy in the kapok of the lifejacket, and in the air trapped underneath it, to support him for a limited time. But something was dragging him down. Recovering from the first shock of immersion, he found, as George Varley had found a year earlier, that his legs were hopelessly entangled in the canopy and shroud lines of his parachute, and that his small one-man dinghy, packed in a case attached to his body, was similarly submerged and entangled.

Struggling to keep afloat, he kicked out violently to release the dinghy from its case, holding his breath as the seas broke over him but swallowing water continually. A despairing glance around him revealed no sign of the escorting corvette.

Taylor's descent by parachute had been witnessed throughout the convoy, and the corvette was hurrying towards the point of his splash-down. But the tiny bobbing figure of the man they hoped to rescue was hidden by the swell.

Exhausted by his efforts to release the dinghy, Taylor was barely able to keep afloat. And as the minutes passed, the buoyancy of the lifejacket was no longer enough. When the next wave came it overwhelmed him, tumbling him far beneath the surface. His head broke clear again in the trough of the wave, but as he gulped and gasped for breath he knew he was drowning.

In the trough of that wave Taylor suddenly glimpsed a lifebuoy. Surely someone must have thrown it to him. Then he realised that the wave that had seemed so bent on his final destruction had been the bow wave of the corvette.

He grabbed the lifebuoy, but it was still made fast to the corvette, and it took him speed-boating through the water, buffeting the last of his breath out of him. In desperation he held on and fortunately at that point the line broke.

Having overshot, the corvette turned back and lowered a boat. Once aboard, Taylor was wrapped in a blanket and a jam-jar of rum was poured down his throat, diluting the seawater inside him. A hot bath on the corvette, dry clothes, and more dilutant for the sea-water, completed his recovery, and at 15.50 he was returned to *Empire Heath*.

For his exploit Taylor was awarded the Distinguished Flying Cross to add to his DFM. Early the following year he applied for the work he had always wanted and he made a career for himself as a test pilot until he was killed in a flying accident in 1948.

XVI
Not a Whimper but a Bang

Following the invasion of North Africa in November 1942, the Gibraltar run was extended to take in Casablanca and Algiers, enabling the men of the Camships to break fresh ground. But at about this time, two *Staffeln* of III./KG 40 were transferred from France to Italy, where they were employed in a transport role and two *Staffeln* of I. *Gruppe* were sent to the Russian front, where they ferried supplies into Stalingrad. One result was that anti-shipping operations in the Atlantic fell right away. For the Camship crews the excitements that winter were mostly confined to the normal hazards of sailing in convoys in wartime and they did not escape their share of damage and sinking by mine and torpedo.

The first convoy to North Africa that included a Camship left Britain on Christmas Eve 1942 and arrived in Algiers on 7 January 1943. Conditions there were completely disorganised and at first the attitude of the French was uncooperative and even hostile. The Hurricat was unserviceable and could not be flown off, so the intention was to off-load it for inspection at Maison Blanche airfield; but the French asked an exorbitant fee to unload and reload it, so it stayed where it was.

Sub-Lieutenant John Pickwell, an FDO who had been one of the first to ride an ice-cream barrow on the lawn at Stanmore, and who had already been torpedoed twice in the Atlantic, writes vividly of one of these voyages to Algiers.[5]

My trip with pilots Joe Lamb [Deryck Lamb] *and Black Max* [Maxwell Charlesworth] *was one of the most amusing. When we first went on board, the two of them asked me why the*

---

[5] In later years John Pickwell was to become the organising force behind an unofficial association of former MSFU men that still flourishes today.

ship was flying a red flag. They thought I was pulling their legs when I told them that it meant we were loading explosives. They weren't so amused when the captain pointed out the bombs, land mines etc.

The most disconcerting thing about being torpedoed, I had found, was the way the ship continued to plough on through the water at speed when all one wanted to do was lower the boats. Now, having got away with it twice, I was scared it might be third time unlucky.

We played poker every night of the voyage, but after we had taken all the money from the ships' officers we had to play between the three of us. Our destination was Bone, at that time the furthest Allied port along the North African coast and we cheered up a lot when we heard it had been changed to Algiers.

The convoy was attacked by U-boats and aircraft the night before we were due at Algiers, and when a torpedo passed right under our stern I was so scared I paid off my poker debts and went to bed fully dressed and wearing a lifejacket. Next afternoon we were just entering the port of Algiers, feeling comfortably sorry for the poor chaps who had to carry on to Bone, when a destroyer rushed up and told us to rejoin the convoy as we had to take the place of one of the ships that had been sunk the night before.

We sat down to 'tea' (really dinner) almost right away, and I had such a sinking feeling in my stomach that I had to force myself to eat. We must all have felt the same as hardly anything was said at the table. But we got through to Bone without any further attacks and then back to Algiers.

We tried in MSFU to forget inter-service rivalries, and pilots and FDOs exchanged top tunic buttons as a compliment to each other. But differences in temperament were not so easily swapped, and this was particularly noticeable in port. The pilots went ashore and stayed there whenever they could, while the FDOs were generally content to remain on board. Unlike the FDOs, the pilots could never think of the ship as their home.

It was not until the spring of 1943 that the Condors that had survived the transfer to the Mediterranean and Russian fronts were returned to *Fliegerführer Atlantik* and before they resumed operations their methods were drastically revised. No longer were they to fly armed reconnaissance patrols, seeking out their prey. Routine reconnaissance duties were assigned to the new long-range Junkers 290A-5s and the Condors were only sent out with a definite target in view. Supplied at last with a sophisticated bombsight, the crews were given a minimum attacking height of 9,000 feet, except where cloud conditions allowed an attack at lower altitude to be attempted with reasonable safety. Another innovation, reserved for occasions when an all-out effort was ordered, was for a number of Condors to fly to the target area in formation, fan out until the target was sighted and then re-form for the attack.

There were fundamental changes, too, in prospect on the Allied side. During the winter of 1942/3, while the bulk of KG 40 was still scattered to other fronts, the dwindling threat to Allied convoys, coupled with the shortage elsewhere of experienced fighter pilots, had inevitably become the subject of further correspondence between the C-in-C Fighter Command (where Leigh-Mallory had succeeded Sholto Douglas) and the Chief of the Air Staff. On 24 February 1943 Portal suggested to Pound that the emergency for which MSFU had been formed was over and that the time had come for the RAF to pull out.

On 1 March it was decided that Camships would not resume on the Arctic run that summer, but would be employed only on slow convoys to Gibraltar and North America. With this in mind and reassured by the paucity of Condor attack in recent months, Pound accepted Portal's suggestion. 'I fully agree,' he wrote on 4 March, 'that this commitment, if it is to continue, should be borne by the Admiralty, since it is essentially naval in character.'

Soon afterwards, with escort and merchant aircraft carriers coming into service in greater numbers, a target date for the complete disbanding of the Merchant Ship Fighter Unit was set for 15 July.

In April 1943 *Empire Morn*, having survived the Arctic run unscathed the previous summer, struck a mine off Casablanca and suffered casualties, among them twenty-one killed. She was carrying explosives and was at once abandoned. But she did not blow up and next day the survivors reboarded her and she was towed back to Casablanca. The Hurricane escaped damage and was flown to Gibraltar. More fortunate in some ways was the Camship *Empire Eve*, which was struck by a torpedo in the Mediterranean seven miles from the African coast off Cape Tenes on 18 May. Four of the engine-room staff were killed in the explosion, but otherwise casualties were few. 'The whole ship was lit up in a huge circular orange flash,' writes the senior RAF pilot on board, Mowbray Garden, 'and there was a colossal explosion. The ship lurched to port and the captain called "Abandon ship".'

The time was 18.30, and the FDO, Johnny Shaftoe, had just gone down to his cabin to get a coat when the torpedo struck. He was flung against the deck-head and temporarily stunned, and at the same time two chests of drawers were thrown across the doorway, blocking his exit. He owed his life to the reserve pilot, Ross Taylor, who had seen him go to his cabin. He at once left the deck, dragged the chests of drawers clear, revived Shaftoe and brought him out. The ship sank in six minutes. 'Had it not been for Taylor's presence of mind, wrote the Station Intelligence Officer at Speke afterwards, 'Lieutenant Shaftoe would without question have gone down with the ship.'

An interesting insight into the enemy's thinking was provided for the MSFU survivors when they sailed for home via military transport on 27 May. The convoy was carrying about 15,000 Axis prisoners, of whom there were 1,900 Germans on the transport. Their general condition was good and their equipment excellent, their discipline and morale were high and their behaviour was correct. They repeated the familiar line of argument – that they had no quarrel with the British and would beat the Russians in the following year and then make a negotiated peace. But their morale was sustained by their own propaganda: their knowledge of the general war situation was extraordinarily deficient and many of them thought that Stalingrad, where surrender had finally come on 2 February 1943, was still in German hands. They were astonished that the convoy was not attacked and they persuaded themselves that its immunity was due to the fact that their omniscient leaders knew it was carrying prisoners.

No enemy aircraft were sighted on the voyage home and it seemed that at last the Condor menace had petered out. Meanwhile the planned rundown of MSFU was implemented. Farewell celebrations of unparalleled abandon even for MSFU were held, leaving their almost indelible mark on station buildings and stores. George Pinkerton was posted to command 56 OTU and granted the acting rank of group captain, a richly deserved promotion. Pilots went back to Fighter Command training units to relearn their trade, some with relief, some, after the long absence, with misgiving. Fighter direction officers, some of them with no other naval experience as officers, left in similar degrees of enthusiasm or perturbation. Sea crews returned to a world of daily routine orders and senior NCOs. All that was retained of MSFU was a nucleus of administrative personnel pending the return of Camships still at sea.

With the perversity of events, however, a recrudescence of Condor activity on the Gibraltar run began to be reported just as the break-up of MSFU was being implemented. Several times in those final weeks, as Camships sailed home for the last time, the only thing that prevented a Hurricat launching was attendant mist and low cloud.

When Convoy SL 133 left Gibraltar on 23 July 1943 on the final leg of its homeward-bound run from Sierra Leone, it was accompanied by the last two Camships in service, *Empire Tide* (a survivor of convoy PQ 17) and *Empire Darwin*. It was nearly nine months since the launching of Norman Taylor on 1 November 1942 and with the knowledge that they were returning home to a disbanded unit where they had missed all the farewell parties, and where postings to unknown destinations would be awaiting them, a certain lack of zeal on the part of MSFU crews might have been excused. Fortunately no such relaxation was discernible. It was known that sailings from Gibraltar were always reported by German agents watching from across the Bay of Algeciras. The pilots, two on each Camship, were all new to the job and keen to prove themselves. The FDOs were two of the most experienced and long-serving on the unit. Recent reports of Condor sightings did not encourage carelessness or complacency and two days out from Gibraltar, warnings were received by the senior officer of the escort of probable Condor attack.

The convoy consisted of forty ships, in eight columns of five. *Empire Tide* was leading the extreme port column, *Empire Darwin* the starboard. At the suggestion of Ginger Ward, the FDO on *Empire Tide*, the MSFU crews were taking turns at standing at readiness. For the first three days, as the convoy headed west into the Atlantic, nothing was seen. But at 20.25 on the 26th, when the convoy was 250 miles off Cape St Vincent and had recently turned north, a four-engined aircraft, flying at about 1,200 feet, came into focus on the port bow at a distance of twelve miles. It was quickly identified as a Condor.

The enemy pilot made no attempt to come to close quarters. He was over a thousand miles from home, and his mission was reconnaissance. With cloud eight-tenths at 1,500 feet, it was useless to launch the duty Hurricane and after the Condor had completed an anti-clockwise circuit of the convoy, lasting about twenty-minutes, it disappeared into cloud.

Next day the escort was reinforced by the cruiser *Scylla*, which took up position in the centre of the convoy to give maximum protection with her anti-aircraft guns. For thirty-six hours SL 133 was left to itself. Then on the morning of 28 July news was broadcast on the convoy R/T wave that a Gibraltar-bound convoy 120 miles to the north-east was being attacked by eight Condors and that more than one ship had been sunk. Consequent on the disbanding of MSFU, this convoy had no Camship protection.

That afternoon, with *Empire Tide* the duty Camship, an unidentified aircraft was picked up on the radar thirty-five miles astern, but nothing was seen from the convoy. Soon afterwards *Empire Tide's* catapult developed a fault and while the firing mechanism was being stripped down, *Empire Darwin* took over guard.

The FDO on *Empire Darwin*, leading the starboard column, was John Pickwell and he was standing on the bridge when he was alerted by a sudden burst of chat coming over the loudspeaker and a reference to an unidentified aircraft. No one rated his abilities as a naval officer more modestly than Pickwell, but if there was one thing he was good at it was aircraft recognition. He soon picked out what to him was the unmistakable silhouette of a Focke-Wulf 200, exactly as depicted in the recognition books, coming up from astern on the starboard side.

The two pilots were sitting on the forehatch just below the port wing of the bridge playing cards with the sea crew, so Pickwell had no need to raise his voice. All he had to do was lean over the bridge and quietly warn the pilot on watch, a young, slow-speaking, unexcitable Scot named Jimmy Stewart. Posted to Speke straight from an operational training unit, Stewart had never been in combat. 'You'd better get in the aircraft, Jimmy,' murmured Pickwell. 'There's a Focke-Wulf 200 over there.'

In his puckish way Pickwell had calculated that this information, imparted without histrionics, almost as an aside, might not be taken seriously. But as the card-players looked up from their game, all Pickwell had to do was point to starboard. In the next instant the action-stations buzzer sounded and the crew ran to their posts.

Simultaneously with the sighting of the enemy plane, however, a United States Air Force B-24 Liberator was sighted dead ahead. The convoy was passing roughly due west of the Condor base at Bordeaux, 800 miles distant and from the experience of the southbound convoy two days earlier it seemed likely that several more Condors were in the area. With scattered cloud at 3,000 feet increasing to six-tenths at 10,000, with many blue patches, conditions for the Condors were good. With this in mind the SOE was content for the Hurricats to be held in readiness for the major attack he had been told to expect, and he asked the Liberator crew to intercept the Condor.

For several minutes both aircraft were lost to sight as the Liberator gave chase. Then the Condor was seen again on the opposite side of the convoy, flying at 150 feet, with the Liberator astern and slightly above and gaining slowly.

The fight between these two four-engined giants began to look like a duel to the death as the Condor pilot, relying on his gunners, held his course. With the rival gunners blazing away at each other, both aircraft suffered hits, but the Liberator pilot, too, showed no sign of flinching. The running battle had lasted a full minute when the port outer engine of the Condor burst into flames and the Liberator began climbing away. In a desperate effort to maintain height the Condor pilot jettisoned his bombs, but seconds later the aircraft hit the sea. It struck at a shallow angle but cartwheeled at once and finished up on its back.

Soon afterwards an SOS was received from the Liberator. Then there was silence. The plane was now twenty miles distant, its position was known only approximately and it was believed to have come down in the sea. But in the harsh economics of convoy protection, no ship was detached to search for it.

The crew had flown straight into action without hesitation. There was one less

Condor to threaten the convoy and the Hurricats remained unexpended. The value of the Americans' sacrifice was underlined within minutes when two more Condors were sighted by the escort some distance away at high level.

On *Empire Darwin* the decision was taken to launch, and the ship was turned fifteen degrees off course to avoid the swell. But before Stewart could be catapulted off, Pickwell spotted yet another Condor at 500 feet ten miles to the north-west. As this Condor began to fly down the port side of the convoy it became apparent that it presented the more immediate threat and the decision to launch, which had been temporarily halted, was reactivated. As the Condor approached the convoy from the beam, Pickwell called Stewart. 'Bandit nine o'clock, flying right to left.' Stewart replied that he could see the target from where he sat, and at 19.38 the first mate pulled the lever and the Hurricane was launched.

'Tally-ho!' As soon as he was safely airborne Stewart got a visual on the Condor and turned to port to give chase. The Condor pilot immediately climbed to 1,000 feet and steered south, keeping on this heading for one minute before turning east.

On the monkey island of *Empire Darwin*, Pickwell was chafing with annoyance and frustration. After more than two years of waiting and at the ultimate moment, the opportunity for which he had been trained had come and his earphones had gone dead. He couldn't raise Stewart and he felt utterly useless. But Stewart had no need of vectors, in the clear evening visibility he was manoeuvring to attack from the west, directly out of the sun. This brought him up on the port quarter of the Condor, and at $6\frac{1}{4}$ lbs boost and 2,600 revs he was making an air speed of 250 miles an hour and having no difficulty in catching up.

At about this time Pickwell's chagrin was not improved by the other two Condors, which began bombing the starboard flank of the convoy from high level. Looking across from the port side, Ward saw Pickwell's ship, apparently straddled by bomb bursts, disappear in a cloud of spray. But it reappeared soon afterwards, more or less unharmed.

As Stewart approached the low-flying Condor he noticed its dark green camouflage, but the ventral gondola he had been taught to look for was not conspicuous. The Condor pilot, like his compatriot earlier, took no evasive action, but as Stewart opened up at 300 yards the return fire was so intense that he could not be sure whether it came from cannon or machine-gun. Somehow the Hurricane escaped being hit and he closed right in, aiming at the cockpit, allowing for deflection, and keeping the firing button depressed down to point-blank range. There was a vivid white flash near the Condor's turret as he broke away.

Turning back for a second attack, he got in no more than a half-second burst before his guns jammed. He had fired about 800 rounds. Breaking off again, he made several more attacks but couldn't get his guns to fire.

As the Condor pilot made for a bank of cloud in the distance, Stewart decided to return to the convoy. The last he saw of the Condor it was slowly losing height. An eyewitness on one of the freighters, however, Second Officer Francis of the *City of Exeter*, kept it in view. Afterwards he wrote:

> The aircraft on the starboard side of the convoy was the first machine to be shot off. This aircraft
> flew off from the convoy then passed ahead of it, chasing a Focke-Wulf to the port quarter in an

anti-clockwise direction. The Hurricane dived on the F.W. 200 which dropped sharply, rose again for a moment, and crashed into the sea.

Confirmation came from Third Officer Nicholson of the *Bactria*, who saw the Condor gradually losing height to the south-west before striking the water.

Returning to the port side of the convoy, Stewart saw bursts of heavy anti-aircraft fire several thousand feet above him and soon realised what the escort was aiming at – a Condor at 7,000 feet which was making a bombing run from west to east. Stewart climbed to the Condor's height and made several dummy attacks; the Condor pilot dropped his bombs on a straggler astern and disappeared into cloud.

Meanwhile yet another Condor was silhouetted on the horizon dead ahead, height 150 feet, distance about twelve miles. The duty pilot on *Empire Tide* was a Londoner named P.J.R. Flynn, inevitably dubbed 'Paddy' Flynn, and he was as extrovert and exuberant as Stewart was reserved and phlegmatic. Like Stewart he had never been in combat. Stamping around with impatience at having missed the chance of a launching, he had been imploring his sea crew to get the firing mechanism serviceable. This they eventually succeeded in doing and at 20.36 the decision was taken to launch. Eighty-four seconds later the second Hurricane was airborne.

The launching was so prompt that Ginger Ward's task of vectoring Flynn on to his target was no more than a formality. Flynn climbed to 200 feet, and using $6\frac{1}{4}$lbs boost and 2,600-2,800 revs he soon reached maximum speed, enabling him to catch up with the Condor in two and a half minutes. As the Condor turned away to the east he saw identification markings clearly visible on a dark grey camouflage.

Coming up astern of the Condor on the port quarter, Flynn opened fire with a two-second burst at 300 yards. There was a short burst from the port lateral machine-gun of the Condor and as Flynn closed directly astern he saw that the gunners in the front and rear turrets were firing at him point blank. He judged from the splashes in the sea beyond the Condor that his own fire was slightly low.

Breaking off he executed a climbing turn into the sun, then began a series of beam and quarter attacks from the port side up sun. As with the other two Condors, the pilot took no violent evasive action but relied on his gunners. On his second run Flynn concentrated his fire on the cockpit and knew he was on target, but he had to fly through blistering return fire and his Hurricane was repeatedly hit, mostly in the wings.

Even the impetuous Flynn realised that he would first have to silence the Condor's guns.

Breaking off again, he began his third run by spraying the fuselage between the rear turret and the lateral gun position on the port side before closing to 100 yards and finishing up with a short burst of fire directed at the front turret. Again he saw his tracer stabbing its mark.

Hoping he had silenced the gunners, he went now for the outer and inner port engines, but the answering fire was as withering as ever. The Perspex of the cockpit hood behind his head suddenly splintered and a gaping hole appeared in the port wing. For compensation he had to be content with increasing spurts of smoke from the Condor's port engines, but in the glare from sea and sun he could detect no flame.

As he closed in for a final attack, a bomb from the Condor fell away right in front of him and he nearly flew into it. Soon afterwards he felt the blast from the explosion as it hit the sea. Then, as the Condor pilot jettisoned the rest of his bombs, Flynn fired a final burst that exhausted his ammunition before dropping back to observe results.

Smoke was pouring from the Condor's inner port engine and the plane was losing height. But in the combat Flynn had driven the Condor round anti-clockwise from north-east to south-east of the convoy, and he was now forty miles from the nearest ship. With a damaged Hurricane to nurse home it was time he headed back. Unable to raise Ward on the radio, he climbed to 3,000 feet and steered north-west, and after ten minutes he sighted the ships.

Waggling his wings, he began a left-hand circuit of the convoy and was at once instructed by Ward to climb to 10,000 feet. Yet another Condor had made an appearance. The Hurricane responded reasonably well and Flynn had reached 6,000 feet when he spotted the latest Condor a further 6,000 feet above him, several miles distant on the convoy's port flank. 'Keep clear of the line of fire, Paddy,' warned Ward. The heavy anti-aircraft guns of the *Scylla* were about to open up.

Stewart had already baled out and been picked up by the convoy, and now Flynn followed. He had been airborne for fifty-two minutes. He was about to hoist sail when, at 21.38, after ten minutes in the water, he was picked up by the escort vessel *Enchantress*. Half an hour later the light began to fail.

SL 133 hadn't seen the last of the Condors even now. A determined attack was delivered next morning, lasting forty-five minutes and bombs were dropped from between 8,000 and 10,000 feet, but never by more than two aircraft at a time. The bombing was noticeably more accurate than on the previous day, but again no serious damage was sustained. The number of aircraft taking part was five in all, exactly reflecting, by simple subtraction, the difference between the eight that had attacked the southbound convoy on 26 July and the three that had since been brought to combat.

At 18.00 on 30 July the vice-commodore of the convoy signalled all ships confirming that three Condors had been destroyed on the 28th. Since none of the Condors was seen to be hit by anti-aircraft fire, it seems that Flynn's attack, too, was successful. If, as was suspected, German Intelligence had reported the disbanding of MSFU, the Condor crews had been given an unpleasant surprise.

For the British this eleventh-hour success, triumph though it was, was something of an embarrassment. The value of the Camships and the advantage of having more than one to a convoy, had never been more convincingly demonstrated. But already the remaining pilots, fighter direction officers and sea crews had left Speke and gone their separate ways. The aircraft had been flown to the training units and MSFU had been officially closed down. 'It will be a great nuisance,' moaned the Air Ministry, 'if we have to start it up again.'

The Air Staff had begun with a vision of 200 seaborne Hurricane fighters poised on their catapults, ready to protect Britain's Atlantic convoys from air attack. Second thoughts had reduced the figure to 35, but in the light of experience on the Russian convoys this was scarcely enough. On the German side the visionary had been Edgar Petersen, who had modestly proclaimed in 1940 that if he could send out forty or fifty Condors every day the blockade of Britain could be really effective. But the number of Condors produced in 1941 was only fifty-eight and even in 1942, when the peak of production was reached, the total was only eighty-four. The potential of the Condor, as the Germans realised too late, was never fully exploited. 'Given suitable aircraft and well-trained crews,' said a German appreciation of March 1944, 'the *Luftwaffe* could in no theatre of war achieve such great successes with such small losses as over the Atlantic.' But Condor production had meanwhile been allowed to taper off and as the long-awaited Heinkel 177 began to appear as a replacement, the Condors were gradually returned to the task for which they had originally been designed – long-range transport – and no more Condors were built after the first few weeks of 1944. Meanwhile the Merchant Aircraft Carriers and the Coastal Command and USAAF Liberators assumed the Hurricats' task of closing the Atlantic Gap.

In a period of just over two years the Camships had undertaken 175 voyages, averaging 3,000 miles per voyage. Of the total of 35 ships, 12 had been lost to enemy action. There were 8 operational launchings, and although enemy aircraft were claimed to have been shot down after only 6 of them, none of them could be called abortive. The notion of a suicidal, one-way-ticket mission, however, proved false. Although there were several narrow escapes, only one pilot, John Kendal, was lost after an operational launching.

When the Condors began their depredations in the Atlantic in the summer of 1940, the potential threat seemed almost as deadly as that of the U-boats. A deterrent had to be found and a vital ingredient of that deterrent was the Catapult Aircraft Merchant Ship. When HQ Fighter Command finally informed Speke that MSFU was to be disbanded, they enclosed the following message from the Admiralty:

> *My Lords would like to express their great appreciation of the services rendered by the RAF in providing this valuable defence for our convoys, and it is with great regret that they are now forced to recommend that this association of the RAF with the Merchant Navy should be brought to an end.*

No balance sheet can ever be struck because, in their positive/negative role, the tonnage the Camships protected, and the lives they saved, must always remain an imponderable. Even on the Arctic run, where they adapted to a somewhat different role, their contribution can never be accurately measured. Suffice it to say that the Condor scourge, so catastrophic for Britain when it first made its impact, was never a serious menace once the Hurricats got started. That, in the final analysis, was their most significant achievement.

Appendix I
Sequence of Events in Firing the Catapult

(for details see Catapult Drill)

States Of Readiness

'*Stowed*'. In harbour when circumstances preclude Catapulting – No Rockets in place, or firing circuits connected. Sentries on aircraft if necessary – All securing gear in place.

'*Secured for sea*'. Normal position when weather is too heavy for launching. All rockets necessary loaded. Firing circuits connected. All securing gear in place.

'*Cleared away*'. Normal position when possibility of launching. Catapult's and aircraft's crew standing by. All securing gear removed. Engine ready to start. Rockets loaded. Firing circuits connected.

'*Ready to launch*'. Catapult and aircraft ready in all respects. Engine running. Personnel under cover. 'Safety link' in place. *Note*. At sea the Trolley and Aircraft should always be secured in the 'Firing Position' with the Breaking Strip in place. In harbour other positions on the runway may be used if desired, consideration being given to the positioning of the securing wires on the aircraft. During periods when the ship is liable to air attack, if the Master and Pilot decide that conditions are suitable for launching, the catapult is brought to the 'Cleared away' position.

The Catapult Firing Officer, after consultation with the Master and Pilot, sees that the correct number of rockets are loaded and the electrical circuits correctly connected.

When The Fighter Direction Officer Reports That An Unidentified Aircraft Is Approaching

(a) *Master* orders 'stand by to launch' and orders the aeroplane flag (F International code) to be hoisted 'close up'.

(b) *Pilot and aircraft crew* start up aircraft engine.

(c) *NCO of aircraft crew*:
   (1) Sees footsteps of aircraft stowed after the pilot is secured in the cockpit.
   (2) Checks that the undercarriage wheels are up.
   (3) Sees runway is clear of all obstructions and that no loose gear, spanners, etc. have been left on the trolley.
   (4) Removes front locking bolt keep pins and stows them in the small rack provided in the Catapult Firing Officer's firing hut.
   (5) Reports to Catapult Firing Officer 'Catapult ready for firing'.

(d) *Catapult Firing Officer*:
   (1) Sees path of the launch clear inboard.
   (2) Sees that the firing switch is open.
   (3) Plugs in the 'safety link'.
   (4) Places himself by the Firing Switch, protected from blast, where he can see both the Pilot and the bridge.
   (5) Holds up his Blue flag as the signal to the Master that 'the Aircraft is ready

for launching'.

(e) *The unidentified aircraft comes into Sight and is identified as Hostile.*

(f) *Master:*

    (1) Alters the course of ship as necessary to the firing course.

    (2) Sees path of the launch clear outboard.

    (3) Orders pre-arranged signal to be sounded indicating to all personnel 'take cover'.

    (4) Holds up his Blue flag, thus ordering Catapult Firing Officer to 'launch as soon as ready'.

(g) *Catapult Firing Officer* circles his Blue flag as a signal to the Pilot to open his throttle.

(h) *Pilot* opens his throttle, and, when ready, holds up his right hand so that the Catapult Firing Officer can see it, and then cuts down his hand.

(i) *Catapult Firing Officer* waits a pause of three seconds, cuts down his Blue flag and at the same time closes the firing switch. *Note*: It is most important that the Firing Switch is closed at such a moment that the aircraft is not launched on the downward scend of the pitch. In general the best moment to close the Firing Switch will be just before the ship passes through the horizontal on the upward scend.

Appendix II
Tactical Notes for Hurricane Engaging Focke-Wulf 200

(Convoy Raider)

Pilots must have an appreciation of the armament and the capabilities of the Focke-Wulf 200 in order to be in a position to appreciate the likely evasive tactics to be adopted by a Focke-Wulf 200.

Armament
1. Downward-firing cannons, one forward and one aft. These cannons are used for strafing ships and it is, therefore, fairly certain that their arc of fire is fairly small and manoeuvrability not great. On the other hand, they are a deadly weapon against a fighter which maintains a steady approach or break-away.
2. Top armament. As far as can be ascertained, behind the pilot's cockpit there is a revolving power-operated turret with either two or four machine guns. It would appear that this turret has an all-round field of fire, including ahead. This is by far the most effective weapon, and the likely evasive tactics will be decided by the capabilities of this gunner.
3. In the dorsal position there is another pair of guns firing astern and covering the tail effectively. It is thought, therefore, that the only blind spot on the Focke-Wulf is under the wings, although it is possible that even this may be covered by machine guns pointing out of the sides of the fuselage. These constitute no real menace, however.

Tactics
4. Assuming that the interception of the Focke-Wulf takes place when it is engaged on attacks on shipping, the height will be somewhere below 500 feet. At this height the Hurricane should have 60/100 mph of speed in hand, and it should thus be possible to do a surprise attack, getting into close range before the attention of the Focke-Wulf is transferred from the convoy to the Hurricane. Under these conditions, the Hurricane pilot should withhold fire until the range is about 150 yards, and maintain this burst as long as possible, but taking care that he does not get into an astern position, where he will be simply throwing his ammunition away on armour plating. If the Focke-Wulf sights the Hurricane before a surprise attack can be made, he is most likely to either climb into cloud, if the clouds are very low, or dive down to as near sea level as possible. It is most likely that this latter manoeuvre will be the one employed. It is unlikely that the fighter will be sent off if the clouds are under 2,000 ft rendering the escape of the Focke-Wulf easy.
5. Once a Focke-Wulf is down to sea level and fully conscious of his danger, destruction becomes much more difficult, and the fighter pilot will have to plan his exact attack. The advantage of speed at this stage will most likely be about 50 mph. With the Focke-Wulf flying at this low height, it is quite certain that if the fighter can hit the pilot, the aircraft will strike the sea before any immediate action can be taken by the second pilot. It is thus advisable that the fighter should attack from ahead if possible, carrying out a curved diving

attack. Great care should be taken by the Hurricane pilot not to break away in an upward climbing turn. He should continue at sea level on a jinking course until out of range. He should then turn and examine the position afresh. If a head-on attack is found to be impossible, either through lack of speed or inability to get the position, then a beam attack will have to be carried out. It is fairly certain that the enemy aircraft will turn in towards any threatened beam attack and this should be allowed for in the approach. Fire should be withheld until the aim is perfect and range close, and the break away should be again erratic and at sea level until out of range. As mentioned before an astern attack should be avoided at all costs on account of heavy armour and armament. Pilots should remember the following points:

(i) The chief aim is to kill the pilot and crew. To stop the engines may be a good thing but there are 4 engines.

(ii) A straight approach assists the enemy rear gunner. A fighter which turns and pulls up immediately after an attack is a 'sitter' for the rear gunner.

(iii) That when his approach is unsatisfactory he should break off and not waste ammunition and the chance of being hit on a hopeless attack.

(iv) A bullet fired at 100 yards is worth six fired at 300 yards.

(v) *Pilots normally underestimate deflection and range.*

(signed)
D. E. Gillam
Squadron Leader,
Air Tactics
21st May, 1941